D1195403

LIVING WHEN
EVERYTHING CHANGED

LIVING WHEN EVERYTHING CHANGED

My Life in Academia

MARY KAY THOMPSON TETREAULT

RUTGERS UNIVERSITY PRESS

NEW BRUNSWICK, CAMDEN, AND NEWARK,

NEW JERSEY, AND LONDON

Library of Congress Cataloging-in-Publication Data

Names: Tetreault, Mary Kay Thompson, author.
Title: Living when everything changed : my life in academia / Mary Kay Thompson Tetreault.
Description: New Brunswick : Rutgers University Press, [2019] | Includes bibliographic references and index.
Identifiers: LCCN 2018047934 | ISBN 9780813594903 (cloth)
Subjects: LCSH: Tetreault, Mary Kay Thompson. | Women college administrators—United States—Biography. | Catholic women—United States—Biography. | Feminists—United States—Biography.
Classification: LCC LB2317.T47 A3 2019 | DDC 378.1/2092 [B]—dc23
LC record available at https://lccn.loc.gov/2018047934

A British Cataloging-in-Publication record for this book is available from the British Library.

♾ The paper used in this publication meets the requirements of the American National Standard for Information Sciences—Permanence of Paper for Printed Library Materials, ANSI Z39.48-1992.

www.rutgersuniversitypress.org

Manufactured in the United States of America

For Elijah Tetreault Braiman, born 2010, and his generation:
May the changes you encounter in life serve you as well as mine have.

CONTENTS

Preface   ix

1 My Life as a Professor Begins   1

2 Going Home and Leaving Home   18

3 Nestled in the Bosom of Catholicism   31

4 Wandering in the Wilderness   56

5 Finding Love and Work   70

6 Becoming the Men We Wanted to Marry   87

7 My Lewis and Clark Chapter Concludes   109

8 A Deanery of My Own   131

9 Second Chance to Be a Provost   154

10 Opportunities and Ambition Overshadowed by Ambivalence   175

11 Shifting My Gaze Forward   193

12 Among the Most Interesting Provost's Positions in the Country   210

13 A Wild Patience Has Taken Me This Far   231

Notes   251
Index   255

PREFACE

This is my story of living through the period that the *New York Times* colum-
nist Gail Collins has characterized as "when everything changed."[1] Her political
and social history of American women since the 1960s provides broad brush-
strokes of all the things that are now different. There are many: the taken-for-
granted assumptions about what women can do, the legal protections against
educational and employment discrimination, the positions on the politics of
housework, and much more. Her vignettes on the effects of the second women's
rights movement on the lives of ordinary women inspired me to appropriate and
extend her title, calling this book *Living When Everything Changed: My Life in
Academia*. In the twenty-four years between 1980 and 2004, I spent my professional life inside colleges and universities. In this book, I hope to illuminate how
those changes for women have played out in higher education in general and in
my life in particular.

An essential part of rooting out the past's truths in my time at the academy was probing the things that had shaped me.[2] How was it possible for me,
an adolescent in the 1950s, a girl who aspired to marry and raise children and
whose identity rested in being Catholic and from Nebraska, to imagine something beyond those origins? I was able to get beyond the repressive culture of
growing up female in the 1950s because first the civil rights movement and later
the women's movement slowly eroded my traditional aspirations and opened up
new ways of seeing the world. Those movements sparked a reimagining of both
my personal life and my professional one.

Attending the University of Chicago set me on a path of intellectual inquiry.
Initially, I was motivated to learn African American history so that I could
enlighten my all black high school students when I was teaching school on the
South Side of Chicago, and later my interest extended to women's history.
The difficulty of locating primary source materials for my students led to the

publication of my first book, *Women in America: Half of History* (1978). That publication, plus earning a doctorate and marrying a man who in time was willing to move beyond traditional gender roles, gave me the credentials and the courage to pursue an ambitious university career.

What was it like to be one of the "firsts" to benefit from affirmative action and join the procession of educated men? Mine is the story of an insider's perspective on the life of an academic on the three campuses where I served, first as a tenure-track faculty member and department chair and later as a dean and provost. All were places where the loftiest ideals held sway: the value of the life of the mind, of liberal learning, and of scholarly work. The early years especially were ones of optimism, when feminists dreamed of transforming their institution into a woman-centered university. I found my campuses to be places where some were receptive to new ways of thinking and behaving. But they were also places with intractable hierarchies fueled by male privilege, white privilege, and the primacy of the liberal arts and sciences.

My behind-the-scenes tale of the workings of academe chronicles my evolution from a newcomer with a naive view of what professors and administrators did to someone who came to understand the benefits and costs of advocating for what I believed was best for an institution. At times in the narrative, I focus on the work of teaching and research, and at others, my attention shifts to the administrative work that enables universities to run smoothly. An important aspect of my administrative life was the day-to-day camaraderie, the "aha" moments and how it felt to achieve something by working with others. I also pay attention to the harder part of being an administrator, dealing with others who have a different idea about how things are "supposed to be," as well as the archetypes—the disaffected faculty member or administrator, the good citizen, the enthusiastic newcomer, the productive scholar, and the committed teacher.[3]

By reading my life story, I hope the reader will come to see what has changed and what has not and relate her or his own experiences in order to do the following:

- Explore the interplay between one's self and one's generation.
- Gain a deeper understanding of the specialized world of higher education, how universities work, and the challenges those inside face.
- Trace the social relations that are shaped by the academic culture and history of a particular campus.
- Decide when gender was a difference that made a difference, or where I was responsible for what happened and where I was not.
- Imagine how colleges and universities can change to prepare our students for the complex futures they will face.

Chapter 1 begins with my first day as an assistant professor in 1980, in the middle of my life rather than with my actual birth date, because that appointment was a defining experience—a new birth into a life that I had idealized and longed for since my student days at the University of Chicago. A greenhorn, I initially thrived in the feminist paradise of Lewis and Clark College, a small liberal arts college in the Pacific Northwest. I relished my newfound popularity as I unwittingly took on risky assignments as an untenured faculty member. Yet at the time of my first review in 1982, I was still told, "You haven't done enough."

In chapters 2 and 3, I turn to a chronological approach to explore the deep Nebraska roots that defined my family as well as the forces that led us to leave. Throughout all our leaving because of my father's military assignments and returning "home," being Catholic consistently defined us. It was our world—church, school, friends, and community. It also determined my college choice.

Chapter 4 illustrates how the church gave me shelter when I was a college graduate wandering in the wilderness of gender-segregated jobs with conflicting aspirations for love and work. In chapters 5 and 6, I focus on changes that were happening in American society in the 1960s and 1970s that affected my life. In 1963, I moved to Chicago, unmarried and without a profession. Ironically, this left me free to benefit from those decades when many traditional ways of doing things were being questioned.

In chapter 7, I pick up my story from where it left off in chapter 1 and delve into how my time unfolded at Lewis and Clark in the 1980s. Learning from my first pretenure review, I walked a tightrope between my new understanding of tenure requirements and continuing to say yes to high-profile assignments, unrealistic about the perils of such work. Unable to imagine spending the next decades in a teacher education program when only the liberal arts and sciences had legitimacy, and thirsting for more administrative responsibility, a chance meeting led me to look elsewhere.

Chapter 8 covers my seven years as a dean at California State University, Fullerton. I learned from observing my mostly male administrator colleagues and our strong black female president. There were fun and satisfaction to be had in helping lead a school that was thought to be unworthy of notice (partly because it contained the traditional female disciplines of education, health, and human services) toward being one singled out for its achievements. Could a committed feminist figure out new and creative ways to be a dean?

Chapter 9 chronicles the circumstances that led to my becoming a provost in 1993. It was a time of pursuing exhilarating university initiatives, such as redefining our mission and goals, and working with deans and department chairs to imagine and implement innovations in academic affairs.

Chapter 10 and 11 tell the story of my search first for a college presidency and later for another provost's position. Over time, I learned that the most critical relationship in higher education administration is that between the president and the provost. My relationship with the president was confounding. We agreed about important institutional directions, but what I experienced as his increasingly bullying behavior ended in my exit from the university in 1998.

The pull I felt to be a president was in conflict with my scholarly work. Who was I—a scholar, a feminist, an administrator, or someone who didn't fit comfortably into any of those categories? I explain my decision to turn down an offer to be a president because I felt no passion for what was needed at that institution.

Chapter 12 portrays my five years as provost at Portland State University (PSU), a position characterized by a prominent leader in higher education as one of the most interesting assignments in the country. The university gained attention for its success in articulating its urban mission and designing an innovative general education program.

Chapter 13 continues to chronicle my work at PSU—namely, the importance of resource and budget management. But there was trouble in paradise. The system of favors and rewards for those in the former provost's inner circle had created a culture of insiders. There was a price to pay for a newcomer reluctant to think and act like the natives.

I conclude by asking, What did I expect when everything changed in the 1960s, holding out the dream of a more egalitarian society? How did living through this time shape my beliefs about how to transform a university for a diverse society? What did I expect as I pursued an ambitious university career, since the talents and values that fueled my advancement later contributed to my exit? As the child of parents who thought of "going home" as visiting relatives in eastern Nebraska, I could not have imagined that my "going home" would not be a physical place but a region of the mind: leading an examined life, publishing ideas I turned over and over, and being an essential part of teams that reimagined a university for the twenty-first century.

LIVING WHEN
EVERYTHING CHANGED

CHAPTER 1

MY LIFE AS A
PROFESSOR BEGINS

"Can a girl from a small railroad town in western Nebraska find happiness as a college professor?" I paraphrased the opening question of the mid-twentieth-century radio program *Our Gal Sunday* to fit my circumstances as I drove up the hill to Lewis and Clark College in southwest Portland on my first day as an academic.

Memories of my graduate student days at the University of Chicago in the 1960s washed over me. Late afternoons, I would see elderly white male professors meandering through the streets of Hyde Park as they walked toward their stately old homes. I imagined them ruminating over some problem in their scholarly work. I wanted to be one of them. My new appointment as the social studies educator in a master of arts in teaching (MAT) program was the first step toward joining the procession of educated men.

I brought my attention back to the road, which climbed through stands of huge Douglas firs, giving me the feeling of entering a deep forest that would go on forever. Monday, August 4, 1980: it was a startlingly clear summer morning in the Pacific Northwest, the sun scattering mottled light through the trees. As my car reached the top of Palatine Hill, I caught a glimpse of the college in the clearing below. The playing fields with their simple wooden bleachers seemed diminutive in comparison to their surroundings, something I hadn't noticed when I interviewed on campus the previous April. The main gate, a former carriage house of the Lloyd Frank estate, and the manor house, where a warren of administrative offices was housed, were perfect reproductions of English Tudor architecture. Yet despite the opulence of the manor house and its 137 acres, the majority of faculty offices and classrooms was housed in prefabricated bungalows put up hastily after the college moved upstate from Albany to Oregon's largest city in 1942.

Pulling into the parking lot opposite the library, an imposing structure of glass and brick that jutted out, I swung into one of the parking spaces and walked down the drive to my office in Bodine Hall. As I entered the office, the department secretary greeted me with a smile and a warning: "You have a lot of meetings for your first day." Her most distinctive feature was a cocoon of thinning, teased, dyed brown hair that stood atop her sixty-something face. "Dr. Eder will be in to meet with you at nine o'clock. And remember that you will be sitting in on his student advising today from three to six. Oh, and don't forget your appointment at human resources at one."

Once in my office, I took in the empty floor-to-ceiling bookshelves on one wall and imagined how I would fill them with treasured objects. From a packing box, I picked up an etching my husband, Marc, had made of Miró-like figures representing our family's connections: Maman, Papa, l'enfant. There was also a drawing our daughter, Chantal, had reluctantly done one Sunday afternoon. She had come into my study at home and asked me to play. "Oh honey, I'm sorry I can't. I need to work on my book. Why don't you sit down here and draw something?" Now in my hand was her portrait of me wearing a wide smile with a green nose, large loop earrings, and red Dr. Scholl's shoes, sitting at a typewriter, its keys flying. "May 25, 1975" was inscribed in large letters at the bottom in her six-year-old hand. My eyes looked up from her drawing toward the windows, a postcard view of Mount Hood in the distance.

Just before nine o'clock, there was a knock on my door. Thinking it would be Sid Eder, the director of the program, I was surprised to see Paul Magnusson, the associate dean for graduate programs, looking as well dressed and bright eyed as I remembered him from my campus interviews. He could have been mistaken for a mannequin recently stepped out of a window display. His jacket, shirt, and tie looked new, carefully coordinated in contrast to the shabbier versions I had seen on others. Even his glasses were the latest designer fashion, with round, tortoise-shell frames. "I just dropped by to welcome you and see if there's anything you need."

Just as I was about to respond, there was another knock on the door. I looked out and saw Eder, a surprised expression on his face. "I didn't realize you two had a meeting." "No meeting," Magnusson said, "just dropped by to welcome Mary Kay." I felt uncomfortable when I saw the tension between them and wondered about its source.

As Magnusson left, Sid sat down at the round glass table. "Let's get right to it," he said. "The first thing you need to understand is that students in this program are already classroom teachers, getting their advanced certificate and a master's degree—a state requirement." Moistening his thumb, he looked inside a slim folder, touched a green sheet of paper, and slid it out. "Here are the education requirements—research methods, secondary teaching strategies, classroom management. You'll see that we have a course to meet each requirement—actually, with the same name, all dictated by the state's Teacher Standards and Practices

Commission, TSPC for short. The other half of the program is courses in a student's subject matter area—art, English, history, social studies, and the sciences—taught mostly by the undergraduate faculty. It's all here on these sheets," he said, splaying out various colors as if they were paint samples—pink for art, brown for social studies, and so on. Tapping a yellow pencil on the folder, he said, "Look these over so you'll have some idea of what is going on when we begin advising students at three."

At one o'clock in the afternoon, I met with the director of personnel, who asked, "When do you plan to retire?" *Retire? I've just gotten here,* I thought. I did a quick calculation, "2005." The surprised look on her face made me wonder if I had overstepped some norm. I felt I owed Lewis and Clark at least twenty-five years, since they had gambled on hiring me.

At two forty-five, the secretary placed a dozen students' folders on my desk. Putting her finger on the top one, she said, "Now *there's* a student from a prominent Portland family. His family is the quality boot maker. People in town were surprised when he went into teaching." At three, Sid and I were seated at the table in my office when the first student came in for advising. A young man in his mid-twenties, he wore hiking boots and a smirk, a look of disdain on his face. He slumped into the vacant chair and said, "Is there any way I can get out of Research Methods? What do research methods have to do with teaching U.S. history?"

"Sorry, pal," Sid said, "It's a state requirement. Why not take it this fall with Dr. Tetreault and get it out of the way?"

"When is it offered?"

"Seven to ten o'clock on Thursday evenings."

"Do you know what that means? I start teaching at seven thirty in the morning. By the time I'd get home, it would be ten thirty at night. Up the next morning at six. to get to school in time for my first class. Can't be done. I need the requirement waived."

A sense of "trouble ahead" washed over me. I was scheduled to teach a course for which I was ill prepared, one that students found irrelevant, one scheduled at the worst time. Suppressing those feelings, I asked, "Would it work better for you to take an elective, possibly my Multicultural Education class, at four o'clock on Tuesday?"

The student looked at me and said, "Multicultural Education? How could that be relevant for my students or me? I teach in Beaverton, the most homogeneous school district in the state." When he walked out the door, Sid said, "Didn't I tell you?"

The next student had a different reason for an exception. "I've finished all the requirements for the program except one course, Secondary Teaching Strategies. Could you waive that requirement for me? I employ lots of different teaching techniques in my five classes. I need to complete the program by December to get my salary increase. My wife and I are expecting a baby in January and absolutely need the money."

Eder's answer was the same, "Sorry, pal."

As the hours progressed, my office seemed to get smaller, the overhead lights brighter. When the last student left that evening at six, my desire to live amid a community of scholars seemed delusional. I said, "Most of the students we've advised today don't seem to want to be here. I guess it's because the degree is required."

"That's right, they don't see it as having anything to do with their teaching; all seven hundred of them. But the reason they come here instead of Portland State is the personal attention, the one-on-one advising. Most of them are graduates of one of the state's universities. They see being here at a liberal arts college as a step up." I suppressed the troubling information about student enrollment. At least they didn't show up at the same time—only one every fifteen minutes. Would I ever be able to connect to the students in a more meaningful way than Sid?

⫸⫷

By the time I finished student advising, it was just after six o'clock; my car stood alone in the parking lot. As I drove home, I felt everything needed to happen at once: find a house to buy, decide where Chantal (who was beginning sixth grade) would go to school, and explore where Marc could find work in the art world. We had an appointment on Friday with the principal of the Portland public school's new magnet middle school, which would be opening in the fall. The student body, drawn from all over the city, was expected to be half black and half white.

I was eager to see how the day had fared for Marc and Chantal, knowing they had spent it in an empty apartment. The minute I turned my key into the door, Marc met me with a horrified look on his face. "Whitey is gone! We haven't seen him for hours; he was here when the movers came, but he seems to have disappeared. Blackie is here but no Whitey."

My eyes darted to a jumble of boxes, rugs, a couch, lamps, crates full of Marc's paintings, and a washer and dryer. The oak table we bought in 1969 sat in the middle. Blackie, one of the two cats Chantal had brought home in the third grade, lay sprawled on one of the chairs, turning to lick his upper front leg. Polar opposites. When friends visited, Whitey would head for the nearest place to hide; within minutes Blackie would be in someone's lap, purring so loudly that conversation was nearly impaired.

"I did everything I could to watch for the cats as the movers went in and out."

"Could he have escaped through those glass doors? He might still be in the yard. You know how he likes to climb up and hide in trees," Chantal said.

Chantal had given the cats fancy names—Sasha and Tasha. The first sign that she had discerned a crack in her parent's perfection was her loss of patience when

Marc and I reverted to calling them by the color of their fur. "Why can't you get their names straight?" Whitey's absence added to my guilt for asking Chantal to leave friends she'd had since kindergarten, friends from her neighborhood school where the children's first question of one another was "Are you Hanukkah or Christmas?"

Dinner was a glum affair—dishes fished out of a box, paper towels serving as both place mats and napkins. Unpacking might help right us. "Let's just unpack the few necessities to hold us over until we find a house," I said.

"The first thing we need to do," Marc said, "is move that rug off those boxes marked 'Kitchen Utensils.'" As he and I grabbed the 8½-by-12-foot rug at both ends, it began to unfold. Suddenly, we saw a patch of white fur. Chantal put her hand to her mouth. Marc continued to carefully unroll the rug, and as he did, we saw a paw. Could it be Whitey? Was he dead? Whitey's flat body appeared, his limp head between his paws. Suddenly, he raised his head, looked up startled, and jumped out of the rug.

That night in bed (a mattress on the floor because the springs hadn't been unboxed), I wondered about the troubling things I had learned on my first day at Lewis and Clark. Maybe wanting to have the life of my University of Chicago professors was a pipe dream. Unable to fall asleep, I thought about the sequence of events that had landed me in this place.

When I completed my doctorate in social education in 1979, the first position I applied for was assistant superintendent for curriculum and instruction of the Newton Public School District, the most highly regarded district in Massachusetts. I was not surprised when, several days after my interview, the head of personnel called and in a solemn tone said, "The pool of candidates was very rich, very experienced. We selected another applicant." But I was disappointed, and I wondered if my newly minted doctorate would ever be the ticket to move beyond my job as an equal educational opportunity specialist for the Massachusetts Department of Education.

By this time, already feeling old at forty-one, I had learned to keep the devil from the door in such circumstances by "doing" something. Hadn't I turned my anger at women's oppression into the project of learning women's history? Libraries were the place of that transition. When I learned of Newton's rejection, I drew on that coping strategy and made the short drive through Cambridge from my office to Gutman, library of the Graduate School of Education at Harvard. Sitting at a long table in the spacious reference room, its dim lighting overhead, I had no idea what to do. My dream of being a college professor flitted into my head. Recently one of my colleagues at the department of education had said, "It's clear this is too small a playing field for all you know, all you've done." *What if? What if I could get an academic job?* I thought to myself. I knew that university positions were published in the *Chronicle of Higher Education*. I went to the reference desk. "Where can I find the *Chronicle*?"

The *Chronicle*, published weekly in newspaper format, covers issues of interest to those in higher education but is mostly devoted to job announcements.
The ads range from full-page notifications of openings for college presidencies to
the briefest descriptions of faculty positions. Once I had the latest copy in hand,
I struggled to master the jumble of entries barely organized into categories:
administration, student affairs, faculty of disciplines and subdisciplines. Eventually I figured out how to locate teaching positions in education. The descriptions in the category "Curriculum and Instruction" left me cold; the course I'd taken
in graduate school on the subject with one of the world's leading scholars in
the field had been mechanistic and boring. The category "Research Methods"
reminded me of how I had hated that particular graduate course. *There's no
place here for me,* I thought. About to give up, my eyes fell on a one-inch ad in
tiny print:

> Social Studies Educator, Lewis and Clark College, Portland, Oregon. Tenure-
> track faculty position in Master of Arts in Teaching Program. Send curriculum
> vitae and letter of application to: [. . .] Deadline: 11/1/79.

Lewis and Clark College, what kind of a place could it be? Oregon? I visual-
ized a map of the West Coast: California to the south, but what was above it?
Oregon? Washington? I had never been to Portland and only knew of it because
my grandmother had traveled there in the late 1940s and marveled at the size
of the roses. I could picture myself in a classroom of social studies teachers, so
I submitted the requested materials and a copy of my book *Women in America:
Half of History,* a collection of primary sources for high school students.

And now here I was, in Oregon. Returning to the present, I turned over on
the mattress and thought of my first contact with Sid Eder. I had been skeptical
of his interest in me from our first telephone conversation. His voice had been
tentative, unenthusiastic as he introduced himself. I'd expected him to say that
I had not made the final cut. He had continued on, however. "Well, you've certainly had experiences the committee likes—a classroom teacher for eight years,
work in a state department of education. I see, though, that you've had little or
no college teaching."

"That's true," I said, "but a colleague and I had full responsibility for the
course 'Introduction to Student Teaching' at Boston University when I was in
graduate school. I thoroughly enjoyed every— . . ."

He interrupted and said, "I worry that you may be a one issue person."

A warning signal went off in my head. "One issue? I'm not sure what you
mean."

"Well, your book and your one article are all about women."

"That's true," I said, "but they are also about race as well. Besides, I understand
that teachers need to be exposed to the full scope of things they face—curriculum

planning, student discipline, teaching methods. . . ." I paused to catch my breath, and he jumped in.

"The committee has selected you and another person to come to campus for an interview. Our secretary will be calling you about travel arrangements."

I arrived in Portland for the interview on a late afternoon in April 1980 and entered the waiting area outside my arrival gate at the airport to find a tall man with dyed black hair, dressed like a professor straight out of central casting: tweed sports jacket, light-blue dress shirt, striped tie, and brown buck shoes. His perfectly clipped nails were cupped around a sign that read, "Dr. Tetreault." As I approached him, he held out his hand and said, "Sid Eder. Dr. Eder."

Once on the freeway headed toward Portland, Sid talked of the pleasures of living there. "You can be reading the Sunday paper and, at eleven o'clock, decide to go cross country skiing on Mt. Hood and be on the trail in a little more than an hour. Downtown Portland went through an impressive revitalization when Neil Goldschmidt was mayor—he got Nordstrom's to stay downtown and pushed to replace a parking lot in the center of the city with Pioneer Courthouse Square. And drinking fountains! There are drinking fountains all over town, and they work! Oh, and we're going to have dinner tonight at Hunan, a new Chinese restaurant that is better than any you'll get in LA."

Any conversation about the college or the MAT program was strangely absent.

On the first morning of a two-day interview schedule, Eder handed me several pieces of paper. "Here's your schedule." I quickly looked down and saw a dizzying list of meetings with the search committee, the program's other faculty member (a science education specialist named Marge Clark), the graduate program directors, and an open meeting with members of the history faculty. There was time set aside with a real estate agent, Associate Dean Magnusson's wife, to check out the availability of houses. Already, I felt in over my head.

My first meeting with the search committee helped offset Eder's tentativeness. As I scanned those around the table, I saw that five of the six were men, some appearing to be "new" men young enough to have been influenced positively by the women's movement. They appeared warm and welcoming. Clark, the lone woman at the table, made me uneasy. When I first learned she was a Catholic sister, a parade of those who had taught me in elementary school, their faces surrounded by white wimples and black veils, flashed before my eyes. It helped somewhat that she was a contemporary sister. The only sign that she was a member of a religious order was the silver band on her right hand with a crucifix embossed on the top.

David Savage, a historian and associate dean of the college, held up a copy of my book and said, "The ways you've creatively organized materials in your book around the stages of the life cycle remind me of the historian Gerda Lerner. She's been on campus a number of times and we all fell in love with her." Savage let out a high-pitched laugh and raised his eyebrows high above his glasses. "I can't say much about it, but we're trying to persuade her to leave New York to teach here. Imagine having a historian of that stature among us." Savage went on to tell us that the college was beginning to develop a national reputation in women's studies and had just received a major grant from the National Endowment for the Humanities to integrate topics and materials on women and gender into the general education curriculum.

I was pleased the interview started off on this note, especially after Eder's charge that I might be "a one-issue person," and I told them how Lerner's theory of women's history had shaped the way I'd organized the book into sections— "Growing Up a Girl," "Following Tradition," and "Leaving Home." I finished by saying, "Her observation that we should organize women's history around the lives of women, not men, had a great influence on me."

Feeling affirmed, I saw that an older man, a political scientist with a grave frown on his face, had a question. "You've had quite a varied educational experience—a modest Catholic women's college; a great university, the University of Chicago; and a run-of-the-mill one, Boston University. What have you learned from all that variety?"

Ah, I thought to myself, *another gatekeeper, and another man to win over.*

"By being a student in these very different institutions, I've learned that quality matters most: the quality of the faculty, the quality of the students. My academic values were shaped at the University of Chicago—the value of the liberal arts, the place of research in a college or university." His nod signaled that he was satisfied with my answer. Sid sat quietly throughout the interview.

My second day on campus, I had an interview with Paul Magnusson. He was the most forthright person about where graduate programs sat in the college. "The liberal arts undergraduate faculty—about one hundred strong and enamored with their 1,800 traditional-age students—is the guardian of the institution. They're uncertain about the place of graduate programs, and some think we compromise the college's identity, especially counseling and public administration. Education is a little better off; our programs have been offered since the college was founded. The law school is on a separate campus and a world apart."

"This worries me," I ventured to say. Magnusson went on to assure me that the centrality of the MAT program to the college was demonstrated by the decision to house the program's offices in the newly renovated Bodine Hall along with the history and biology departments.

Late in the afternoon of the second day, when my campus interviews concluded, Eder drove me to the town Lake Oswego, where I was staying. Here was my last chance to win him over, to convince him I was the best choice. He broke the silence by asking, "Well, how did it go?"

"Very well, very well," I said. "It was such a pleasure and so informative to meet faculty in the liberal arts and in the MAT program. The blend of liberal arts and education courses is one that I have valued since I was in graduate school.

There are a lot of interesting possibilities here, building the program in social studies and working with the liberal arts faculty in the college." I knew better than to say anything about what excited me most—being in an environment that valued women's studies.

Sid nodded but said nothing. Just after we turned right on A Street in Lake Oswego, the wealthiest town in Oregon at the time, he stopped the car outside a restaurant, Amadeus, and said, "Here's a good place to eat. I need to get home and won't be coming in with you. I've barely seen my family during these two days. Keep the receipts. A taxi will pick you up at the motel in time to make your flight tomorrow morning." Once my suitcase was on the sidewalk, he drove off, leaving me standing as I watched his car moving up the street, becoming smaller and smaller.

Slinging the strap of my garment bag over my shoulder, I walked into the restaurant, empty at five o'clock, and took a table near the window. Small vases of trillium on each table cheered me. Hadn't someone told me that they only bloom every seven years? I doubted that I'd be in Oregon for the next bloom. I had overheard mention of the other candidate, an assistant professor at the University of Arkansas and former Stanford basketball player. How could I compete with that?

Too tired to read a book, I picked up a menu while images of interviews from the past two days distracted me from clearly seeing the evening's offerings. I ordered the boeuf bourguignon. Too exhausted to eat, I took a few bites and signaled the waiter for my check. There was no one on the sidewalk as I waited for my taxi. *How different from the bustle of Boston*, I thought. Back in the motel, I finished packing, laid out my clothes for the return trip home, got ready for bed, and settled back on my pillow, ready for one of the best moments of each day as I lit my single, customary cigarette and thought about how much I wanted this job.

Several weeks later when I picked up the phone in my office and heard Sid Eder's voice, I stifled a small gasp. "I'm calling to offer you a tenure-track position as an assistant professor, beginning August 1. The salary is fourteen thousand dollars." My heart beating quickly, I said, "I can't accept that. My husband will be giving up a job at a gallery on Newbury Street. We won't even be able to afford piano lessons for our daughter. I can't come for less than twenty thousand."

Sid cleared his throat. "Let me talk to the associate dean and see what I can do."

When a counteroffer of seventeen thousand dollars came two days later, I accepted it.

The week before fall classes began was full of welcoming events: a reception at the dean's home, a faculty luncheon, and a picnic for newcomers and their families. Dinah Dodds, a professor of German who was assigned to be my host, escorted me to the dean's reception. We drove there in her small, aged BMW along a freeway that, after Boston, seemed free of cars on a Sunday afternoon. Glancing over at me in the passenger's seat, she said, "It's great to think we have another feminist on campus. And in teacher education!" Her voice registered surprise. "There's a group here that you might want to join. We call ourselves WIGs, short for women's interest group. We're organizing to try to get more female faculty and to design a women's studies program. We have individual courses, but that's all."

"I'd be interested in being a part of that," I said.

On Friday, Dinah escorted me from my office to Templeton Student Center for the lunch for new faculty. As we walked through the glass doors into the dining room, a stocky young woman wearing a baseball cap and dark glasses handed Dinah a small brown paper bag. "Here's the latest," she said, avoiding eye contact with either Dinah or me. "I didn't expect to get it so soon," Dinah said. Leaning toward my ear, she whispered, "This is the latest Amanda Cross mystery, *Death in a Tenured Position.*" Dinah went on to explain that Amanda Cross was the pseudonym for Carolyn Heilbrun, the first tenured woman in the English department at Columbia, who wrote a series of fourteen mystery novels. Kate Fansler, the protagonist, is a bright, witty literature professor in a prestigious New York university. A master at satire, Heilbrun captured the secret life of such "firsts." "You can chart your status in the feminist hierarchy here," Dodds whispered, "by how soon you get the hard copy of Heilbrun's book that Leslie circulates among feminists." Later, when it came to me, I read it with the same identification I had read Nancy Drew mysteries as a preadolescent.

Dinah and I hadn't gone more than a few feet when she stopped. "Here is Susan Kirschner from the English Department, one of WIG's most active members."

With that remark, Dinah hugged a tall, attractive brunette whose hair, precision cut, fell at an angle over the right side of her face each time she moved. A long, gauzy floral designer scarf was wrapped around her neck. "Glad to finally meet you," I said. "David Savage was singing your praises when I was on campus for an interview this spring."

"David," Susan said smiling. "Did he talk with you about the women's studies seminar? I hear that you've published a book in American women's history. You might want to consider applying."

"Would I love that," I said. "I learned from doing my book that the real challenge was how to organize readings according to women's lives instead of men's in the public sphere."

Susan raised her right index finger and cocked her head in a way that signaled I might have said something interesting. "You sound like the historian Gerda Lerner. We tried to get her to join our faculty, but she went to Wisconsin instead." We were interrupted by the deep voice of the dean summoning everyone to find a table.

"Let's have lunch soon," Susan said.

Signs announcing the table for each department hung high above people's heads. When I lowered my gaze, I saw a sea of men, men strikingly alike: white, dressed in khaki or tweed jackets and oxford button-down shirts. The only diversity I could see was in the color of their ties. A few women sat here and there: one at the English table, one at psychology, one at anthropology, two at communications. There were none at mathematics or any of the sciences. The only table with a small cluster of women was the one for graduate programs: one woman in counseling psychology, another in special education for deaf and hard of hearing, and Marge Clark and I in the MAT program. Heilbrun's idea of firsts seemed writ large here.

Once the dishes were cleared, the dean, a historian with a Stanford PhD, stood at the podium, a warm smile peeking out from under his mustache. "Welcome to the beginning of another academic year. Let me introduce our three incoming faculty. It is my pleasure to present first Mary Kay Thompson Tetreault, assistant professor in the master of arts in teaching program. Mary Kay is a historian with degrees from the University of Chicago and Boston University. A scholar, she recently published a book, *Women in America: Half of History*, which approaches history from the perspective of women. She is an excellent addition to our faculty." Restrained clapping ensued.

As I listened, I almost believed everything the dean said about me, except that he was telling a slanted version of the truth. True, my book was a history of American women, but it was a textbook for high school students. Only my undergraduate degree was in history. I had a master of arts in teaching and an EdD in social education. Was education so demeaned at Lewis and Clark that my introduction required Brown's obfuscations? Or was it that Magnusson, given to exaggeration, had written the dean's remarks?

~≈≈≈≈

The first week in October, two months after I had arrived on campus, Marc and I attended a college reception for a visiting scholar. How I loved the intellectual stimulation of such events and the congenial faculty community. When we walked into the room and headed for the wine bar, the first person I saw was Magnusson, who gave me a welcoming smile. His wife, Candy, stood near him. Knowing that Magnusson, the most powerful man among the graduate faculty, was important to my success, Marc struck up a conversation with Candy as Paul and I stepped away. "When the dean and I interviewed you last spring, we agreed that you would be a good person to replace Sid as program chair. He doesn't want the post any longer, and you do."

Surprised but elated that he had such confidence in me, I said, "You're right." We both laughed. Magnusson's offer made my mind race. I relished the idea of addressing the problems intrinsic to the program: too many students; only two full-time faculty, with adjuncts and liberal arts faculty from the undergraduate school teaching a course or two; an unimaginative program of study that mirrored the state's certification requirements; and a class schedule inconsistent with teachers' work life. Sid, Marge, and I set aside several mornings during the academic year to identify ways of improving the program with more imaginative course offerings or group advising—we agreed that we gave essentially the same advice to individual students every fifteen minutes. Sid, who increasingly felt pressure to concentrate on his work as director of continuing education and summer sessions, would say, "Do what you want. I don't have time for such things. My other assignments eat up more than half my time." Here was a chance for Marge and me to shape a higher-quality program.

Magnusson wasn't the only male colleague who sought me out. The phone call to serve on a search committee within the history department came from the chair, *Robert Wilson. "We've an important search this year in the department, the first since I was hired in the 1960s. We have no tenured women in the department and need to hire one." I hung up the phone, flattered at Robert's invitation but not sure what was involved. By serving on such an important search in the college, I figured I might be able to build bridges between undergraduate and graduate programs.

Needing to talk to someone after Wilson's call, I walked down the hall to Michael Stark's office to tell him of my invitation. The sign on his door read, "Chair, Counseling Psychology." Stark had been on the search committee when I was hired and was someone I had come to like and trust. He reminded me of Sigmund Freud, with a shock of black hair framing a face capable of the most sympathetic look when he raised his head and smiled a smile that seemed born from some deep suffering. "Ah, Wilson," Stark said, "he's a master of campus politics, counting his votes on every issue he wants to influence. Be wary. His veins aren't full of blood; they're full of ice water."

I only had time to return to my office and look out the window before I heard a knock on the door. Flashing a smile and widening his eyes, Wilson asked, "Have a second?" In his late thirties, he eased his lanky body into a chair at the round table in my office. Robert's thin face, long nose, and dark-brown hair that he often brushed away from his eyes gave him the look of a charming scamp.

"Glad you're willing to consider serving on this important committee," he began. "We need to raise the quality of the department; too many slackers. Too many who don't do their work—hell, who have no work." He leaned forward and laughed. "One of my colleagues just returned from a sabbatical where he spent the year learning to throw ceramic pots. A man with a PhD, a full professor." He frowned. "Too many come here and just want to hike and ski. I talk about this so much at home that my young daughter says to her stuffed bear, 'Have to get them to do their work.'" He continued, "This is also an opportunity to hire someone to develop a course in women's history. There is only one woman faculty member in the department, and she's not on the tenure track—doesn't yet have her PhD." Here was an offer too appealing to resist.

The several meetings the search committee spent narrowing down the applicant pool to the seven or so candidates that Wilson would interview at the annual American Historical Association (AHA) meeting in January gave me a sense of how search committees worked and how well prepared our members were. Meeting their standards, I soon learned how much time the assignment demanded: reading through more than two hundred applications and making a case for a person's advancement to the next level took time away from grading the stack of papers that needed to be returned to students.

The morning after his return from the AHA meeting, Wilson stopped by my office. He was enthusiastic about an American historian about to finish her dissertation. "She's bright, has lots of potential, and is more than prepared to teach a course in American women's history. I definitely think we should interview her. She's originally from the Northwest so that's a plus in our favor. The problem is going to be selecting another candidate. Bringing in two for interviews should be enough."

During her campus interview, the candidate spoke to the committee about her research and elaborated on how she used diaries, letters, and other first-person documents, in addition to public and organizational records, to reconstruct the everyday lives of ordinary women living on the frontier. Equally important, she had a well-developed philosophy of teaching, one centered on student learning.

The other candidate was a Thoreau scholar, stiff in his three-piece black suit, looking as if he had just completed a walk around Walden Pond. He lit up at every opportunity to share the good reviews his first book was receiving. The search committee spent hours deliberating which candidate was a better fit. Who would be the better scholar? Who showed the best promise of future "work"? Who would be the better teacher? Did the department really need a woman?

The evening before the committee's final meeting to settle on recommendations to the dean, Wilson called around nine o'clock to say he was dropping by for a chat. The two of us sat in my living room across from one another on the white sectional sofa. One of Marc's paintings hung on the far wall: a six-by-five-foot canvas whose underpainting of yellow, green, and tan caused the bold red squares of various shades of encaustic paint to pop out. Wilson didn't take long to come to the point. "I really think the Thoreau scholar is what our department needs—bright, lots of potential, and he's already published his book."

"But what about the department's need for a woman, a feminist scholar?" Where had his enthusiasm for hiring a woman gone?

"Well, that's only one need we have. Someone else could teach women's history—perhaps me, perhaps one of our part-time faculty." I wondered how long our circular conversation would continue and glanced at my watch. Robert noticed and said, "Can I count on your vote for my candidate tomorrow?"

Certain that the woman was the strongest candidate, I calculated the fallout of standing up to the most powerful faculty member on campus. I knew I could not live with myself if I sided with Wilson. "I'm afraid I'll have to vote for her. She's more mature, and she'll bring a needed area of specialization to the department." Wilson gave me a strange look and said, "It's late. I appreciate knowing where you stand, but I really need a colleague, someone I can talk with."

The next day when the search committee met, each of us made a case for our favored candidate. Except for Wilson, all the men and I supported the female candidate. I felt a sense of relief when I saw that Robert didn't seem to hold my vote against me. Was it because he was the kind of politician who moved beyond disagreements to the next high-stakes issue? The woman was hired.

As the year progressed, I took pride in gaining my stride. I went into the office every morning at nine o'clock, prepared and taught classes, advised students, and served on committees. The history department's search wasn't the only one; the administration had decided to offer a new graduate program in educational administration, and I was on the committee to design the program and gain approval from the state's certification agency. Later, I was on the search committee to select the program director.

My teaching assignment for my first academic year was two courses per quarter, for three quarters. The pair of courses would alternate among Research Methods, Secondary Teaching Strategies, and a new offering I designed, Multicultural Education. I was enthusiastic about the third but worried about the other two.

When I interviewed at Lewis and Clark, Sid had asked if I could teach Research Methods, a course for which I was woefully unprepared—in my doctoral studies, the only B I'd received had been in Research Methods. Fearing that a negative response would torpedo my chances of being hired, I gave an enthusiastic, "Yes!"

Twenty-eight students enrolled in Research Methods for the fall quarter. The class was held in a theater-style room, its seats ascending. As I stood at the lectern introducing myself, I felt diminutive looking up at them, a Christian gladiator facing menacing patricians who lusted for my death. Had fear not clouded my vision, I would have noticed how tired they looked, dark circles under many eyes, their body language mostly that of fatigue. Students were courteous in the beginning, not challenging my stumbling explanations. But one evening around nine forty-five, midway through the quarter, one of the male students, his body much too large for the desk he occupied, raised his hand. Before he spoke, he looked at another of his male classmates, who fought to keep a smile off his face. "Can you tell me what a null hypothesis is? It says in our text that it is an assertion that the things you were testing are not related and your results are the product of random chance events. I don't understand."

"Well," I said, casting my eyes over my notes to find what I had written about the null hypothesis. "In statistics, the only way of supporting your hypothesis is to refute the null hypothesis." I looked up at him as feelings of panic and inadequacy surged through my body. I read on. "Rather than trying to prove your hypothesis right, you must show that the null hypothesis is likely to be wrong; you have to 'refute' or 'nullify' the null hypothesis."

"I still don't get it," he said.

"I see it's nearly ten," I said, as the image from Roy Lichtenstein's pop art painting, *Drowning Girl*, came to mind. "Let me think about this and see if I can give an explanation next week that helps you understand." Try as I did the following week to explain the null hypothesis, I never felt I had adequately answered his question.

I passed out student evaluations of the course in the final class. No proctor was around at ten o'clock at night to submit and collect the forms, so I took them. When the last student had left the room, I stole a peek—not good. On a scale from one to five, with five as the highest, too many students had marked a three or lower. One student had even circled a one. Skimming the evaluations before I dropped them on the secretary's desk, I quickly slipped the lowest ranked one into my briefcase, thinking, *This process has made me a liar and a cheat.*

On more solid ground in my own course, Multicultural Education (because I had spent more than fifteen years reading, writing, and thinking about it), I took pleasure in designing my syllabus. I assigned fiction—Maya Angelou's *I Know Why the Caged Bird Sings* and Maxine Hong Kingston's *Woman Warrior*—along with articles on the topic. Believing this was a course where I could make my mark at Lewis and Clark, I was disappointed to learn that only four students, all white women, had enrolled. Once we overcame our self-consciousness at being such a tiny band, these practicing teachers talked of the possibility of providing an antiracist education to their mostly all-white students. Our like-mindedness had the feeling of a lovefest. My student evaluations in Multicultural Education were all fives.

I had scant knowledge of what readings to use for my course Secondary Teaching Strategies. I had learned to teach while a student at the University of Chicago's MAT program by observing John Patrick, my supervising teacher at the university's Laboratory School. He engaged students in a variety of activities: writing exercises, small group discussions, and field trips. He never called them strategies. Because of his modeling, I came to love teaching, to search out innovative materials, and to spend hours devising creative activities to help students engage with ideas.

I saw my role as encouraging my Lewis and Clark students to reflect on the educational, social, and political contexts of their teaching. With this purpose uppermost in my mind, I selected Maxine Greene's book *Teacher as Stranger*, a critique of schools and their practices that asked teachers to look at their classroom as a stranger might. Written in the academic style of the 1960s, Green drew on what philosophers had thought throughout the ages, jumping from one to the next, often on the same page. One rainy evening made darker by the hour, in a gray, barren classroom, I attempted to get my dozen or so students to discuss Greene's book. "By now, you should have read the first half of Greene's book. Do you agree with her analysis of the deficiencies in K–12 education, especially for minority students? Do you agree with her ideas on how to repair them?"

Silence bounced off every surface in the room. A female student looked at me and asked, "Who is the stranger here? I don't feel like a stranger in my classroom; we have no minority students." Most believed race did not matter, especially their own as white. But their resistance had a point—Green's philosophical reflections, rather than helping them to be more successful, seemed overly critical of teachers. Not only was my choice inappropriate, but I never succeeded in getting them to examine the contexts of their classrooms and the world beyond.

Later, when I described my Secondary Teaching Strategies course to Dan Duke, who was on campus to interview for chair of Educational Administration, he said, "Oh, you must use Bruce Joyce's book, *Models of Teaching.*" I remained silent, never having heard of it. I immediately sought out the book and discovered that Joyce and his coauthor, Marsha Weil, had identified more than eighty distinct models of teaching from which a teacher could choose: some designed to help students grow in self-awareness or creativity, others to foster the development of self-discipline or responsible participation in a group; some stimulating inductive reasoning or theory-building, others leading to mastery of subject matter. The next time I taught the course, using Joyce's book, I felt less of a stranger.

During our first full Oregon summer, Marc, Chantal, and I rented a house several blocks from the Pacific Ocean for a week. Lying on the beach, unwilling to dip a toe in water that was only fifty-eight degrees, I finally had time to reflect on the past year. I bought my first journal and opened it with the following:

Manzanita, August 4, 1981

Beginning now, I am going to write for thirty minutes each day in this journal. I want to record my thoughts and feelings in this, the forty-second year of my life. Yesterday was the anniversary of our first year in Oregon. It has been a much better year than I expected. Marc has a job at Augen Gallery and a show in November at the University of Portland. Chantal did superb work at Harriet Tubman Middle School, although she had to learn to stand up to bullies. She has only begun to speak of the loss of her Massachusetts friends. I was promoted to department chair, and I'm worried about directing the program, but I will succeed. My biggest worry is my upcoming review, which is coming up in the fall. Get Robert Wilson to help prepare my file.

Untenured assistant professors at Lewis and Clark were reviewed for continuation of their contract and eventually for tenure in their second, fourth, and sixth years. The purpose of which was, the promotion and tenure document declared, ". . . to determine whether they [faculty] are making satisfactory progress toward meeting the institution's standards . . . in the areas of teaching and scholarly or creative activity."

Each faculty member under review was required to prepare a file that began with a self-assessment of their teaching, research, and service, and to include supporting materials: course syllabi, student teaching evaluations, articles or books published during the period, and evidence of service both on and off campus. I tackled my teaching first, wondering how I could put a positive spin on some of my misjudgments. Yet still, my teaching evaluations had improved, Research Methods would be taught by someone else, and I had thankfully found Joyce and Weil's text for Secondary Teaching Strategies.

My two publications, my book and an article in *Interracial Books for Children*, wouldn't count toward this review because they were published before I signed my contract at Lewis and Clark. I had begun an evaluation of the women's studies seminar held at Lewis and Clark that summer, but it was in such an early stage that I decided not to mention it.

But hadn't I spent a great part of my first year in institutional service? I would emphasize that—I would even ask to be accelerated because I had done so much. I made an appointment to talk with Wilson about how to present my work. When we met, I made my case to him. "There have been improvements in my teaching, but my greatest contribution has been service—two searches, designing the program in educational administration, and being appointed chair in my second year."

"Service, hmmm," he said. "Let's see how we might present this. And you think you have a case for accelerated advancement?" Something about the tone of his voice, the look of skepticism on his face, made me feel that he was willing to play along but incredulous that I could be so naive.

The following April, I received a letter from the dean regarding my second-year review.

Previous levels of review noted that you are a thoughtful instructor and working to improve your teaching. They also noted that your service was extraordinary for a first-year faculty member. Regrettably, your scholarship is not sufficient to warrant accelerated advancement. In fact, you have not done enough. You will need to improve in this category before your next review.

When I finished reading the letter, I felt the blood rush to my face. Not done enough? I had never before been told that I hadn't done enough.

CHAPTER 2

GOING HOME AND
LEAVING HOME

We were, as Chantal said, "one whole happy family" as we drove from Massa-chusetts to Portland in July 1980. As we headed west along Interstate 80, I was reminded of how car trips every several months during my childhood to visit grandparents, aunts, uncles, and cousins in eastern Nebraska were the setting of my parents' stories of their early lives. We always left late, after my father, a sales-man (first of Chesterfield cigarettes and later of automotive parts), had returned from work and we had eaten dinner. There was never a question of eating in a restaurant; there were too many of us for such an expensive venture. We had a shorthand way of referring to ourselves: Dad, Mom, Mary Kay, the boys, and the little girls. The advantages of birth order gave me, the oldest, a name. The boys, Dan and Mike, two and five years younger than I, were a pair. Patty and Peggy, born in 1946 and 1949, respectively, trailed me by eight and eleven years.

The drive northeast from North Platte to the place my parents still called home was in our secondhand Packard along dark, two-lane highways, travel-ing more than five hours. We started out east along Route 30 to Columbus, paralleling the Platte River. We then headed north through Norfolk, and once we got to Plainview (where the 2014 film *Nebraska* is set), we had to decide to take either the road fourteen miles northwest to Creighton, where my father's family, the Thompsons, lived, or the road ten miles east to Osmond, where my mother's family, the Haselhorsts, farmed. My parents, born fewer than twenty miles and twenty days apart (both of them in January 1917), met at a dance in one of the farming towns near Norfolk when they were nineteen. They mar-ried quickly at twenty-one, at the time the respectable thing to do with a baby on the way.

We children always argued for driving to Creighton, where cousins abounded. (My father and his nine siblings would go on to produce forty-four grand-children.) Most often, our plea to visit the Thompson cousins would win out, and because the hour was so late, we would spend the night in Creighton at

Figure 1. Marc, me, and Chantal, off to Oregon, July 1980

the house of Aunt Dorothy, my father's middle sister. She lived with Grandpa Thompson; her husband, Brad; and eventually their five children. No matter what time we arrived, the lights were on and the sink and the counter near the water pump were covered with dirty dishes. Montgomery Ward and Sears catalogs and coats and scarves and magazines spilled over in disarray from the table and chairs. Aunt Dorothy, who always wore a faded housedress with a slip hanging irregularly below its hem, was in sharp contrast to my mother, who knew exactly where a hem should hit on the knee or calf each season. At first I felt ill at ease, but a second look around Dorothy's kitchen often revealed a pan covered with a dishtowel on a chair. Cinnamon buns were rising. They would be ready, warm and yeasty and sweet for us in the morning.

Once breakfast was over, we would head along narrow country roads to see my favorite cousin, Rose Marie. Her father, Michael, my father's oldest brother, lived on a rented farm with his wife and their nine children. Rosie was the fifth born. As preadolescent girls, we had the freedom to make our own fun, running barefoot through the cornrows, although my tender city feet complained the minute I hit the first clod. We would coast down their lane on a bicycle until I felt moisture in the seat of my pants, terrified that there might be a link between that and frightful rumors of something called "a period." All the while, we were willing apprentices to her older sisters' knowledge of female culture. After noontime dinner, we girls would stay in the kitchen to do the dishes after heating water from the pump. Claire, the oldest, would wash, dipping the dishes of twelve people into a sudsy basin while Ellen Jean rinsed them in clear water and dried them with a patterned feed sack towel. One day, Margie, sitting at the table and reading the instructions on the back of a Toni Home Permanent kit, looked up and said to no one in particular, "Do you know that eating the pith of oranges will improve your complexion?"

What each town offered was of little concern to us as children. Osmond and Creighton in the 1940s (with populations of 800 and 1,300, respectively) were small compared to North Platte (a railroad town of 12,500), and the differences were writ large in the movie houses. North Platte boasted two sumptuously decorated theaters, the Paramount and the Fox, diagonally across the street from one another. The Paramount was finer, with ornate ceilings, a large lobby with a brightly lit concession counter, lush carpets, ushers who used flashlights to seat those arriving late, and a women's restroom with a bank of mirrors that always startled me when I saw myself reflected dozens of times. Kenny's Karamel Korn, tucked in next to the Paramount, was a child's dream, oozing an odor of caramel corn almost ready and displaying a heady array of candy bars, nuts, and soft drinks. One could buy a bag of caramel corn—sweet, sticky, and salty all at once—to take into the theater. In contrast, the movie house in Osmond would not have been distinguishable from the other one-story buildings on State Street except for its modest marquee. Showing films only on Wednesday and Saturday, which were shopping days for people from the surrounding farms, its interior was bare and unadorned.

There were other differences as well. Dominating the movie houses in North Platte was the eight-story Pawnee Hotel, the tallest building between Omaha and Denver, with a subtle marquee announcing the entrance to the White Horse Bar. A world away in Osmond was the pool hall, a low building with only a bar and several three-quarter-size billiard tables, where Grandpa Haselhorst lingered while Grandma saw a movie, commiserating with other farmers about the uncertainty of weather and crop prices. But the most striking difference between Creighton and Osmond was how quickly the streets in Osmond ended and cornfields rose up, making me fear that the land might swallow Grandpa's new Ford as we drove along the narrow country roads.

On the return trip to North Platte, our conversations eventually turned to how much better off we were than our relatives, particularly the Thompsons, who lived in what my father called "the rural ghetto." It wasn't just the visible differences between North Platte and home that gave him this perception; it was the lack of jobs for the generation leaving the farm and the ways dysfunction played out—anger, more children than financial or emotional resources could bear, barroom fights, and alcoholism.

"It must be tough," my father would begin, first reflecting on his sister Dorothy. "Brad is out of work again. Shirley told me Joe had to fire him from his construction crew. He just can't do the work; he's never learned how to work. And did you hear him defending Roosevelt? They're all after a handout."

"If that weren't enough," my mother said, "Dorothy is pregnant again. They're lucky to have Grandpa's Social Security check, small as it must be."

"And Dottie seems more nervous than ever," my father would continue. "Even though she has a college degree from the University of Wisconsin, she is totally ill equipped to care for those babies that seem to appear every year or so. You wonder what she was thinking when she married my brother Jim."

≪≪≪≫

Our close quarters during these car trips and our dim headlights that were often the only ones lighting the road set the stage for tales of education pursued and education denied, of survival through the agricultural busts and booms of the early twentieth century and the Great Depression. The narrative of education pursued was my father's: "When I finished eighth grade, in a one-room school-house about a mile from our farm, I was ready for high school, which meant St. Ludger's Academy in Creighton. My dad had to find a family in the parish where I could board; living eight miles from town, often on impassable roads, made that a must. The only possibility Father Windolpf could come up with was Annie Dowling's. Annie was a single woman who had adopted a son, Tommy, off one of the orphan trains from the East."

My father never told us who Annie was but explained that orphan trains transported children whose parents had died or couldn't take care of them from eastern cities to the Midwest, where they would work as extra hands on farms and other places where there were food and shelter. Notices would go up about the arrival of an orphan train, and on the expected day, families that needed labor would show up at a local church or the town hall. The available children, all decked out in new clothes and wearing nametags, would be introduced to the crowd. If one of them appealed to someone, the adult accompanying the child would arrange for the child's placement.

"You'd better behave, Mike," Dan always joked, "or we'll stop at the next station and put you on a train."

Our father would continue. "Annie's house was so small that she didn't have a place for me to sleep but said to my parents, 'If John needs a place to stay, and this is the only place you can afford, he can sleep in a tent in the backyard.'" He would then begin to sing "Oh Danny Boy," moving on to "I'll Take You Home Again, Kathleen," his tenor voice expressing nostalgia for an Irish immigrant's experiences he never knew, his ancestors having emigrated nearly a century earlier. While the light from the dashboard was too dim for me to see my father's face, his singing left me to imagine what it might have been like for a thirteen-year-old boy to be alone after dinner in a tent during Nebraska's cold winters. I was too afraid to ask if Annie ever let him sleep inside when the temperature went below zero. Was he allowed to stay in the house until bedtime?

There was also the story of education denied. When my father was about to graduate and he thought he'd be valedictorian of his class, Annie talked of moving to Austin, Texas, so that both he and Tommy could attend university. This dream was cut short when Annie died unexpectedly days before his graduation. He went back to working for a dollar a day on someone else's farm and eventually got a job teaching in a one-room schoolhouse.

My mother harbored a secret she believed too dangerous to tell her children on car trips, sharing it with me only in private once I was in first grade. She was twenty-seven at the time, and my brother Michael, born in March 1944, was sleeping in a bassinette nearby. My mother stood over the dining room table, carefully moving a pattern up, down, and sideways over a piece of plaid material, its wool soft to the touch. I sat at the table, worrying that she might not get the dress finished in time for my best friend's birthday party. "You've got to make sure the plaid matches at each seam. Otherwise, it looks like some amateur did it." Her perfection, most often pressing up against some deadline, paid off in clothes that made me feel almost as pretty as Shirley Temple, minus the ringlets—a houndstooth Chesterfield coat with a velvet collar, for instance, or a pale-blue polka-dotted dress with a sweetheart neck and three-tiered ruffled skirt. My brothers wore pint-sized men's wool suits she had tailored.

Looking up from the pattern, she said, "I'm going to tell you something, but you must promise not to tell anyone else." I nodded, not knowing what else to do. "I wanted to go to high school more than anything in the world. I loved school; I dreamed of being a scientist. I was the best student in my eighth-grade class." I looked at my mother, who seemed to have forgotten that she was talking to me. She looked down at the pattern again and stopped moving her hands. "Grandpa refused to let me go. No matter how much I argued with him, he wouldn't budge. A stubborn, bull-headed German, there was no changing his mind." She lowered her voice to mimic his. "'How do you think you're going to get into town every day, a twelve-mile trip along muddy roads in the spring and through blizzards in winter? There's no place for you to board in town, and besides, we can't afford it. Why does a girl need to go to school when she's just going to marry and be a farmer's wife?'" Almost whispering, she said, "I was never able to go to high school." Now, looking at me, she said, "That is why, when I first laid eyes on you, I said, 'This child is going to college.'"

I kept my promise never to tell anyone of her secret, knowing that her greatest disappointment contributed to a deep sense of inferiority. And although I didn't know what she, a woman who had never been on a college campus at the time of my birth, imagined the experience would be like for me, it became clear that going to college was something she imagined for herself. One of the first things she did in the late 1960s, after moving to California to be near her sons while her husband was in Vietnam, was to get her GED and two associate of arts degrees, one in waste management and the other in medical technology. When Chantal was born in 1969, attending classes trumped coming to Chicago for the birth. I felt resentment that I had no mother to advise me on the care of a newborn but admired her decision.

<center>~~~</center>

My parents' family stories on both sides were a narrative of factors beyond their control, although my mother's side believed hard work and persistence might make a difference. Their American story was laced with crop failures, uncertain weather, pests, and inflated—then depressed—farm real estate values. But theirs was also a story of single-mindedness: being a successful farmer mattered most; both husband and wife did whatever needed to be done. My mother's parents, Frank and Emma, were preceded by the generation that had emigrated from Germany, Czechoslovakia, and Switzerland in the 1870s and 1880s, seeking fertile farmland. As a young couple in the 1920s, my grandparents saved for a down payment on a farm and traveled around eastern Nebraska and South Dakota looking at properties, eventually buying a farm in Burke, South Dakota, at cripplingly high interest rates.

At first things went well; the drought ended briefly during the 1920s, crop yields were good and so, too, were prices for corn. But then the trouble began. South Dakota is known for grasshopper plagues, which have a cycle of about seven to ten years. "Oh, it was terrible," my mother would say. "We would be out in a field and suddenly the sky would darken, and huge swarms of grasshoppers would descend out of nowhere and devour everything." Her vivid description left me feeling hopeless. "And if that weren't enough, the drought returned. There was no rain for months. Dad would plant the crops and they would dry up before they had a chance to peek up above the ground. The fields had huge cracks in them, and because the soil was so dry, dust storms made visibility nearly impossible."

At this point, my father would add, "And then the bottom fell out of farm prices. If you had a good crop, you couldn't get anything for it. The value of farmland fell 30 to 40 percent." My mother would again pick up the narrative. "If it hadn't been for Mom's garden and her chickens with their eggs, we would have starved. She was able to sell eggs, as well as cream, to the hotel in town." They held on for eleven years but finally couldn't meet their payments; they lost their farm to foreclosure. "That was the only time I saw my father cry," she would add. It was hard to imagine Grandpa Haselhorst crying over anything.

Grandma was the one who took action. Fed up with their failures, she visited her relatives in Nebraska, near Osmond, and saw that farmers were doing much better there. She came back determined that they return to Nebraska. They did so in the fall of 1933, driving cattle and a team of horses pulling a hayrack and a wagon filled with furniture and personal belongings. "My dad drove our car, carefully planning and scouting the route. We camped out during our trek—a long week. We were most afraid of meeting up with gypsies." In the end, the Haselhorsts' story was one of success. Farm prices shot up with the increased demand for crops during World War II. While visiting in 1944, I woke up and looked out the window one night to see a dim light from my grandfather's tractor moving up and down the cornfield.

On my father's maternal side, the Boyles, my great-great-grandfather, Charles Boyle, was among the sixty or so settlers who left Dubuque, Iowa, in 1856 to establish the first Catholic parish in Nebraska. Mostly Irish immigrants, the colony was led by Father Jeremiah Trecy and settled one mile north of Jackson, Nebraska. By 1858, its population had grown to nearly two hundred. In 1860, Trecy went to Washington to seek permission to establish a mission among the Ponca Indians, but once the Civil War began, he became an army chaplain and never returned to the colony. Had he come back, it is uncertain what he would have found; the original settlers eventually became dissatisfied with the location because of flooding, and its gradual depopulation continued until every resident had moved away.

Andrew Thompson, my great-grandfather, had made his way west from his birthplace in New York State, first to Wisconsin and then to Nebraska in 1874. His Civil War records show that he was twice wounded while serving with the Wisconsin Iron Brigade. Andrew's westward movements seemed not to have translated into material success for future generations.

In the early 1900s, my paternal grandparents, George and Mabel Boyle Thompson, farmed land owned by others, with Grandpa taking the odd job breaking prairie for someone else. His oldest daughter, Leona, in a handwritten account (my extended family's first memoir), observed, "Families like ours rented and gave a share of the crop as rent. I do not recall any stigma attached to that method, but sharecropping was what it was, if not in name, then in deed." At Grandma Thompson's urging—she kept insisting they should get a farm of their own—they bought a relinquishment, a homestead in eastern Nebraska that the previous owner had given up, and met the requirements of the Homestead Act: living on the land for four years (1912–1916) and building a tiny house, fourteen by twenty-eight feet. They never made a profit; the soil was sandy and unsuitable for farming. Over time, the reality of their isolation seeped in. There were neither roads to their homestead nor fences marking their property. It was twenty miles to the nearest train; they never were able to attend Mass. The most telling evidence of the absence of community was that Grandpa delivered the two children born during those years.

The greatest motivation for leaving their homestead was that the local school was open only three months a year and their children, now numbering six, weren't getting any religious instruction. So they loaded all their worldly goods on a hay wagon and moved to Creighton. These choices and the values underlying them fed the Boyles' and Thompsons' aura of certainty and superiority. What mattered most was that you were smart, able to cut someone down with your quick wit or a cutting remark. They were educated for their time and place—all their children, except for Leona, completed high school, a distinction few other families in the community achieved.

There were lessons for me in the difference between how each branch of my family weathered hard times. From the Haselhorsts, I learned single-mindedness, persistence, and that success wasn't something ethereal—it was bushel yields, prices paid, chicks hatched each spring, and jars of vegetables and fruit canned. From the Thompsons, I learned that being smart was best and to care about things larger than yourself. From both, I inherited a combination of values deeply internalized, values that would serve me well over time. One of those values, mostly unconscious, was that strong women could take the initiative and argue for decisions that benefited their families.

Even though we saw ourselves as much better off than our relatives, the recession of 1948 and our economic insecurity pushed my parents in a new way to leave home. Moving to California, as many Nebraskans did at that time, was out of the question. Despite my parent's dysfunction—my father's binge drinking from time to time when he "fell off the wagon" and my mother's debilitating "nerves"—they construed California as the place that only failures chose. My parents knew they could endure hardship and were sensible, with both feet on the ground and no need for psychiatrists. Unlike Californians, who ate only salads for dinner, we had well-balanced meals: meat, potatoes, a vegetable, and always a salad and a homemade dessert. My father had utter disdain for, as he said, "people who work up a false appetite by having a cocktail before dinner."

But these feelings of superiority and disdain didn't alleviate the financial uncertainty of selling automotive parts in western Nebraska. My father sought and found financial security by enlisting in the United States Army, believing, as he signed his enlistment papers and shook the recruiting sergeant's hand, that he had been accepted into Officer's Candidate School (OCS) at Fort Riley, Kansas. Secure in how well he had tested ("My score on the army's intelligence test was well above the ninety-fifth percentile"), he now saw a path to some security, a chance for advancement, and retirement benefits. I never learned specifically why things didn't work out but did overhear a conversation my father had with a friend who was in OCS: when he had reported for training, my father was informed that he did not meet the age requirement, being too old by several months. Instead of a career as an officer, he would be Sergeant Thompson during the twenty-five years he served.

In the late summer of 1948, we moved from Nebraska for the first time, believing we would someday return to the place where we had roots. And return we

did over the years, to our house on West Fourth Street in North Platte, a rental
when we were away but our home nonetheless. Our departures and returns were
a microcosm of U.S. military engagements and how they shaped one soldier's
assignments:

1949–1950: Fort Riley, Kansas
1950–1952: Korea; wife and children in Manhattan, Kansas
1952–1956: North Platte, recruiting duty
1956–1959: Germany; wife and children there for two of those years
1959–1967: North Platte, recruiting duty
1968–1969: Saigon, recruiting duty; wife and sister Peggy in California
1969–1971: Madison, Wisconsin, recruiting duty
1971: Lincoln, Nebraska, to retire

How did this leaving and returning contribute to me becoming me? Despite
my parents' thinking of us as middle class, socioeconomic differences were writ
large in the military. Once in the army, there were people around us unlike any
we had known: Southerners who "talked funny" and men who kept a baseball
cap on while they ate dinner. These strangers, with their unrefined behaviors, fed
our belief that we were somehow apart, especially from enlisted men and their
families.

In the spring of 1950, we were assigned housing at Fort Riley. "Finally, we'll
have enough bedrooms for everyone," my mother said. When I first ascended the
stairs to our second-story apartment, carved out of renovated World War II bar-
racks, I imagined soldiers' combat boots moving up the narrow wooden stairs.
But once inside, the space was sunny, if sterile. My mother had ways of making this space more familiar: in our picture window, she centered a lamp with
the silk shade she had made; the matching couch and chair, with doilies to protect the arms and back cushions, and a copy of a still life by Max Streckenbach
were the things of home. She "settled" the kitchen first and made our favorite
comfort foods: roast beef, fried chicken, and pork chops. The first night or two,
we would have to eat ice cream, dour looks on our faces. It would be a few days
before she had the time to make a lemon meringue pie or devil's food cake.

For the first time, I attended a public school, Fort Riley Elementary School on
the main post. Riding the bus for forty-five minutes each way from Camp For-
syth, the outpost where we lived, I looked around for another sixth-grade girl. No
one; there was no Kay Rodney or Judy Hansen to walk the mile to school with as
we had done in North Platte, gossiping along the way. Even the new schoolhouse
seemed strange: a one-story white-frame building with a cupola and a bell that
rang to call us into class, looking as ancient as the schoolhouse on the cover of
the *Saturday Evening Post*, which my father read from cover to cover the day it
arrived. The building sat out in the open, unprotected by trees and looking alone,

forlorn. A ravine, wooded and dark, sloped down from the back of the building. I longed for the three-story brick building that housed all twelve grades at St. Patrick's School in North Platte, a sturdy fortress with a basement where, some Friday afternoons, we children and the nuns watched religious movies—*The Song of Bernadette, Our Lady of Guadalupe*—and Shirley Temple films. I missed the traffic noise from East Fourth Street that came through our classroom windows in the spring.

Now, instead of a crucifix hanging high above the blackboard at the front of the classroom, there was only a large American flag off to one side. There were no prayers at the beginning of class, only a standing recitation of the Pledge of Allegiance first thing in the morning. Watching my teacher, Mrs. Brown, was like watching a Technicolor movie: bright henna hair, dark-red lipstick, polished nails, and suits offset by brightly colored blouses. No more black and white nuns' habits.

Sitting in my new classroom, I felt self-conscious, wondering if I'd ever have a friend again. But miraculously, I began exchanging looks with the most interesting girl in the class, Martha Seitz, who sat close by, off to one side. Every time one of the boys said something foolish, she'd look at me. Martha was attractive; her dark-brown hair in a classic pageboy with straight bangs cut just above her eyebrows was offset by luminescent white skin. She was the friend I wanted.

One day, when the bell rang for lunch, Martha approached me and said, "Let's go eat on the back steps." There, with the warm Kansas sun on our faces, we opened our lunch bags. When I saw that Martha had only a peanut butter and jelly sandwich and an apple, I offered her one of my chocolate chip cookies. The lunch my mother had packed—a roast beef sandwich with lettuce and mayonnaise, potato chips, celery sticks, cookies, and a pear—was abundant in contrast.

"Thanks," Martha said, accepting the cookie. "I can think of ten places I'd rather be than cooped up in Mrs. Brown's class."

"Like exploring the ravine down there," I said, pointing to the wooded land that sloped away from the back steps.

"Or reading what I want to—my favorite book, *Anne of Green Gables*," Martha said.

"Anne of what? I've never heard of that book."

"Oh, no. You must read it. I have two copies. I'll bring one for you tomorrow."

"Did you ever read the Mary Rose books?" I asked.

"Never heard of them," Martha said.

I'd read the Mary Rose series in fourth grade, the year I read more books than anyone in class. Once I had finished an assignment, Sister Rebecca would let me go to the narrow cupboard tucked into one wall of the classroom and take down one of the books in the twenty-volume series. Within the dark-red hardcovers of each book was the life of a girl such as me—Catholic, the oldest in a large family; the girl I aspired to be, obedient and pious; or the woman I imagined becoming, the mother of a large and loving Catholic family. I owned only one book of my own: *Alice in Wonderland*, the tale of a strange girl who kept falling into holes. *What was the point of such a gift?* I thought when I unwrapped it on Christmas Eve. Once I read the book, it would just sit on a shelf.

But *Anne of Green Gables* was different. Two weeks later I returned Martha's copy. "I finished it. I loved it," I said. "And guess what? My mother said that you could sleep over at my house Friday night. Do you think your mother will let you come?"

The next Friday evening, once we'd finished a large slice of my mother's chocolate cake, we went to my room. Sitting on the single bed, we talked about Anne's life—Anne, whom we now called Annie as though she were real. "Wasn't it terrible when she became an orphan and was sent by mistake to a farm on Prince Edward Island?"

"Scary. Sometimes I hate my father, and of course my brother," Martha said, "but I'd feel alone if I were an orphan. What helped save her was her best friend Diana."

"Every girl needs a best friend." We both laughed.

"You know what I hated? I hated the way Diana liked boys, especially that awful Gilbert Blythe."

"Yeah, he was as dumb as the boys in our class. But Annie was smart. She even did better than Gilbert, the teacher's pet, in exams sometimes." The more Martha and I talked about the book, the more we became Annie. She was strong and opinionated like us. Annie was our age, but more importantly, she was a girl with a sense of her own strength, her own empowerment. She, like us, believed she could do anything.

A week or so later, Martha passed me a note in class: "My mother said you could sleep over next Friday night. The only thing I have to do is go riding with my father Saturday morning at the stables on the post. Have you ever ridden horses?" The thought of riding a horse made me nervous, but I wasn't going to let that get in the way of sleeping over at Martha's.

As my father drove me to Martha's, he said, "She must be Colonel Seitz's daughter. He's the commander of the Fifth Infantry Battalion, had a distinguished record during World War II, and helped liberate Buchenwald." The tone of my father's voice suggested that being a colonel was better than being a sergeant. As we entered the section of housing for officers' dependents on the main post, I clutched the paper with the number for her house in my hands—7 Shofield Circle—and, looking up, saw that we were already on her street. "I think her house should be about two more blocks," I said. My father had a terrible sense of direction and became furious when he got lost, usually blaming my mother. Since she wasn't with us, I knew I was closest to his line of fire. I looked up and saw huge elm trees and large, two-story limestone homes with wraparound porches set back from the street.

Martha's mother answered the door, looking just like her daughter only older. "Come in, come in," she said. "Sergeant Thompson," my father said, holding out his hand. Once inside the front door, I saw a wide-open hallway with a stairway going up to a second floor. There was a rack for hanging coats, a chest with a bouquet of fresh flowers, and on the floor, a rug of faded beige and maroon and green colors. The portrait of a stern soldier looked down upon us. There were large rooms off to each side—a living room with books stacked on every table and a dining room with a large table and upholstered chairs. I began to feel embarrassed as I heard my father say, "Yes ma'am, yes ma'am." He sounded like one of those Southern sergeants my mother looked down on.

"Let's go up to my room," Martha said. As we ascended the stairs, an older boy ran down, glancing at Martha and saying, "Stupid."

"Who was that?"

"My brother, who thinks he's God."

When Martha and I dressed for riding on Saturday morning, I put on my jeans, my new short-sleeved plaid shirt, and brown loafers. I began to feel insecure as I watched Martha put on jodhpurs and a black velvet jacket and tuck the traditional black riding hat under her arm. We sat in the back seat of her father's car as he drove to the stables that, once inside, revealed a cavernous space. Along the perimeter was a track with one lonely rider bouncing up and down as her horse trotted at a slow speed. Martha's father looked at us and said to me, "Stay here. Have you ever ridden a horse before?"

"I haven't," I said weakly, feeling I had somehow failed him. In a few minutes, he returned, leading a horse in each hand. "Here, sweetie," he said to Martha. "I was able to get your favorite. And the other should do for someone who has never ridden a horse before. Now, come around to the left side of the horse," he told me. "Careful you don't get too close to her back legs, or she'll kick." I felt any self-confidence drain from my body as I imagined a horse's hoof in my stomach.

"Now put your left foot in the stirrup, and throw your right leg over the saddle."

How was I ever going to get my leg up over an animal that towered over my head? It took six tries before I was in the saddle. With each of my attempts, the face of Martha's father turned a deeper shade of red. I had never had anyone look at me with such disgust. Once Martha saw I was on my horse, she clutched her reins and galloped around the track. Her father and I looked at one another through her dust.

When I got home, my mother asked, "How was your time at Martha's?"

"You won't believe what her mother served us for lunch. Nothing but a peanut butter and jelly sandwich."

"That's all? No vegetables or fruit?"

"Nothing. Only a glass of milk."

I didn't tell my parents about horseback riding; I was afraid it might hurt their feelings.

Figure 2. Thompson family photo, December 1959

Did leaving Nebraska and living on an army post, the only place where the designation "army brat" and my father's rank were felt, matter to me becoming me? For the first time, I sensed a difference between a friend's social class and mine, a difference unknown at St. Patrick's School in North Platte. My mother's admonition not to tell anyone about her lack of education began a pattern of being selective about what I told friends such as Martha. Were the costs of such a reserve, clear in hindsight, higher than those of staying in Nebraska? If my cousin Rosie's family was any gauge, the costs of staying were high. Her oldest brother, Philip, died young of alcoholism, and a younger brother, George Michael, committed suicide.

Living in Germany nearly a decade later would matter much more. For me, it would be a defining experience. My siblings also each have a story of how they benefited from leaving Nebraska and how they especially benefited from attending a school for military dependents in Germany. Dan discovered aeronautical engineering; Mike gained a foundation in photography that led to success in that profession; and Patty, who renamed herself Trish, learned that she had artistic talent. Peggy, who was eight when we arrived in Germany, attributes her careers in the helping professions of alcohol counseling and, eventually, school psychology to her position in a mildly dysfunctional family rather than schooling.

CHAPTER 3

NESTLED IN THE BOSOM
OF CATHOLICISM

North Platte's Catholic parish, St. Patrick's, which we attended until I was eleven (and returned to when I was fourteen) was our world—church, school, friends, the Knights of Columbus for men, the altar society for women, and the Catholic Youth Organization for children. Being Catholic defined our family, even though Catholics were less than 20 percent of the population in the 1940s and 1950s in Nebraska, a predominately Protestant state. We were secure, however, knowing that we belonged to the one true Church; church doctrine affirmed our sense of superiority. Pope Pius XII's encyclical "Mystici Corporis Christi" (1943) asserted that the mystical body of Christ and the Roman Catholic Church were the same thing. There was no salvation outside the Church.

Rituals marked our growing up: first confession and communion at seven ("the age of reason") and confirmation at eleven. We began each school day attending Mass and receiving Holy Communion. Rows of children filled the pews. If you sneaked a glance backward, you could see the nuns interspersed among the children, including Sister Juliana with her combined first- and second-grade class of sixty children. She carried a small noisemaker in her pocket, a "cricket," that she would press—one chirp to kneel, two to sit, or three to stand. Sister Thomasine and the third graders followed, and so on, all the way through to the high schoolers, with girls singing a Requiem Mass for the dead in the choir loft most mornings.[1] Altar boys of various ages assisted the priest.

The nuns' white coifs were tight around their faces, revealing only eyebrows, eyes, nose, mouth, and chin. Their starched white wimples formed a sort of dome that held their black veils. Communicating with their God, they looked composed until one of the children committed an infraction—talked to her partner, slumped on the pew, dozed off. Suddenly, the sister was all presence, scowling at the child, snapping a finger. Occasionally, a wisp of hair would escape at the edge of a coif. We would look away, embarrassed by this hint of humanness.

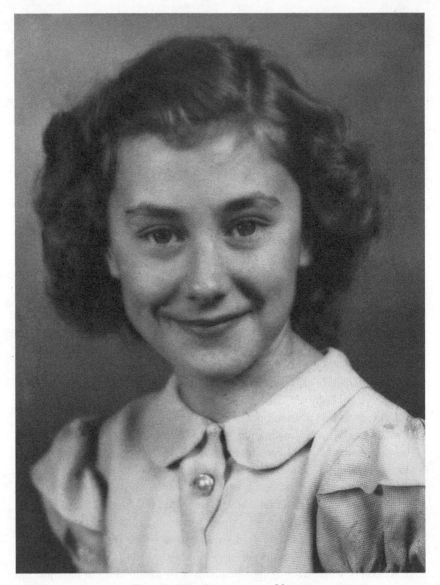

Figure 3. Mary Kay, ten years old, 1948

Our first class of the day was religion. Each year we read the Baltimore Cate-chism, a paperback with a green cover about the size of a *Reader's Digest*. It began:

Why did God make you?

He made me to know Him, to love Him, and to serve Him in this world, and to be happy with Him forever in heaven.

Before we began any assignment, we wrote "J.M.J." at the top of the paper, for Jesus, Mary, and Joseph. We wore our religion on our bodies: Miraculous or St. Christopher medals were cold against my chest until they warmed up. Holy cards showing the Sacred Heart, the Blessed Virgin Mary, or saints in the ecstasy of their adoration kept the places in our textbooks. It gave me comfort to know I had a personal God to whom I could tell my troubles or ask for special favors. My guardian angel was always with me, an assurance against harm.

St. Patrick's was a mission church of Ireland, and the priests from my child-hood and adolescence were both Irish, first Father McDaid and later Monsignor Murray. Both spoke with a brogue. "Now what have ye been doing to get such paar grades?" Father McDaid would ask Fritz Dodson, when he came to our class to distribute report cards. "Young people must resist the sin of farnication," Monsignor Murray would intone during one of his sermons. If your last name was Fitzpatrick or Doyle, the priests gave you a special smile, a pat on the head. My surname was never Irish enough to get such treatment. The fact that my paternal grandmother was a Boyle was lost.

Despite being an Irish mission church, we students were profoundly ignorant of any aspect of modern Ireland. In high school, during the formation of politi-cal parties for Cornhusker Boys' and Girls' County Government Day, my party struggled to find a name. Eventually we turned to Sister Berenice, a diminutive and soft-spoken nun. She looked out innocently, face framed by her starched, white wimple, and asked, "Why not use Sinn Féin?"[2] "Shin fain, shin fain," we repeated, oblivious to Sister Berenice's radical politics. Soon, signs urging sup-port for Sinn Féin's candidates were posted throughout the school. I chose the image of a cheerleader's megaphone that blared, "Hey, hey, what do you say? Let's all vote for Mary Kay! Sinn Féin's choice for County Surveyor."

We were quietly taught the dangers of sexuality, first by nuns and later by priests. The commandment that trumped all others was the sixth: "Thou shall not commit adultery." Sister Casimir was particularly obsessed with that one. She would cast her eyes heavenward and flutter them as she warned, "The near occa-sion of sin is everywhere. God sees everything you do." She then spun out stories of saints who had resisted sexual temptation. Was this different than stories that were whispered about uncles and aunts who "could not control their feelings"? Was my mother one of those people? I became suspicious, counting the months on my fingers between the date of her wedding, February 27, and my birth, Octo-ber 27. Didn't it take nine months for a baby to be born?

"I'm an illegitimate child," I told my mother, with the certainty of half knowledge.

"No you're not!" she scoffed. "Your parents are married. What kind of non-sense are those priests and nuns putting in your head?" From that moment on, I suspected that my mother was not truly religious. How could she be if she had committed "farnication"?

When my father left for Korea in the fall of 1950, we no longer qualified for dependent housing at Fort Riley. My parents decided that we should live in Manhattan, Kansas, where there was a Catholic school. I had turned twelve that year, and during the long evenings when my mother and I were alone, after the kids were in bed, she taught me to play canasta. I listened to my mother describe the rules, but I had other things on my mind.

"I'm not going to get my period," I said.

She laughed. "You certainly are."

A few nights later, I was standing in the kitchen after we put the canasta cards away and said, "I'm not going to get my period." She walked right up to me, came close to my face, and said, "I'm tired of hearing you say that. I don't want you to say it again." There was something frightening in her response, an anger I hadn't seen before. I backed up.

"I'm not, I'm not," I said, "I'm not going to get my period." I began taking steps backward; she kept walking toward me.

We kept up this dance as I backed into the makeshift bathroom installed in our basement apartment, the shower drain flush to the floor and the flimsy shower curtain pushed aside. Right as I said "No I'm not," I fell backward into a basin of cold water, the baby bath left over from my sister Peggy that morning. I gasped at the cold water that hit my back, at falling backward, at being prostrate before my mother. "I'm not," I sputtered. The shock of the water couldn't dampen my resistance to becoming a woman. Now I wonder if I subconsciously wanted to escape my mother's life.

At that time, my mother was living alone with her five children, ages twelve years old to barely one, while her husband was in Korea. Despite this, she asked little of me. Doing housework on Saturday mornings was her only expectation. I never cooked and can't remember ever changing a diaper. Did she free me from those obligations because she wanted me to have the friendships and activities she had been denied because she was unable to attend high school?

If my behavior was any indication, I showed little enthusiasm for women's traditional roles. I hated housework. When I was in junior high, each Saturday morning I would ask my mother, "What do I have to do before I can go meet my friends?"

She replied, "I can't tell you. Let's just work until the work is done." I would look around our cluttered living room and feel utter defeat.

"Just tell me what to do. Why don't you make a list of what needs to be done and give jobs to the boys and me?" It was ten o'clock in the morning, and they were still in their pajamas. "If you won't do it, I'll make up a list and assign jobs." Defiant looks passed over the faces of my brothers, aged ten and seven, at the slightest hint of any direction from me. None of the men who later reported to me were ever as resistant.

I couldn't wait to get out of the house to meet my friends. We were brought together by a sports-centered culture. The summer after seventh grade, my best friend came by on her bicycle every day at half-past noon, and we'd pump our way to the community pool (which, in Manhattan, was sadly for white people only), making sure we were in line the minute it opened at one. We were serious about swimming, taking a junior lifesaving class and practicing our dives and strokes for the annual swim meet. Once the swimming pool closed in the fall, however, basketball permeated the very air we breathed and bound us together. We played "H-O-R-S-E" for hours; I aspired to be one of the Harlem Globetrotters. The Kansas State University Wildcats had made it to the Final Four in 1948 and would do so again in 1951. While tickets to football and basketball games were usually scarce, we always had them, since Anne, the daughter of the university's athletic director, was in our friend group. A framed *Saturday Evening Post* article featuring Anne's father, Larry "Moon" Mullins, who had played football at Notre Dame in the 1930s, hung prominently on a bedroom wall in their house.

Figure 4. Junior class officers, St. Patrick's High School, 1955. Seated: Secretary, Mary Kay Thompson; President, Dean Arensdorf. Standing: Treasurer, Larry Drost; Vice President, Mike Fitzpatrick.

When I was fourteen and a freshman in high school, I had not yet heard Freud's saying "Love and work, work and love, that's all there is." Yet my desire for both resided within me as a muddled stew. I imagined that I would leave college after a couple of years to meet my generation's expectations that women marry, stay at home, and raise children. But I harbored a desire, mostly unconscious, to achieve other things—things that only fed my ambition to excel. A picture in our junior yearbook of the class officers, three boys and me, foreshadowed where my ambition would place me: often as the lone female at the table.[3]

My "credits" in our senior yearbook, with numbers referring to the year in high school, read as follows: Sodality 1,2,3,4 (Prefect 4);[4] 1, 2, 3, 4; Cheerleader 3, 4; Class Secretary 2, 3; Class Play 4; Homecoming Attendant 4; Lettermen's Sweetheart Attendant 2; Orchestra 2, 3; State Music Contest 2, 3, 4; County Government 3; Diocesan Oratorical Contest 3, 4; Annual Staff 4.

Success in swimming also fed my desire to excel. There were several activities for me to join at the North Platte Municipal Swimming Pool, including diving, lifesaving classes, and water ballet. Before the annual swim meet, which was held in late August, I toyed with the idea of entering the diving competition. Afraid of the answer, I asked the head lifeguard, "How many dives do I need to compete?" I barely qualified for the three dives requirement. Though unable to master a flip, from the three-meter board I had been practicing a front dive, a jackknife, and a cutaway, which was a backward jackknife. By the time the diving competition began, it was dark. I decided to do my most polished dive, a jackknife, first. I stood perfectly still midway up the three-meter board, took the required three steps, flew through the air, and shot down into the water. I pushed myself off the bottom of the pool, came to the surface, and looked up at the judges' cards: 9, 9, 8. A nearly perfect score! My next two dives were also highly ranked. That night at the Third Annual North Platte Swimming Meet, I took first place in the Senior Division Girls' Diving. But it wasn't only achievement I had on my mind—I was about to embark on my first foray into love.

Earlier that day, a boy I had recently met was standing outside the pool's high fence beckoning to me. Tom Austin, two years older than me, was nearly six feet tall, with well-developed shoulders, dark, curly hair, and a broad, handsome face set off by a cleft chin. I was a little worried that he might be "rough." He was, after all, from the public high school, drove his own car, and had a friend, Frank, who was a boy of mixed race, Asian and white.

"Hi," Tom said with a smile that sent a funny feeling to my stomach. "I'm coming to watch the meet tonight. Can I give you a ride home?"

"Sure," I said, trying to look calm and nonchalant.

When the meet was over, I got dressed and walked outside the pool to see Tom and his friend waiting for me. Tom put his arm around my shoulder and said, "Way to go. First place! I'm going to give Frank a ride to the Tastee Freeze, and then I'll take you home." I sat between him and his friend in the front seat, feeling the heat from Tom's body.

When Frank got out of the car, Tom said, "Want something to eat?"

"I'm not hungry," I said, and I stayed close to him in the middle space.

"Good, let's go for a ride."

Tom drove out west of town along the irrigation ditch. When we came to a grove of trees with a clearing large enough to park a car, he pulled in, turned off the ignition, put his arms around me to draw me close, and kissed me—a kiss that felt like the most natural, warm, deeply satisfying, connected thing in the world.

"Your hair is like silk," Tom said, putting his fingers on the back of my head.

"Corn silk," I whispered.

"No, no, the softest silk in the world." I felt his warm breath against my ear.

When Tom walked me to the front door, I believed I had it all: a boyfriend and a blue ribbon. My scrapbook records the dates—probably exaggerated—of our relationship: August–October 1953 and August–December 1954. The reason for the break in dates was his family's move to Missoula, Montana, and later to San Luis Obispo, California, during Tom's senior year. He revealed nothing important about himself—that his father was an alcoholic, what it was like to be "new" in his senior year—only how remarkable it was that he was recruited for the basketball team in Missoula when he'd never played before. When Tom and his family returned to North Platte less than a year later, he was different—worldlier and not so interested in me. In subtle ways, he let me know that he didn't have time for a Catholic virgin, that girls could be found who weren't so rigid. I justified my loss and grief by reminding myself that I couldn't marry a Protestant anyway.

But I hadn't just been grieving over Tom's absence the year he was away. Bob Mueller, a senior and the captain of the basketball team, his blond crew cut and perfectly formed white teeth adding to his allure, called me for a movie date in January 1954. Within a week, we were going steady. My election to the Lettermen's Sweetheart Court, a reign lasting three hours at the school's Valentine's Day dance, and my wearing of his senior ring (kept snug on my wedding ring finger by tiny strips of adhesive tape, carefully put on layer by layer) were an affirmation of my success as the girlfriend of a popular athlete.

Six weeks later, Bob pulled his 1948 pickup up in front of a seedy, dimly lit neighborhood grocery that had the advantage of being within sight of my front door yet still out of sight of a father who might come onto the front porch for a smoke. Instead of embracing me as he usually did, he tugged at his class ring, saying, "I need my ring back." Was there another girl? Had I done something wrong? Was I suddenly unattractive? I asked for no explanation, and he gave none.

The answer came several days later in the girls' restroom, as I was standing at the sink washing my hands. The sun shone brightly through the octagonal wire mesh encased between the window's inner and outer glass. A classmate, Judy Hansen, walked up close to me and said, "I know what happened with you and Bob Mueller. He is thinking about going to the seminary and talked to Father Courtney. Father told him he should date someone to see if he had a vocation to be a priest. Together they decided you would be 'the girl.'" A look of pleasure crossed Judy's face.

My feelings of being used and publicly humiliated kept me from talking about what happened with anyone, including my best friend, my mother, or even the beloved young curate who seemed to like me. How could Father Courtney have betrayed me so? Nor did it even occur to me to ask Bob for an explanation. As was the case in my relationship with Tom Austin, Bob and I never talked about anything of importance. It might have been less heartbreaking if he had told me, as he was pulling his ring off my finger, of his vocation. It was unthinkable that a Catholic girl would attempt to stand in the way of a young man's call to the priesthood; I would have understood. Instead, I was left to wonder. Bob turned up in my life more than six years later, but even then, I didn't ask him about what he was thinking at the time of our teenage breakup. These silences seem now to be emblematic of many aspects of gender relations in the 1950s.

Once we were teenagers, our local nuns and priests fell silent about the dangers of sex. Instead, the out-of-town priests who led our yearly three-day religious retreats were the ones who talked to us. The retreat my sophomore year, with its imposed silence and utterly boring theme, "Where will your soul be a thousand years from now?" was halfway over when Kathy Swanson whispered to me, "You won't believe what Joan just told me in the hallway." Joan was Kathy's older sister, a senior, who had a steady boyfriend.

Later, I met Kathy outside the church. "So, what did Joan say?" I asked.

"I can't tell you. She swore me to secrecy. Father Boudern, the retreat master, a Jesuit from Creighton University, swore them to secrecy. But he's supposed to come back for our retreat next year, and he will tell us then what he told them this year."

What can be so terrible that you can't talk about it? I wondered. *Could it be about the secret of Fatima?* The secret of Fatima was supposed to be revealed in 1960. *By that time,* I thought, *I'll be twenty-two. Will that be the end of my life, martyred, tortured by Russians, my children ripped from my arms?*

The next year at our retreat, we were ushered into the sacristy on the last day. Neither I nor the other girls had been there before because we could not be altar boys. It was surprisingly sparse and cool. The sun reflected off the stucco walls. Father Boudern stood at the front of the room wearing a close-fitting black cassock. He looked very old to me. "Sit down on the floor. There isn't room here for each of you to have a chair." We looked up at him, scarves covering our heads.

"It won't be long until many of you enter into the holy sacrament of marriage. It is time you knew about the pleasures of that holy sacrament." I swallowed.

Father continued. "I am friendly with a married couple, a couple who were united in the holy sacrament of matrimony more than twenty years ago. Theirs is a marriage of connection, of communication through touch, touch of their most tender parts." He paused and looked at us. "Sexual joy. Intercourse and what precedes it is their vehicle for mutual pleasure."

There was silence in the sacristy. "In the afterglow of that holy act, in their nakedness, they achieve a level of togetherness that parallels that of Christ and his Church. With her head resting on his stomach, they connect in a way that is only possible in the holy sacrament of marriage." Virgins (well, mostly—one girl would marry a month before graduation because she was pregnant), we had little knowledge of our own bodies and even less of the male one. Father Boudern continued with other images of the couple in their postcoital bliss as my mind shut down.

Minutes later, I heard him say, "And now let me give you my blessing for a long and satisfying marriage." His eyes swept along the cluster of silent girls. "Remember—you are not to tell anyone of our talk, to discuss it with anyone. It is yours to think about and use once you are married. Let us pray to the Blessed Virgin. Hail Mary, full of grace . . ." We took his demand for secrecy so seriously that we did not discuss it with one another.

My choices for college were limited. In the mid-1950s, the bishop of the Grand Island Diocese wrote a letter, read from the pulpit, decreeing that if parents sent

Figure 5. Capturing female friendships before high school graduation, 1956. Back Row: Ann Still, Judy Hansen, Diane Ericksen, Kathy Swanson, Willa Jean Pease; Second Row: Kay Rodney, Mary Anne Broderson, Barbara Fitzpatrick, Phyllis McGrane, Joan Gannon; Front Row: Patricia Mady, Kathleen Clinch, Mary Kay Thompson.

their children to a non-Catholic university, they would be excommunicated. I did not find this troubling, as I aspired to attend a Catholic school anyway. (The bishop's threat was long forgotten a decade later, when my sisters Trish and Peggy attended the University of Nebraska, a public, non-Catholic university.) A chance conversation with a boy I met at a diocesan oratorical contest presented a possibility when, in the midst of telling me how he had been bored with school but into sports, he mentioned that the best thing had been his acceptance to St. Benedict's College, in Atchison, Kansas. "There's a woman's college there, Mount St. Scholastica. It has a great reputation. You should think about going there."

"I'm certainly going to college, but I haven't decided where. One thing's for sure, it will be Catholic. But a women's college? I don't know."

"Oh, don't worry about that," he replied. "The Mount and St. Benedicts do everything together. There are tons of mixers and sports events. All on weekends mostly. Classes are separate."

I applied only to the Mount after his ringing endorsement. I was awarded a full-tuition scholarship of two hundred dollars per semester. To keep it, I just needed to maintain a B average.

Midway through our senior year in high school, Judy Hansen proposed that she and Barbara Fitzpatrick host a slumber party before we graduated and went our separate ways. Avid horsewomen, Judy and Barbara groomed horses for a local rancher in exchange for the opportunity to ride regularly. "Mr. Kanealey is usually in Arizona this time of year, so we can use his house for a night, and I'll get my mother to chaperone."

On the appointed night, Judy chauffeured me and four other friends to the ranch, east of town. Just as we were about to turn onto Route 30, Kathy said, "Wait a minute. We don't have anything to drink."

"Does Mr. Kanealey have any booze we could use? You know, and then we'll add water to the bottles to cover up what we take?" I asked.

"No way," Judy said. "He's doing us a favor to give us his house, and Barbara and I can't risk making him mad. He might take away our riding privileges."

"What are we going to do now? We can't go into a liquor store. We're not even close to twenty-one," Kathy said.

"Who looks the oldest?" Everyone looked at Willa Jean, a buxom girl with glasses who always wore loose-fitting clothes. "Willa," we said in unison.

"Maybe I do look the oldest," she said, "but how am I going to carry this off?"

"I know what you can do to look older—turn your class ring around, so the clerk will think you're married." Laughter filled the car.

Judy pulled the car into the parking lot in front of a liquor store. "OK, everybody needs to give me a dollar." She handed the money to Willa. "Just go into the liquor store, pick up a bottle of Jim Beam, and put down your money." We laughed with a nervous sense of anticipation as Willa left the car and opened the door to the store. We could see her talking with a clerk. Within minutes, she was back empty handed. "That damned salesman looked at me and said, 'Where's your ID, little girl?'"

There were murmurs of "Damn. Now what do we do?"

"Wait a minute," I said. "Cliff—isn't he the guy who buys liquor for the boys? Maybe he'd buy some for us. Fritz said he was an alcoholic, but if he's drunk he couldn't harm us. Besides, there are six of us."

"My dad knows him," Mary Anne Broderson said. "I think he lives above the Platte Storage something-or-other. You know, on Chestnut Street. Let's go find him." Judy drove slowly down Chestnut Street. Tall streetlights cast a weak illumination on each corner. "There it is," Mary Anne said as we approached a large, darkened building. There were no lights on downstairs, but I could see some on the second floor.

"OK. Who is going to go?" Judy asked. "You, Thompson—you were the one with this bright idea."

"I'll go if Barbara and Mary Anne come with me." I looked up to the second story window and continued, "Uncle Cliff, we're coming for you." We walked up to the door, giggling to hide our nervousness as we tiptoed up the dimly lit stairs. There were five doors, a light coming from one that was slightly ajar. I knocked weakly, and a male voice said, "Who's there?"

Before we could answer, a man dressed in a sleeveless undershirt that revealed the sagging flesh of his exposed arms appeared at the door. "What do you want?" He had no teeth.

"Are you Cliff?" Mary Anne asked.

Slurring his words, he said, "I sure as hell am," weaving even though his hands were on either side of the doorframe.

"We're on our way to a party and don't have any bourbon," Barbara said.

"Well, goddamn, that's not a problem. I'll get you a fifth if you give me the money. Give me a minute to put my shoes and coat on." We returned to the liquor store where Willa Jean had been spurned. Cliff weaved back and forth as he entered. "Get down," Willa Jean said. "If the clerk sees us, he'll call the cops." After a few minutes, Cliff returned with a brown paper bag.

Once we dropped Cliff off, we drove toward Kanealey's farm in a heightened sense of excitement. "Can you believe what we just did?" I asked. "Found Cliff, got him to buy some booze. . . . Whatever will we do if we get caught?"

"Imagine the headlines in the *North Platte Telegraph Bulletin*—'St. Pat's Senior Girls Arrested for Possessing Liquor,'" Barbara said.

"'Said that they were transporting it to Monsignor Murray for a Knights of Columbus meeting,'" Kathy said. We collapsed on one another, laughing.

When we pulled the car into the driveway, we saw that Judy's mother had already arrived. She was different than most of our mothers; she had only two children and worked alongside her husband in the shoe store he managed. "Let me show you what I have in the kitchen," she said, "Cokes, 7Up, and chips. I'm all set up in the back bedroom, so let me know if you need anything."

We spent the early hours of the party drinking 7Up spiked with bourbon and singing love songs. One of us would shout out a title, and we'd begin:

There's a somebody I'm longin' to see
I hope that he, turns out to be   ·
Someone who'll watch over me

From there, we'd move on to other favorites: "I'll Get by as Long as I Have You," "Too Young," and "Sentimental Journey"—all love songs that expressed our yearnings, our dreams of being swept away by romantic love. Despite my short-lived teenage romances thus far, I clung to the 1950s belief in romance.

Voices began to grow dim as I felt the room spin. "I think I'm drunk," I said.

"Sober up, you space cadet," Barbara said, "and don't barf. It's time to sober up when Thompson thinks she's drunk."

"All you need to do is drink some milk," Kathy said. "It makes the alcohol evaporate." Kathy weaved her way to the refrigerator and poured six glasses. I drank mine and felt no different. The room moved as I looked at her.

"What we need to do is get some fresh air," Willa Jean said.

"But I don't have any shoes on," Mary Anne replied.

"You don't need shoes on to get fresh air."

We all walked outside, some with shoes on, some without. I felt the melting snow quickly soak through my socks as I walked in circles, hanging onto Kathy's arm. Once inside, our laughter got louder as Judy said, "Well, another remedy that failed."

Suddenly, Judy's mother shot out of the bedroom. Her hours of being a permissive parent were over. The minute she saw the state we were in, she gasped, "Look what you have done to me. I trusted you. What are your parents going to say when they learn how drunk you all are?" Much to my surprise, my parents didn't punish me or threaten to ground me for thirty days, as they sometimes did when I talked back to my mother.

⟨⟨⟨⟨⟨⟩

To speak of the Mount as having a campus in 1956 is an exaggeration. On an afternoon in late August, my parents and I drove up the hill to the college and turned onto a circular drive. An imposing, tan brick building with a cross above its façade stood out as an impenetrable fortress. I counted the stories: one, two, three, four. Off to the left was another cross, atop a structure that jutted out—certainly the chapel. Beyond that, I could not see. Off to the right was a modest white two-story building. My mental image of a college campus had been shaped by Kansas State University, which I had known as a preadolescent. This looked so small.

Young women wearing badges that read "Orientation Leader" stood in the drive, flashing smiles and calling out, "Welcome to the Mount! Here—let me help you with that luggage." I hoped my three-piece white leather Skyway set, purchased with my employee's discount at O'Connor's department store on the layaway plan, signaled my good taste. Already I missed my friend Barbara, St. Patrick's most accomplished clotheshorse. "You need at least one pair of Bermuda shorts, enough skirts and sweaters so you don't wear the same things to class in one week, and of course, special dresses for those hot dates." She'd then belt out our rendition of the song "I Get Ideas": "When we are dancing and you don't have any clothes on, I get ideas, I get ideas."

I was brought back to the front steps of the Mount. Raising her hand upward, an orientation leader said, "Here is the main building, where you'll have just about everything you need and won't have to worry about going outside in our ever-changing Kansas weather. Freshman dorms are on the fourth floor, classrooms on the second, administrative offices and an auditorium on the first, and most importantly, the dining room is in the basement."

"You forgot the high school academy on the third floor," another leader said, "and the smoker—it's outside on the fourth floor and overlooks the bluffs and the river. And there's also one in the basement, just off the gymnasium."

"Let's get your stuff up to your dorm, so you can settle in before Sister Imogene welcomes the freshmen in the auditorium at four thirty. Let's see. What was your last name again?"

"Thompson."

"Ah, yes. Mary Kay. St. Rose's dorm."

Once off the elevator, I looked down the pristine hallway, its beige walls seeming to go on forever, interrupted only by a nook that contained a rocking chair, floor lamp, and small end table. "That's where Sister Scholastica keeps watch over the freshman dorms every night. We're almost there. Your dorm is halfway down the hall." *Is there anything cleaner than a convent?* I wondered.

I imagined my own dorm room with a mate or two—funny, I hadn't been given their names ahead of time. We came to two large doors under a wooden sign topped with a cross. When the doors opened, I saw a huge room with sixty iron beds, sixty dressers, sixty small wardrobes, and sixty curtains that could be pulled around each space for privacy, all in straight lines. Large windows graced the south side of the dormitory. My "room" was in a middle row.

As I watched my parents' car disappear down the circular drive, I walked back up the front steps, unsure of which way to turn and feeling unbelievably alone. Where would I ever fit in here? At four-thirty there was an assembly in the auditorium; I slipped into one of the seats in the back row, under the balcony, reaching up to make sure my freshman beanie was still in place. A nun with a welcoming face, ruddy cheeks, and a mouthful of teeth stood at a podium on the center of a large stage that had seen much use. She exuded confidence as she tossed back her veil.

"Welcome, class of 1960!" She smiled and leaned forward on the podium. "You are on the cusp of a remarkable journey. You are now officially Mount-ies, part of the Benedictine tradition that began with St. Benedict and his sister, St. Scholastica, twins born about 480 AD—he the founder of the Benedictine monks and she the Benedictine sisters. Both followed the Rule of St. Benedict, which guides our lives here at the Mount, a rule that balances prayer and work and that emphasizes the relational nature of human beings. I urge you to achieve a balance between your work—being a student—and your spiritual growth. I also urge you to become a full member of this community, taking advantage of all we offer—stimulating classes, student clubs, music, and acting; the gift of par-ticipating in the liturgy as it changes throughout the year; singing in the *schola cantorum*, and of course, attending daily Mass."

She shifted her weight to the other foot and placed her hands higher on the podium. "But we offer you more: the best of the liberal arts tradition; the chance to study history, literature, languages, mathematics, and the sciences; to explore worlds that you never knew existed. We hold out to each of you the prom-ise of becoming a whole man. That is the promise of a liberal arts education."

A whole man. A chord had been struck. I was being offered something bigger than myself, something beyond the material, something beyond college as a place to find a husband—my first imagining of an examined life.

I thrived on the routine: daily Mass at seven o'clock in the morning; breakfast of hot chocolate and freshly baked rolls (I was surprised when I went from 115 to 125 pounds); classes in introductory German five days a week as well as fresh-man English, psychology, and elementary physical education; dinner at six in the evening followed by supervised study hall for freshmen from seven to nine o'clock; and lights out at ten o'clock, except on weekends. I portioned out my study time by course, staying away from the dorm until late in the afternoon. For the first time, how well I mastered my classes mattered. I considered piano lessons, imagining myself in one of the practice rooms and feeling my heart soar as I played Beethoven or Chopin, but decided in the negative. I joined no clubs. I tried out and became a cheerleader for St. Benedict's College, surprised when a dormmate said, "You won't want to do that after this year." My high school values were already passé.

Each semester, students' grade point averages were posted on the main bulle-tin board, ranked from highest to lowest. At the end of my first semester, I joined the crowd clustered around the freshman list, expecting at best to be where I had been in high school, within the top quartile but no better. When I finally worked my way up to the list, I started with number one, stopping at number seven: Mary Kay Thompson, 3.80. Was I a better student than I thought? Had there been some mistake?

But the aspiring intellectual had brought the good-time girl along with her to college, and those of us in St. Rose's dorm with a rebellious streak soon found one another. We called ourselves "The Sinful Seven" and had individual names: mine was Grace, an offhand remark after some clumsy stumble that had stuck. Others were Betty Bitch, Boozer, and Booger. Our rebellion was progressive—initially sitting on the wide windowsills of our dormitory and blowing cigarette smoke toward the windows after lights out, then hiding in the shadows of the fourth-floor smoker on warm fall evenings after Sister Scholastica had already called out, "Everyone back to your dorms." We made late-night raids of the kitchen, until a padlock on the ice cream freezer signaled that the nuns were on to us.

By the end of my freshman year, I was happier than I had ever been. I had a rich network of friends, the luxury of attending classes and studying while the nuns provided meals and kept our dormitory clean, and dates with upperclassmen from St. Benedict's. However, my smooth trajectory forward at the Mount wasn't to last. "I'm not coming back next year," I told my friends, waiting until their surprise subsided to continue. "My father is in the army, stationed near Mannheim, Germany. I can't pass up the opportunity to spend a year there." My family had dreamed of traveling, and this seemed too valuable an opportunity to squander.

Once in my family's apartment in Germany, lying on the bed in my room—narrow and small but mine nonetheless—I felt trapped. It was June 1957, and I had no job and didn't know where to begin. Even though I still had my tuition scholarship, I needed at least one thousand dollars to return to the Mount and be able to afford room and board. I began to think I had made a mistake in planning to spend the year in Germany. I made a list of options:

- Stay here and rot on this bed.
- Return to U.S., live with Aunt Irene and Jim in Ohio, work, save $1,000, and return to the Mount second semester.
- Get job here and save $1,000—but where? How? Help!

My mother's inquiry about my living with her sister Irene got a quick response: "We don't want to take responsibility for an eighteen-year-old. Regrettably, we have to say no."

In late October, help came from our Catholic chaplain, Father Gorsky, who said, "We've got to do something about Mary Kay." I gulped. Had he recognized my voice from the confessional? He continued, "She needs work. I could use some help in the office, typing and filing and such. I can't pay her much, but I can find something."

For the next several months, I sat outside Father Gorsky's office in a small room with little to do except calculate what I was earning, knowing I would never reach my goal of one thousand dollars. My hopes rose when, after failing it the first time, I passed the U.S. Civil Service stenographer test and qualified for a position. Assigned to a procurement center, I spent most of each day as the only American in a huge, open room with more than twenty Germans, typing orders for munitions headed for the Middle East. Eight copies of each order were required. One mistaken number and I would have to fold carbons and copies forward, erasing each, the last first, until I reached the original slip and typed the correct number. With this new job, my financial goal was now within reach.

My days were excruciatingly dull, but my nights were not. With the draft in full operation during the 1950s, there were 8,500 GIs on the Mannheim post and few—if any—young women except for wives among the dependents. A date with Father Gorsky's assistant once more shifted my world. As I was leaving Mass one Sunday in June, Dimitri, standing at the back of the chapel in perfectly pressed summer khakis, his brass Chaplain Corps insignia sparkling, motioned to me. "I was thinking of driving through the Black Forest later this afternoon and wondered if you'd like to come along." He didn't look dangerous, but he also didn't look very interesting. I said yes anyway, just to be with someone close to my age for a while.

When Dimitri picked me up, he behaved in a safe way, carefully opening the door to his Volkswagen Beetle for me and keeping both hands on the steering wheel. Except for a drive through the hills of Pennsylvania, I had never been in a forest. From time to time, I could see people hiking on paths, dressed in their Sunday best. I began to relax. Shortly after a sign indicated we were nearing the center of Baden-Baden, Dimitri slowed the car down and parked. We walked to a square in the city and suddenly saw a full orchestra, its members, all male and dressed in tuxedos, playing Beethoven's Fifth Symphony. I felt my heart stop. There in the June sunlight were families clustered at tables surrounding the orchestra; some drinking beer, others wine; some dipping spoons into tall glasses oozing ice cream, fruit, and sauces. What was it that struck me so—the power and beauty of the music? Or was it the glimpse into a life that I yearned for and could now imagine for myself?

As I sat at the desk outside Father Gorsky's office, a parade of chaplain's assistants dropped by to introduce themselves—Catholic boys, schooled in the same catalog of sins as I. Rarely a night passed that I didn't go out to drink beer or sometimes dance or have dinner. There was Tom from Chicago, who called me his "funny Valentine" and took me to a Modern Jazz Quartet concert in the Stadthaus in Heidelberg. Afterward, we descended a narrow spiral staircase at a

Figure 6. An evening in Heidelberg with Jack Lange, 1958

nearby *ratskeller* to hear the quartet's informal concert, sitting at a small, round table so close I could have reached out and touched the musicians. There was Jack Lange (French pronunciation, please) from New Orleans, who wore a signet ring with a crest, and Leon, the son of wealthy Kansas farmers, who, much to my surprise, enrolled at St. Benedict's College once he was discharged from the army. He lasted less than a semester; I wondered to what extent I was responsible for his decision to attend, because I had spoken so glowingly of the colleges. Even Tom Austin, my old flame, someone my father had enlisted and who was serving as a helicopter mechanic in Heidelberg, showed up. My high school, teenage self could never have imagined the romantic dinner we shared in Heidelberg, the rose he purchased from a gypsy, or our walk along the Neckar River on a summer's evening.

Daily life in Germany and traveling throughout Europe brought up questions I hadn't before imagined. One of our first family trips was to Rothenburg ob der Tauber, the well-preserved medieval city in Bavaria with its walls and gates, red-colored roofs, and yellow-and-brown half-timbered buildings. The scene set me to wondering, *Who had walked these streets in the tenth century? What did they think about?* Visiting cathedrals raised questions about the place of the Catholic Church in European history. Shouting "Viva il Papa!" as Pope Pius XII waved from the balcony of his summer home in Castel Gandolfo gave me a feeling of a deep connection to Catholicism. Trips to Holland, Italy, Austria, Paris, and London added other layers to my questions. Walking through the American pavilion at the Brussels World's Fair, I felt glamorous, sophisticated, and worldly. The year

I spent in Europe proved important to my evolving consciousness even after I
returned to college.

≪≪≪≪≫

As the taxi from the Atchison train station drove up the hill, my heart pounded at
the first sight of the Mount. The administrative building still stood out as a fortress, but a diminished one, smaller and barren, now that I had seen cathedrals
in Europe. As I was unpacking in St. Catherine's, a residence hall with double
rooms, Pat Ward, a tall, lanky woman with a pronounced New Jersey accent,
stuck her head in my open door and said, "We're going over to the junior class
meeting. Come along with us." Her group of friends was different from mine
freshman year—more serious now that they were juniors. Once inside the classroom where the meeting was held, shrieks of recognition and hugs greeted me.
"You actually came back; you said you would. How was Germany?"

"Wonderful, wonderful."

"I can't wait to go to Europe," *Marlene Schneider said. "What did you think
of Rome?"

"I loved it. It was one of our favorite places—the Coliseum, the Sistine Chapel, the pope's summer palace."

"I'm planning to go to Europe after I graduate, when I'm able to earn enough
money."

"Don't take a trip to Europe; live in Europe. They are such different experiences," I said as I slid into one of the few seats left in the classroom where we
were meeting.

Sister Imogene called the meeting to order, saying, "Well, juniors. It doesn't
seem possible that you entered as green freshmen only two years ago. And look at
you now—upperclassmen, serious students." A ripple of laughter filled the room.
She went on. "Our first order of business is to elect class officers."

When nominations for vice president were called for, I was surprised to hear
Pat say, "I nominate Mary Kay Thompson." Someone shouted, "Second!"

Sister Imogene got up from her chair, flipped her veil back from her face, and
said, "I'm sorry, Mary Kay is not eligible for the office." I raised my head and wondered, *Had the nuns kept some secret record of my behavior freshman year, someone
informing them of all the beers I drank at the Hilltop Café?* I was the only one left
among the Sinful Seven because all the others had dropped out.

"Mary Kay is not a junior."

All I had imagined about returning to the Mount while in Germany shifted.
I had imagined coming back and resuming my college life right where I'd left
off. Instead, I now lived among juniors, but I was not one. The Mount's campus
seemed smaller than I had remembered, the hours more restrictive. To cope with
my disappointment, I began what would become a pattern in my life: following

a new passion as a way to escape being sucked into smothering despair. My new passion this time was European history; I switched my major from elementary education to history. I wasn't troubled that my courses—Greek, Roman, medieval, modern European (two semesters), and Russian history—were all taught by Sister Juanita, the one history professor at the college, a woman with a PhD who gave lectures that closely resembled a textbook.

Late February and early March are cold, gray months in Kansas. I became obsessed with leaving the Mount. Jack Lange had convinced me, when I knew him in Germany, that New Orleans was the most romantic, human, creative city in the universe. I latched onto the idea of transferring to Xavier University, but I couldn't see how I could get from the Mount to there. I did not know that Xavier was the only historically black Roman Catholic institution of higher education in the United States. My solution: pour on the credits and graduate in three and a half years.

But before my pals graduated in 1960, my inner good-time girl and her friends began to chafe against the strict rules at the Mount: no drinking and a weekend evening curfew of eleven o'clock. One bright hope in our otherwise dateless lives was the Mount's annual Sweetheart Dance; we could invite a man of our choice. I settled on *John Haverford, the student body president at St. Benedict's, after we had spent an evening at the Hilltop Café dancing to a steamy rendition of "There's a Summer Place." John was well liked, round faced, and short, barely taller than me. He was planning to go to law school after graduating.

Marlene (now my roommate and an aspiring writer, who impressed me because she read Susan Sontag) invited someone she knew from home who was attending Kansas State in Manhattan; he brought along a friend. Taking advantage of the motel room they had rented, we held a cocktail party there before the dance. By the time we got to campus, our loud laughter signaled that we were all clearly drunk. "We're having such a good time, I don't want this to end," Mary Jo Monahan announced loudly.

"We'll all be Cinderella in less than an hour."

"Let's go back to the motel."

"Are you crazy? We won't be able to make our curfew unless we leave right now."

"That's not what I mean. Let's go back to our house, check in, and then sneak back to the motel."

"Shut up. Someone might hear of our wild scheme."

By the time the dance was over, we had all agreed to Mary Jo's plan. John Haverford said to me, "We'll meet you at the bottom of the hill at half past midnight. Be there."

"How are we ever going to get past Sister Dunstan?" I asked Marlene. A philosophy professor, Sister Dunstan was the prefect at St. Catherine's Hall, alleged to be the most brilliant nun on campus, and the daughter of a judge.

"Well, we'll listen for her steps when she goes from the parlor to her room upstairs and hope she runs the water forcefully." I laughed at the thought of Sister Dunstan doing something human.

Marlene and I changed from our formal dresses into something more appropriate for a night in a motel in the 1960s. About ten minutes later, we heard the steps creak under Sister Dunstan's substantial weight, waited five minutes, and got out of bed. I slipped into my black suede high-heeled pumps. Marlene opened the door and saw the dimly lit hallway was clear. We tiptoed past our suite mates' room and exited through the side door.

My heels sunk deep into the snow as we ran down the lawn that sloped to the street. The moon was full, illuminating the waiting car. "We've escaped, we've escaped," I said, laughing and collapsing into John Haverford's arms. The motel room was crowded with five couples. We spent the hours from half past midnight onward drinking and talking. Eventually, couples began to drift off to find a place to lie down. Somehow John and I managed to get a bed, or at least a part of one. "What's the combination for this dress?" he asked, fumbling near my collar.

"There isn't one," I said. Turning away, he fell asleep.

The next morning, hung over, looking around at the detritus of empty glasses, cigarette butts, and bedding falling over the sides of the two beds, I asked, "What time is it?"

"Ten past eight," someone answered.

"We've got to go back at a time when no one will be around, before people start streaming from the chapel after nine o'clock Mass to breakfast in Scholastica Hall. Thank God the dining hall is now in one of the new dorms. That will give us some cover."

"I've got it!" Marlene replied. "We'll go back after nine, after everyone is in the chapel. No one will see us, since it is at one end of the campus and our house is at the other."

When Marlene's date drove us back, the campus was deserted. We got out of his car, went up the walk to our dorm, and opened the front door. All was quiet. Trembling with fear and laughter, we went into the safety of our rooms.

Several days later, Marlene came into our room, quietly shut the door, and said, "Haverford's been campused."

"Did the priests catch him?"

"No, Benedict's has an honor system. Someone convinced him he had to turn himself in. He's student body president, after all. So the student discipline panel decided that being confined to campus for a month was an appropriate punishment." As the weeks progressed, it seemed too good to be true—we had escaped being discovered. But a month later, on March 15, the Ides of March, I met up with Mary Jo. "They know," she said. "Someone told on us."

"They know?" I felt fear seize my body.

"Yes, we each have a scheduled time to report to a hearing in the Formal Parlor. Mine is at seven o'clock this evening. Sister Dunstan will be waiting for you to tell you when you have to show up."

When my appointed time came, I was ushered into the parlor. The light from the chandeliers was dim, and the oriental rug and large mahogany table in the center of the room gave it an aura of formality. "Sit in that chair," Sister Imogene said, pointing to the one in the center of the room. I faced a semicircle of a dozen Benedictine nuns, all looking down, their hands hidden behind their cowls.

"In the 112-year history of the Mount, we have never had such egregious behavior as yours. Your violations fly in the face of what it means to be a Mountie. I need not reiterate what you five have done."

"Yes, Sister,"

"We sisters in this community have deliberated about what would be a fair and just punishment, beginning with expulsion." My breath caught, fearing that my goal of a college degree was about to slip through my fingers.

"But because everyone but you is a senior and you are all students with acceptable records, you are suspended for six weeks. You are to leave campus by the end of the week and return to your home. Each of your professors knows of this decision and is prepared to give you assignments for that period. It is your responsibility to contact them. You are now excused."

"Yes, Sister."

I left the parlor and ran down the steps thinking, "Oh my God, oh my God." Blinded by my tears, I slipped on the sidewalk and sank into a snow bank, weeping.

On Friday, I took the train from Atchison to North Platte, a trip of more than six hours, worrying all the way there about my parents. I had told them exactly what had happened. I distracted myself from what I believed I would face at home by reading *Rally Round the Flag, Boys!* by Max Shulman, imagining I might find salvation by marrying a salesman from Connecticut. When I arrived at the North Platte train station, only my father was there to meet me. Giving me a hug, he said, "You look like you've grown, hon."

When I returned to campus six weeks later, the first person I saw was Marlene, who said, "There's an assembly at four-thirty today, and we are required to attend." I slipped into a seat in the back of the auditorium, approximately where I had sat during my first freshman assembly and been electrified at the idea of becoming a "whole man."

Sister Imogene took the podium and began, "We have called an assembly today to iterate our expectations for those of you privileged to be here at the Mount. As you know, your every action is a reflection on the college and the Benedictine community. Our expectations are that you will always behave as a representative of the Mount, as a representative of young Catholic womanhood. In practice, this means no drinking of alcoholic beverages, no instances of putting yourselves in danger of mortal sin." She then proceeded to reiterate our exact violations of the college's code of behavior.

I had never imagined that a college assembly would be held upon our return to humiliate us as a negative example. Had the nuns ever considered giving us the same punishment as Haverford? Why was ours so much harsher? Did this difference arise from the patriarchal belief that women were more responsible for upholding Catholic morality?[5]

By my last semester at the Mount, in the fall of 1960, those I considered my classmates had graduated. I felt as though I were living among strangers. I barely knew anyone in the class of 1961. As a way of dealing with my loneliness and uncertainty about my future, I would go to the college library, sit at one of the long wooden tables, and pore over references such as *Choosing Your Career*. I sent off an application to Voice of America, the U.S. government-funded international news source that serves as the government's official institution for nonmilitary broadcasting, to spread the good news of American democracy as a German speaker. About to earn a minor in the language, I pictured myself back in Germany, sitting in a sound booth and speaking into a microphone, and in Heidelberg, sitting at a classical music concert or driving with a date through the cultivated countryside, with houses clustered together in small villages among green fields stretching as far as the eye could see. I recalled the art; the musty smells of churches, castles, and museums; and the taste of beer, wine, and bread—tastes that lingered in my palate's memory.

The rejection letter took little time to arrive. "Your voice audition is not of the quality we require at Voice of America." I blamed my failure on my German pronunciation, which was not that of a native speaker. The fact that female voices were rarely heard on broadcasts escaped me.

~~~~~

I had spent the previous summer in North Platte, living at home to save money and working long days as a lifeguard and director of the city's swimming program. One Sunday in early June as I knelt in a pew at Mass, I saw Bob Mueller walk up the central aisle to the communion rail, his body a little less lean, his blond hair still worn in a crew cut. I felt my old attraction to him. I remembered how it felt to be in his embrace and recalled going steady with him when I was sixteen. Now all my best friends were married: Kathryn Swanson to a physician, Barbara Fitzpatrick to a recently commissioned army lieutenant, and Mary Anne Broderson to a highway patrolman. I felt like I was the only single one left. I looked for Bob after Mass, not knowing what I would say to him.

Later that day, Bob called, and we began seeing one another. In cryptic snippets, it came out that he had spent only a year in the seminary before deciding he had no vocation. He'd then attended Kearney State College for a semester but was now back in town working for the telephone company. "You know those guys who climb poles to install telephone wires? That's me, that's what I do all day." I felt uncomfortable at how defeated he sounded. Bob's mother had died several years earlier. He never once mentioned her.

It was comforting to have a boyfriend, though—someone I saw regularly. On nights when Bob wasn't playing basketball in a city league or having dinner with his father, we played Hearts and drank beer with Bob's older brother and his wife. In these simple routines, I could imagine what it would be like to be married to Bob, to have children together, to be a part of his family. These fantasies were subjected to a reality check as I saw their lives up close: signs of little money with a world limited to family, St. Patrick's parish, and North Platte. When Bob's brother raised his cards to arrange them, his nails were bitten and raw. I suppressed any thoughts of the future, knowing deep down that a life of cards and beer was not enough for me.

The night before I was to return to the Mount, Bob said, "I'm going to miss you. Are you sure you have to go?" I pulled away from him as I said yes, feeling something hard against my body. Could this be the same thing one of my Mountie friends reported in horror after a date? He said, "I don't know if I can wait until you come home for Thanksgiving. I may have to come to see you in Atchison."

Bob kept his promise. When I answered the door to St. Catherine's Hall the Friday night of homecoming weekend, Bob and my brother Dan stood in the porch's dim light. The eerie quiet of the house—everyone was at a pep rally—surrounded us. Bob's loose winter jacket hung on his body. *Had he even brought a sports jacket?* I wondered. From that moment, I knew that marrying Bob would be a terrible mistake. After the homecoming dance, as Bob and I necked in the front seat of his car, he said, "I love you. I think it's time we got married."

I felt my body tense. I became as mute as Bob had often been. How could I tell him that I no longer saw him as a future husband and that the life we would have together in North Platte would be suffocating for me, similar to being buried alive? I couldn't tell him that marrying a college dropout and a telephone lineman was beneath what I aspired to. Telling him would have violated our tacit beliefs about social class—that we were all middle class. In the 1950s, a women's social class status derived from her husband. And being sexually compatible wasn't enough. Instead of being honest (perhaps because I was incapable of that), I decided it was best to answer his proposal with a letter:

Dear Bob,

I would like to accept your proposal for marriage, but I find I can't. I think I have a vocation to be a nun.

Sincerely,

Mary Kay

Figure 7. College graduation

What a twist of the knife! My lie was so freeing that I wanted to laugh out loud. Even though I was lonely and uncertain about my career possibilities, I could not bring myself to see marriage—especially to the wrong person—as an escape.

I sat on the stage in May 1961 among the other graduates, in the same auditorium where I had been moved to become "a whole man" and where, later, I had fought to suppress my disgrace and anger as Sister Imogene had ticked off the infractions of the Benedictine way that my friends and I had committed after the college's Sweetheart Dance. My parents were in the audience, after earlier having said how proud they were of me, the first on either side of the family to graduate from college. Only later would my sister Peggy tell me of my father's resistance to my decision to go to college.

My goal of a college degree now completed, I felt hollow. What I couldn't foresee was the way I would wander in the wilderness seeking love and work in the next several years and how the church would provide a refuge.

CHAPTER 4

WANDERING IN
THE WILDERNESS

CHICAGO—JANUARY TO SEPTEMBER 1961

When the door closed on a career with the Voice of America, I took another look at *Choosing Your Career* and saw that Encyclopedia Britannica hired college graduates to do research. The company's national offices were in Chicago, where I could imagine living. Optimistic about my future, I wrote a letter of inquiry, recalling that I had begun college certain that I would drop out to get married. That hadn't happened after all, so it was now time to concentrate on work, not love. I also knew a former college classmate, a social worker for Cook County in Chicago, who suggested I live, as she did, in the Catholic women's residence, which was located on the top floors of Loyola University's downtown building on Michigan Avenue, on Chicago's Magnificent Mile. Things seemed to be falling into place, as I was within reach of my first "college graduate" job. I could taste the promise of being someone.

My optimism was dashed when a slim envelope with "Encyclopedia Britannica" embossed in the left-hand corner arrived after I had interviewed with the company; my score on the general knowledge test was too low to qualify. The next morning, I sat across from a counselor in an employment agency and said, "I'd like to find a job that puts my degree in history and my year living abroad to use."

"History major, hmmm? That sounds like a good major for someone who wants to be a teacher."

"I'm not interested. That's what women do. I took one course in secondary school methods in college and decided it's not for me." Whatever happened, I wondered, to Sister Imogene's promise of becoming a whole man?

"Do you have any marketable skills? You know, can you type and take shorthand?"

"Yes. I was a stenographer for the U.S. Army in Germany, a civil service job."

"Well, that gives me something to work with. There's a job at R. R. Donnelley and Sons in Chicago, one of the most highly regarded printing companies in the country. Their clients include *National Geographic*, *Time*, *Newsweek*, and the *New Yorker*. They also produce AT&T's telephone directories. The position is secretary to the director of marketing. Now, it's on the South Side of Chicago, but I think that neighborhood is safe in the daytime. Would you like me to set up an interview?"

When I got off the "L," the elevated train, at the Cermak Road Station, looking around to spot any danger, I saw an imposing eight-story redbrick building ahead, R. R. Donnelley and Son's corporate headquarters. Atop that, a tower of several more stories jutted up into the cold February sky. On the exterior of the building, near the doors where I entered, were ornamental plaques depicting the history of printing, giving me hope that there might be work of value here, something that might engage my mind.

After my interview, the director of personnel said, "Well, it's time to take you up to the tower where marketing is located. It's a pretty exclusive place—executive offices and two departments, marketing and design. Marketing makes a point of hiring college graduates." Several young men waited at the elevator, dressed in sharply tailored suits, radiating an energy that signaled their importance and privilege. Once inside the elevator, the director whispered, "Those young men you saw in the lobby, they're sales trainees, part of a yearlong program where they learn the ins and outs of sales. They're college graduates on a career path that leads to high salaries and, for some, executive positions in the corporation."

I spent the next seven months as the secretary to the director of the marketing department. The department, with only four employees, was the antithesis of the ad agency depicted in the television series *Mad Men*. Instead of the scheming, hard-driving Don Draper, our director, an elderly man who lived in Indiana, came in only a couple of times a week. He was working on a book on wildflowers, *Glory by the Wayside*, designed to demonstrate the company's quality printing. My desk faced the elevator; the few times it opened each day, only Bill, the associate director whose slouching posture suggested deep depression, and Gladys, whose sole responsibility was to update the mailing list, stepped into my office.

Mornings during my coffee break, I would glance across the cavernous employee cafeteria, not noticing that most tables were segregated by gender but only wishing there was some way to interact with the sales trainees clustered together at a table. My desire sprang more from wanting a boyfriend with a promising future than imagining such an opportunity for myself. I never thought of approaching the trainees' table; it would have been too bold a step, breaching the rules of gender-appropriate behavior in the early 1960s. A closer look would have revealed class segregation as well. We secretaries, sitting at one of the women's tables, were high school graduates drawn mostly from ethnic neighborhoods on the South Side, with few exceptions. The men who clustered together in suits were in sales or management. Those who worked in the printing plant, identified as such by their gray work uniforms, sat together.

The only manager who approached me at work was the director of design, a corpulent older man whose vest buttons strained against his stomach and who offered to give me a lift to the Near North Side one evening after work. I accepted because I had broken an ankle while skiing and found it exhausting to navigate the snow and the Chicago "L." Once in his car, he suggested we drop in at his club for a drink. The interior of his club had all the hallmarks of exclusivity— wood paneling, reproductions of nineteenth-century paintings lit from below, and waiters quietly moving in and out of private dining rooms. Drinks progressed into dinner, and before the meal was over, he was telling me of his chronically ill wife and proposing we make such dinners a regular affair. When I understood what he was asking, I suggested it was time to go.

My experience at the employment agency revealed the gendered expectations of the early 1960s: a female college graduate with a history major might teach or be a secretary if she had the necessary skills. Sales trainee programs such as the one at Donnelley and Sons were for men only. Classified ads were announced as "Help Wanted Men" and "Help Wanted Women."

But as Bob Dylan sang in 1963, "The Times They Are a-Changin." In 1961, President John Kennedy established the Presidential Commission on the Status of Women. The final report, issued in 1963, documented workplace discrimination and recommended affordable childcare, equal employment opportunity for women, and paid maternity leave. That report, along with the 1964 Civil Rights Act, which made it illegal to discriminate on the basis of gender, would become the legal undergirding of the changes Dylan signaled.

The neighborhood where I lived, on the Near North Side, was full of flight attendants instead of the eligible, professional men I had hoped to find. At that time, stewardesses were hired for their good looks; they were white women strikingly attractive all in a similar way—regular features, radiant complexions, small noses, and large breasts. Our "beach" on Lake Michigan consisted of large rocks jutting out from the shore, perfect for sunning and slipping into the water. Stewardesses congregated there like clusters of colorful seals. As I dozed and read in the warm sun, I heard fragments of their conversations and laughter. ". . . got really drunk last night. . . . went out with some pilots after we landed at O'Hare. . . . I can't count how many. I was lucky to get home in one piece. A pilot from United . . . take no for an answer. . . . Isn't he married?" This cheerful banter gave no indication that the first complainants to the U.S. Equal Employment Opportunity Commission would be female flight attendants contesting age discrimination, weight requirements, and bans on marriage. Company policy mandated retirement when they either married or turned thirty.

I lay there, feeling alone among these women, taking pride in my flat stomach and thin body and ignoring the fact that the perfectly formed breasts that filled out my two-piece bathing suit were falsies. I felt like an immigrant in the flight attendants' world, an innocent alien from a small Catholic women's college who was unfamiliar with the culture of their fast-paced lives and practices that seemed dangerous, riddled with mortal sins. My confidence and positive sense of self were in danger of being drowned by what my life said I was: a secretary with a college degree, dating a Montgomery Ward salesman I had met several months before in a course on diplomatic history I was taking at Loyola University. The thought of a future with him was off-putting. I made few female friendships, as I had little in common with the other secretaries at work and no time to meet like-minded women outside of the office. Being Catholic, though, gave me some sense of self-worth. It would be the church that eventually presented an escape.

⁂

A potential way out of my lonely, boring routine came in the person of Marlene Schneider, a former Mount roommate who visited in the summer of 1961. Once I told her about my life in Chicago, dwelling on how much I loved the course I had taken at Loyola but how unhappy I was with my lackluster boyfriend, she clasped her arms, squeezed them, and said laughing, "This doesn't sound like much of a life to me."

Knowing she was correct, I changed the conversation: "And what have you been up to?"

"I've been in Oklahoma City this past year at Sacred Heart Parish—it's the largest in the city—working as a lay catechist in the Extension Lay Volunteer program."

"A lay catechist? What's that?"

She went on to explain that John Sullivan, an Oklahoma priest deeply concerned about the marginalized position of the church in Oklahoma, had hit on the idea that the youth, energy, and faith of recent Catholic college graduates could be put to good use in the dioceses of his state, where Catholics were second-class citizens. Marlene recounted, "I've heard his effective recruitment pitch so many times, I can recall it verbatim. He'd gaze at someone with his beautiful blue eyes and say, 'Imagine what it is like to live in a place where the only other Catholics are your relatives, where a Bible Belt mentality pervades and controls all activities in the town, where going to movies and playing cards are sins, where drinking and dancing are the work of the devil, and where Catholics are off-limits as friends.'"

But it was the young curates who particularly appealed to Marlene. "You won't believe how cool they are. Father Dan Allen is brilliant, interested in existential philosophy. Father Bill Skeehan, a convert to Catholicism, is a former New York ad man. He still looks like one even though he wears a Roman collar—crew cut, argyle socks, the whole bit." Images of the priests of my youth—immigrants from Ireland—popped into my head. This must have been a new breed.

"We spend a lot of time talking about the promise of Vatican II for reforming the church. Both Allen and Skeehan are psyched that Pope John XXIII said it was time to throw open the windows of the church. Let in some fresh air. They believe the upcoming Vatican Council has the promise of bringing about real reform in the church."

"Oklahoma. It sounds so far away."

"But it's not. It's where true reform in the church will happen."

"What would I need to do if I wanted to sign up?"

"Contact the Extension office in Chicago. Our national headquarters are here."

What did I have to lose? My life in Chicago was disappointing at every turn. I could not imagine staying at R. R. Donnelley and working my way from a secretarial position to a professional one, as Peggy Olson did on *Mad Men*.

⤞⤝

Oklahoma—September 1961–1963

By the time I signed up to be an Extension Lay Volunteer in the fall of 1961, there were fifty-seven of us teaching in Catholic schools, serving as nurses, working in Newman Centers[1] and as catechists, and doing work the parish priest deemed important, such as conducting a census or providing religious instruction. When a letter announcing my assignment as one of the latter in Skiatook, Oklahoma, arrived, I looked at a map of the state and saw that the town, about twenty miles northwest of Tulsa, had a population of 2,500.

My introduction to life as a volunteer was not as I imagined or what Marlene promised. Once I arrived at St. William's Parish in Skiatook and stepped into the rectory—I had never been in one before—the stuff of ordinary life surprised me. The dark wooden china cabinet was filled with Hummel figurines. A large dining room table, covered with a white tablecloth, took up most of the room. A harmonium sat in the living room next to drawn window shades. Brandy, the rectory's St. Bernard, the "son of Bourbon," was slumped in the doorway between the kitchen and the dining room, ignored.

Instead of one of the "new" priests that Marlene had touted, the pastor at St. William's Parish, Father Elmer Schwartz, barely thirty years old, quickly set the record straight. Leaning against the kitchen door, holding a cooking fork, he said, "I'm sure you've heard about this new breed of Oklahoma priests, those who latch on to every reform that they believe will rejuvenate the church here—especially the promises of the supposed Vatican II. I grew up in a community of farmers in the western part of Oklahoma. German was my first language. I favor keeping the Mass in Latin; Gregorian music makes my soul soar."

I was seated at the table with three other volunteers as the smell of frying chicken drifted into the dining room. My partner was Mary Ann Banta, a graduate of Duquesne University in Pittsburgh. Her simple white blouse, plaid skirt,

Figure 8. Extension Lay Volunteers, Skiatook, Oklahoma, September 1961—Raja Shaheen, Mary Ann Banta, Patsy O'Grady, and me

clear plastic glasses, and hair shaped in a bob gave her the look of a convent schoolgirl. She also looked safer and more reliable than the other two volunteers assigned to Collinsville, a nearby parish. Patsy O'Grady and Raja Shaheen were graduates of Manhattanville College, located north of New York City. Their New York accents made them seem edgy, and Patsy was smoking at the table. They were quick to let me know their college was also Joan Kennedy's alma mater.

Father Schwartz walked into the dining room with a platter of chicken in one hand and a bowl of mashed potatoes in the other, setting them down and returning with a bowl filled with canned green beans. He had taken off his suit jacket but kept his Roman collar on, held down by a *rabat*, the piece of black cloth fitted to the collar. The back of his white T-shirt was drenched in sweat. "You all think I'm preparing this meal as part of an Oklahoma welcome. But it's my way of softening Mary Kay's surprise when she sees where you'll be living." He let out a high giggle. Glancing around the table, he looked down, closed his eyes, made the sign of the cross, and began, "Bless us O Lord and these thy gifts. . . ."

When dinner was over, we walked out into the warm Oklahoma air. "Those two small houses to the west are where you'll be staying," he said, pointing. "The one to the left is yours. Mary Supernaw, a white woman married to an Osage Indian, lives in the one to the right." Both were modest one-story bungalows; their exterior paint had aged from white to a gritty gray. We four volunteers followed Father Schwartz along an uneven walkway, up two steps onto a concrete slab of a porch, and through a door without a screen. The living room barely had space for a faded beige couch pushed against one wall, a cigarette burn marring one of the cushions; a coffee table with a long history; and a green Naugahyde chair. I could see a small kitchen behind a waist-high divider. A Formica dining room table and four chairs sat in the corner just outside the kitchen. The space, absent of any pictures or plants or personal effects, with the early evening sun shining through dirty windows, was bleak. A hallway to the left led to the bathroom and two bedrooms.

"Woo," said Patsy. "I've never seen anything like this, even in the Bronx." She walked down the hallway to the bedrooms and shouted back, "Raja and I will take the bedroom on the right. One closet? How can two women share one closet?" Mary Ann, Father Schwartz, and I made eye contact. Father Schwartz said, "She should have seen this before the parishioners painted the rooms and furnished them with castoff furniture. I guess that means you two will share the bedroom on the left." Gradually, I came to see that our living quarters were not so much unlike other places I'd seen before. What was new and strange to me was the world of the Oklahoma church and its priests.

That evening, Mary Ann and I sat on the twin beds in our room, looking straight ahead toward one small window. "So," I said, turning to look at her, "what's the real story about renovating the house?"

"Our house was supposed to be finished before we arrived, but Lordy, Lordy. I got my first clue that that was not the case when I couldn't stay there the first night I arrived in Skiatook. Father Westerman gave me a ride from the liturgical conference in Oklahoma City. I was supposed to spend the night with one of the parishioners. By the time we got out of the city after a late Mass on Thursday evening, drove the hundred miles to here, and dropped two seminarians off in Tulsa, Father Westerman was sure Mrs. Neal would be long asleep."

She paused and looked directly at me. "So he put me up in his rectory in Collinsville. But the crazy thing was that no one seemed to notice. What set them off was that I ate meat for breakfast on Friday!"

"You're kidding," I said.

"When Father Schwartz showed up to take me to Skiatook, the first words out of his mouth were, 'What did you have for breakfast this morning?'"

"Breakfast," I said. "The works—bacon, eggs, biscuits."

"The whole parish is talking about how the new volunteer eats meat on Friday!" he exclaimed.

Mary Ann looked at me and shook her head. "I explained that both Father Westerman and I forgot it was Friday when we ate at his neighbor's across the street. She's not Catholic. We ate cheese sandwiches at lunch but never even remembered the breakfast bacon. Father Westerman said he would have given us a dispensation if he'd remembered."

We both shook our heads. Mary Ann continued, "What I really wanted to say to Father Schwartz was, 'Isn't it amazing what constitutes a scandal in a small town? A young woman spends a night alone in the rectory with a good-looking young priest and no one seems to notice. But eat meat on Friday!'"

Soon, Mary Ann and I took up the challenge of doing a parish census, Father Schwartz's top priority. His instructions to us were brief: "Find out who is in the parish and where the fallen-away Catholics are. If you meet non-Catholics interested in knowing more about the church, I'll be happy to go out to meet them." Midmorning, most days, we would pile into the 1950 Volkswagen that the parish provided and drive to a section on the map in one of the four towns of the parish—Skiatook, Barnsdall, Sperry, or Avant. All were in Osage County, which had been designated an Indian reservation in the 1870s. The Barnsdall Oil Company corporate headquarters, vacant since the company moved it to Houston in 1960, towered above the low bungalows in the town.

Signs of poverty met the eye as each town announced its city limits. Small houses were set irregularly at various angles in overgrown yards, showing off flaking paint and often a scattered array of cars on the property. Dogs with the hackles raised on their backs sat on many of the porches, barking. A curtain would be drawn back, and a face would peek out, shouting the dog's name: "Killer, shut up!" The occasional well-manicured yard with trees and flowers and other plants was a rarity.

From the mostly elderly women who answered the doors, we would hear stories of hard times and human loss—sons lost to drink or life in faraway places, daughters living nearby whose lives were constricted by unplanned pregnancies and divorce. Father Schwartz's words at our first dinner often came back to me: "Talking to parishioners, or better yet those who should be, those who are fallen away, about reforms in the church won't bring them back. You've got to understand their lives, how that early marriage outside the church and then a divorce make a difference."

When we did stumble on a Catholic, we would check to see if, by chance, we had a card from the earlier census. Sometimes we had only an address. If we found no card, we would make one and jot down notes. A sampling is as follows:

Mary and Ickey Supernaw. 10/01 Both baptized, both fallen away. Married outside the church. 11/20 Dropped in to see if we could get to them through their daughter-in-law, who sells cosmetics. Parish owes us each $1.99 for a tube of lipstick. Seems worth the cause. 3/17 Went over for a St. Patrick's Day nip. More than buying lipstick needed here.

Liz Burton. 12/4 Dropped in on the parents of two boys in K–4 catechism class in Skiatook. The boys aren't baptized, and Mom is married outside the church. Dad seems to be the obstacle to fixing up the marriage. He works for Shell, nice person.

Mary Alexander. 2/15 A fallen away nobody knew about. Not sure what problem is.

Bob Ross. 4/2 Been away from the church since he was six years old. Talked until 11:30. A rather successful man who poured forth some most unusual ideas about celibacy and transubstantiation.

These parishioners were so unlike the restrained ones I knew in Nebraska. Their twangy Oklahoma accents were markedly different from our standard speech, and I could never predict what would come out of their mouths. Yet generosity unlike any I had ever experienced could be found wherever we turned. Dinners in the home of parishioners would often begin with Manhattans served in a water glass filled to the brim and end with an offer of food to take home: Typical was a parishioner who asked, "Will one chicken be a mess?"

"It will be no trouble at all."

"Well, then will two chickens be a mess?"

Finally, understanding that a "mess" was enough food for a meal, I said, "Ah, yes."

A rich bachelor whose family owned a lot of land near Avant, who we discovered sitting near the cash register in his family's general store in town, showered us with bottles of good Scotch to drink while playing bridge with him, tickets to the Tulsa Opera, and dinners at Jamil's Steak House in Tulsa, where we had to pour Scotch below the table.

It was not only in Father Schwartz's rectory that we saw a priest's life up close but also in Collinsville. The pastor there, Father Westerman, was cold and reserved, the opposite of Father Schwartz. An efficient handyman, he built the rectory in Collinsville himself, ranch style, a temple to the self-sufficient male. Since he was a tall, thin man with a youthful, tanned face, Patsy and Raja came to privately call him "Prince Philip." Once he discovered we played bridge, he invited us to travel to his parish most days off, attend the Mass he celebrated, enjoy the breakfast he prepared, and then deal out the first hand of cards, playing until long after dinner.

Besides our census work, we taught catechism classes once a week in each town in various spaces—a parishioner's living room, a vacant storefront, the parish hall. The rest of our schedule, we made up as we went along, reveling in the freedom of being our own bosses most days. The project that engaged us the most was Father Schwartz. Before our first week in Skiatook had ended, I said to Mary Ann, "Father Schwartz is our first problem. He's too intellectual for the job. He seems lost."

"I don't know how much we can help," Mary Ann said, "but we could start by getting him to do what we think should be done—visit folks in the parish, be more organized, stop playing the organ at midnight, get to Mass on time.

He says we can do anything as long as it doesn't depend on us to continue. If only he knew." We both laughed at Mary Ann's ironic suggestion that we deliberately assume a woman's traditional role of helping a man in a leadership position actually take the initiative and lead.

One afternoon, as we drove back to our little house through the Osage Hills, which were bright with fall foliage, Mary Ann broke the silence: "Every now and then I wonder what it must be like to be in the Peace Corps. It's hard enough to accept this strange place in our own country. Imagine what it must be like in another part of the world. And we have the advantage of doing it for God. I wouldn't do it for any other reason."

"You can say that again," I agreed. "We're certainly not doing it for the money, since our pay, besides room and board, is fifty dollars a month." But looking back, I wonder if I *was* doing it "for God." I think I was doing that work because it gave me a way to enact my Catholic identity. We saw our purpose as connecting with parishioners, something Father Schwartz found hard to do; bringing "fallen away" adults back to the church and, in some cases, seeing that their children were baptized; and providing religious instruction to children. It was a safe place of refuge, far from my postgraduate ambivalence about what I wanted and outside the constricted gender scripts of the early 1960s working world. Ironically, I just ended up supporting male celibate priests instead of male bosses in an office environment.

To leave after our first term was over or to spend another year in St. William's Parish was the source of endless conversations between Mary Ann and me in the spring of 1962. In April, the conversation changed when Monsignor Luecke, the field director of the program, called. He was beloved by the volunteers, mostly because of his warmth and his nonjudgmental character. He was an Oklahoma boy and, at fifty, elderly to me. He had the broad hands of an Oklahoma farmer, and his nails were poorly cut and often dirty. His black suits looked as though he had slept in them, and the ties of his *rabat* were wound around and tied in the front below his extended stomach. His cowboy boots signaled his Oklahoman identity as well.

"I want to talk to you about next year," the monsignor said. "More than 150 volunteers are expected. I'm going to need some help coordinating all that human energy. I'm also going to need a secretary to help with managing the office. It would be good to have one of you girls travel with me to the states where we'll have volunteers—Oklahoma, Texas, Colorado, Wyoming, Illinois, and possibly even Louisiana. They're more likely to tell another volunteer their problems than an old monsignor. And if it weren't enough to be the pastor of the largest church in Oklahoma City and the field director of you volunteers, the bishop has just appointed me his vicar general."

At the time, I didn't know what a vicar general was except that when the word came up, the expression on the faces of young priests changed. I thought it must be about power. A vicar general, second in command to the bishop, assisted in the administration of the diocese, so it turned out I was right.

"Now, you're the girl who seems best for this job. What do you think?"

"Well," I said, surprised at this offer out of the blue, "let me think it over. I haven't decided if I'm coming back for a second year or not."

"Take your time, take your time," he said. "You'd live here in Sacred Heart Parish in Oklahoma City with other volunteers."

When I asked Marlene if she knew why Monsignor Luecke selected me, she laughed and said, "He knows quality when he sees it."

"Did you have anything to do with this?" She squeezed her arms and laughed again.

⋙⋙

I moved to Oklahoma City in the fall of 1962 to take up my post. A new Plymouth sat in the driveway, ready for the trips I would make into the field. Monsignor Luecke believed that he and I should visit each group of volunteers at least once. My car sat mostly idle because he preferred his new black Oldsmobile. At short notice, he and I, always accompanied by another woman (most often Lois, an older volunteer from Ohio who was working in his parish), would take a day to visit volunteers in Oklahoma and bordering states such as Texas, Arkansas, and Missouri. These were places that could be visited in a long day's drive, leaving after 7 a.m. Mass and often returning after 10 p.m.

Our pattern was to travel to a parish, giving the pastor less than a day's notice that we were coming. Once there, Monsignor Luecke would head off to the rectory to meet with the pastor, and Lois and I would meet the volunteers. Their "issues" were similar—a sense of not being sure of what they were doing and not getting along with their fellow volunteers or, less frequently, the pastor. There were also dangers that no one knew to warn volunteers against. A volunteer teaching in an orphanage died when a gas heater malfunctioned and asphyxiated her. Once, Mary Ann and I, along with four young siblings whose home was in open-range country, nearly drowned. We were driving them home after catechism classes when I drove our Volkswagen onto a low-water bridge[2] that had become a raging stream. Just as the car was about to stall and I felt the current shift the car sideways, I gunned the motor, and it sputtered onto dry land. Shaken, we crept along until we dropped the children off.

The trips weren't all serious work though. That fall, when the magnificent aspens were in full color, Monsignor Luecke, Lois, and I headed out for a long drive through Colorado to check on volunteers in a town called Pagosa Springs. Occasionally, another volunteer and I would drive the Plymouth to a distant site—for instance, New Orleans, where breakfast at Brennan's and dinner at Antoine's were a must, or Gunnison, Colorado, where we would ski and check out how things were going up there. It was during one of those trips that

I dropped in on my high school friend Kathy Swanson, who was living in Little
Rock, Arkansas, where her husband was a physician. Her tiny home was not what
I expected. Pregnant, sitting on a bed with her two babies squirming nearby, she
said, "I'll soon have three children in less than four years. Most days I don't know
what hit me." This was not the romantic future she and I had imagined as we
talked late into the night in high school. For the first time, I saw the real costs of
actually achieving our adolescent yearnings.

A closeness began to develop between Monsignor Luecke and me as we
worked in his office by day and drove around often late at night. One day, the
office phone rang, and I handed it to him. I saw his forehead wrinkle. When
he hung up the phone, his face was drained of color. "I have some bad news. One
of the volunteers in Wyoming is pregnant. She's expecting in less than six weeks.
Her pastor and I agreed that she should come to Oklahoma City and live in the
house with you and the other volunteers until she has her baby. I'll call Sister
Clarita at the Little Shepherd Home for Unwed Mothers. She'll be able to arrange
an adoption once the baby is born."

I was standing off to the side of his desk filing papers when I said, "I resent
volunteers who put such stress on you." He laughed. Once I said it, though, it
felt false. I remember thinking, *This is like something you would say to a husband.*
I was once again falling into the traditional gender role of comforting a man
under stress.

The volunteer lived with us until the baby was born, returning for a few weeks
afterward. She was nearly mute throughout. By chance, I bumped into her several years later at the Chicago Symphony. We recognized one another but did
not speak.

It was in Oklahoma City that I finally spent time with the activist priests Marlene had promised, those with a zeal for church reform and the church's social
mission. By then, Marlene had joined an organization of laywomen who made a
promise of celibacy and dedicated their lives to working to achieve the promise
of Vatican II. I first heard Father Dan Allen hold forth at dinners in the laywomen's home. In his early thirties, he was a curate at Sacred Heart Parish in
his first assignment after ordination. A poster in his office at the rectory spoke
volumes: "Give a Damn!" Small in stature, with the flat, broad nose of a boxer,
he was always impeccably dressed in a black suit and a Roman collar, its white-
ness striking against his dark hair. A burning cigarette often dangled from his left
hand. He held a glass of Scotch in the other. These were the same graceful hands
that held up the host and chalice at morning Mass.

Speaking with an Oklahoma twang, his eyes flashing, he would begin an evening by throwing out his ideas about the church. "The facade is beautiful, but the
guts—the guts are full of cancer." The worst cancer was that the church did not
address the real needs of the people. Instead, it prohibited eating meat on Friday
and made the faithful fast from midnight before receiving communion. He loved

to joke about the church's relics and miracles, distractions for the faithful. Once, at dinner, he claimed there was more than one church that claimed to have a relic of the Blessed Virgin's breast milk. His dark eyes connected with mine.

"We need to make the church more accessible to people here in Oklahoma," he said as he got up to refill his glass, "frontier Catholics, people who haven't been to Catholic schools, who may be in a mixed marriage or prevented from receiving the sacraments because of divorce, whose children aren't attending Catholic schools because there are none."

"It's true," Marlene said. "Pope John's message, which stresses the pastoral, not the doctrinal, nature of the church seems particularly relevant in Oklahoma."

Allen then went on to imagine what a useful church would do: form grass-roots organizations that cared for the poor but with a twist. If someone needed help, they would get it. In return, that person would volunteer to assist others and gain self-respect in the process. But he didn't stop there. He proposed opening a free health clinic and area food banks, even desegregating the schools. He paused, flicked the long ashes off his cigarette, and took another sip of Scotch. "The church is useless if it won't take a stand with the defenseless—the poor, blacks, Indians." His anger at injustice reminded me of my father's family.

"But how can the church be a part of this American agenda for social change?" someone asked.

"How can the church take such a stand?" I interjected.

"Form grassroots groups," he said, looking up. "Neighbor to neighbor, call them that. The church needs to move more intelligently toward greater justice. There are truths that can be known and worked into the texture of institutions; there can be the hope of founding a society in which men can dwell in dignity, justice, well-being, and freedom."

Father Allen's ideas for social reform eventually came to the attention of the bishop. One afternoon, the phone rang at my house, and Father Allen's voice said, "I just got off the phone with the bishop, and he said my remarks at the last diocesan priests' meeting had set him to thinking."

"That's wonderful," I said.

"He thought it might be about time for me to have a parish in Tulsa, in one of the poorest sections of the city, to try out some of my ideas. Wouldn't that be wonderful! I could experiment with social reform."

As I lay on the floor by the telephone, listening to him share his aspirations and success in gaining recognition from the bishop for his understanding of both the new theology and the possibilities of reform, I thought to myself, *This is like a conversation between husband and wife.* But I repressed such thoughts as well as my growing attraction to Father Allen.

I knew when my year in Oklahoma City concluded that I needed to move on, even though Monsignor Luecke had asked me to stay another year. But where might I go? I asked Father Sullivan to check out some work opportunities tied to the church in Chicago. I wanted to live in a city, and that was the only one I knew. The cheapest airfare to North Platte, where I planned to stay until I found work, was one from St. Louis. I would spend a night there to make an early morning flight.

Lois offered to drive me to the airport. "Maybe I can get one of the other volunteers to go with me. It's not much over 500, say 550 miles." An hour later, she came into my office and said, "I didn't have to look very far. When I told Father Allen I was looking for a volunteer to go to St. Louis with me, he said, 'I'll go.'" We three drove to St. Louis, found a motel near the airport, and sat in the dwindling light drinking Scotch and laughing at an elderly Oklahoma priest's doctrines on how to pour Scotch over ice so as not to bruise the sacred liquid. Father Allen and Lois departed about eight to make the long drive back to Oklahoma City. I never knew or really understood why Father Allen made that journey.

I grew up believing that one of the worst sins a Catholic woman could commit was to seduce or be seduced by a priest. Since sixth grade, I had held images in my mind of the young curate at Seven Dolors Parish in Manhattan, Kansas, and one of the high school girls walking together, deep in conversation. Later, after they both disappeared, even we sixth graders knew that he had not been talking to her about a religious vocation; she'd had to go away to have their baby. The Extension Lay Volunteer Program continued until 1971. I wonder now if Father Sullivan and the other priests in Oklahoma worried about the risks of putting young women seeking to make a difference in the church into close relationships with some of the most desirable but unavailable men in the Catholic communities. Ironically, these activist Oklahoma priests were the kind of men I desired—nonconformists who were intellectual, had a passionate social consciousness, were sexy, and possessed some of the best of male qualities. But they were men ordained to a life of celibacy. Here was one of the ironies of the Catholic Church: priests, men who represented the ideal male, were off-limits. I couldn't have been the only volunteer who thought this way.

When I left Oklahoma in the fall of 1963, changes were already forming in the frozen world of priests' celibacy and the repressed and unnatural antisexuality of the Catholic Church. It was all there under the surface; some priests left in order to marry. There was a precipitous decline in vocations over the decade of the 1960s. But most of the Oklahoma priests I worked with stayed: Fathers Schwartz, Westerman, Allen, Skeehan, and Monsignor Luecke (even though he attempted a kiss the last time I saw him).

The values these reformers sought to instill in the church had also become a part of me. At the time, I had no idea where all this would take me.

CHAPTER 5

FINDING LOVE AND WORK

"The Eleanor Club, in Hyde Park."

The taxi driver pulled away from Union Station in Chicago. It was October 1963.

Within minutes, we were traveling south along Lake Shore Drive, resplendent in all its energy and beauty: high-rise buildings lined up along the waterfront, and the neoclassical buildings of the 1893 Chicago World's Fair loomed large once we were beyond the Loop. I remembered them from my first stay in Chicago—the Museum of Science and Industry and the Field Museum of Natural History. Here was the city I had almost forgotten during those two years in Oklahoma. But the South Side was different from the North: instead of the gleaming high-rises, I saw the backside of tenements—six wooden porches, side by side, two on each of the three floors, looking worn and near collapse—the only thing visible block after block.

As I looked out of the window, I wondered if this would be yet another wilderness. I had accepted a secretarial job at Calvert House, the University of Chicago's Catholic student center, without the knowledge of a place one gains from an interview. This possibility seemed to promise more than the other job Father Sullivan had suggested—working for the Confraternity of Christian Doctrine, a publisher of children's texts, especially catechisms, on the North Side. Being at a university won out. I chose a place of learning, with a chance to maybe even attend graduate school, and hoped to find eligible men.

The taxi stopped in front of a sprawling two-story brick building with windows lighting up the first floor. An occasional window cast out light on the second floor. Looking up at the Eleanor Club, a women's residence, I was suddenly struck by how little I knew of what lay ahead in my life. The next morning, I walked along the Midway to University Street where Calvert House was located. On the way there, I saw buildings that reminded me of Europe: Rockefeller Chapel was reminiscent of the great cathedrals—a massive stone structure with statues gracing the front of the building and a huge tower pushing against the bright blue sky. Music rang out from a carillon in the chapel; there was a colorful announcement on the door: "Handel's Messiah, December 4 and 5." Hutchinson Hall, one of many collegiate Gothic buildings, was modeled after the colleges at Oxford. In the early morning quiet, I felt I was on sacred ground, ground that held out the promise of an intellectual life, a life beyond the emptiness of material things. My yearning to be a "whole man" was still there below the surface.

I had yet to learn that Woodlawn on the South side of the Midway was a predominately black neighborhood that had been mostly left to deteriorate once a white flight had occurred in the 1950s. Turning onto University Street, I saw Calvert House, one of a long string of brownstone buildings. As my eyes adjusted to the dark foyer, I saw a woman looking out from behind a glassed-in partition at the end of the reception area. She rose slowly from her chair and emerged from an office that resembled a cage to say, "You must be Mary Kay, the new secretary. I'm Helen. So happy to greet my replacement! Let me buzz Father McDonough. He's expecting you." Helen was a slight woman, dressed professionally in a suit and low heels. Her face was covered with heavy makeup. She reminded me of the legions of Catholic women who had devoted their lives to serving the church and its priests. Now she was retiring.

Seconds later, a middle-aged priest bounded down a large open stairway. The top of his balding head and horn-rimmed glasses glistened in the dim light; his clean-shaven face, broad smile, and extended hand radiated warmth. I could smell his shaving lotion. "Welcome, welcome," he said. "I see you've met Helen." He smiled broadly as if something of great significance had just happened. "I'm Tom McDonough, the head chaplain. Rollins Lambert, my assistant, is off attending a diocesan meeting on how the church should respond to what they're calling the 'civil rights movement.' Rollins was the first Afro-American ordained in the Chicago diocese, so he's deeply involved. I'm rushing off to a meeting of ministers and rabbis—ecumenical stuff, you know—at the Divinity School."

Hurrying toward the door, he struggled to get his arms through his jacket sleeves. He paused, turned around, and said, "Today's the first day of the fall quarter, so we'll be mobbed for noonday Mass, but you and Helen can get started. Oh, and one of the perks of the job is a free lunch. Maria, our cook, should be in soon. You'll be eating lunch with her in the kitchen most days, but today"—he paused, took a breath, and bowed—"in honor of Helen's soon-to-be departure and your arrival, you can both eat in the dining room with me."

For most of the morning, Helen showed me the workings of the office and tried to explain her individualistic and byzantine bookkeeping system. She filled me in on the specifics of the house residents. McDonough was a University of Chicago Law School graduate. "He doesn't practice law, per se," Helen said, "but he has multiple theories of how to creatively look after your self-interest while staying within the law. For example, he says there are three institutions you can cheat: insurance companies, the airlines, and the IRS." She laughed. "More scandalizing though is the argument he spins for using contraceptives. If the Vatican ever gets wind of his theories . . ." She broke off and mimed a short gasp to make her point.

She continued, "Rollins is a single child, very close to his mother. Never heard him mention a word about a father. He graduated from the college, one of the first Afro-Americans. Oh, and our cook, Maria. She has her problems—grandchildren to rear, problems with garnished wages, the result of some settlement over an unpaid loan, which is a major challenge to someone who makes forty dollars a week. I've suggested to Father McDonough that he pay her more, but he says that's the going rate for a cook and he doesn't want to upset the local economy."

I felt awkward the first time I sat in the kitchen with Maria, suppressing the thought that she and I might be thought of as the "help." This was not the church in Oklahoma; a young woman eating at a table with priests was not in keeping with the church's norms surrounding celibacy. My education regarding what it meant to be black in white America began that first day at Calvert House.

As McDonough had predicted, students began to stream in for noon Mass. Most of these were adult men, mostly graduate students. Within a few days, I could connect their attire with their disciplines: scientists and mathematicians wore short-sleeve sports shirts and loose-fitting, nondescript pants; law students and doctoral students in the humanities and social sciences wore dress shirts and ties and tweed jackets, some with patches at the elbows. Some took one last drag on their pipes before going into the chapel, looking to see if they were out before sticking it in their jacket pockets. That first day, though, my breath quickened at so many attractive men, men with futures. *There must be someone here for me*, I thought. The irony of seeking to become a "whole man" by marrying the perfect man escaped me.

In that promising stream of potential husbands, I spotted a dark-haired man with olive skin, symmetrical features offset by a cleft chin, and nostrils that curved in the most seductive way. He was a study in contrasts—sexual magnetism muted by an erect posture and no eye contact. His black horn-rimmed glasses cast a protective shield over his face. *Gorgeous*, I thought. Catching sight of him as he left the chapel after Mass, I saw him ease into an MG convertible parked in front of Calvert House. My heart sank. I could imagine the beautiful women who sat in his passenger's seat, the wind blowing their hair. I protected myself by thinking he was too fast for me.

Several days later, I looked out from my office and saw the MG man walk into the lobby. Seeing this as an opportunity too important to squander, I stepped out from behind the glass partition and extended my hand saying, "Hi, I'm Mary Kay, the new secretary." He nodded his head and said, "I was just dropping by for a visit." (A visit is the Catholic practice of going to a church or chapel where the Eucharist is displayed to pray or meditate.) He quickly disappeared behind the curtain that served as a door to the chapel.

Calvert House had a tradition of serving Thanksgiving dinner to students. My sister Trish, a freshman at Rosary College in Chicago, spent the holiday with me. With no invitation to dinner elsewhere, I put our names on the sign-up sheet at Calvert House.

Thanksgiving Day, Trish and I and her date, a freshman at Northwestern, descended the stairs at Calvert House to the basement. A long table was set up to accommodate the twenty or so attendees. Just as we were deciding where to sit, I looked up and saw the MG man. He was alone and quickly took a seat. There were three places to his right, just enough for my party. Would I dare sit next to him? "Trish," I said, "you sit here," pointing to the seat next to the MG man. Her date took the spot next to her. I had just engineered seating that put me two places away from a man I wanted to come to know. Much to my chagrin, just across from him was an attractive woman in political science. He began to talk with her. Afraid to appear too forward, this opportunity slipped through my fingers.

When the MG man invited me to an opera several weeks later, I was surprised. I dressed carefully the night of our date, wearing a dark-green boucle wool suit with a matching sleeveless V-neck top, offset by a gold star pin. I felt confident and sophisticated as we descended a winding staircase in Orchestra Hall during intermission. However, my attempts at conversation yielded only disappointingly monosyllabic answers.

"How was it? How was it?" a friend asked when I returned to the Eleanor Club.

"He's the coldest fish I've ever met," I said. To my chagrin, I later learned that the MG man, a lover of classical music, had a subscription to the Lyric Opera and invited a different woman to each of the performances.

⪡⪡⪡

The growing realization that I was more than three years out of college and still not married, and the subsequent thought that I might never get married, drove me to action. In the spring of my first year at Calvert House, I decided I needed a profession; I was tired of working for low wages as a secretary. Perhaps I could become a high school guidance counselor. I liked people, didn't I? I made an appointment with an advisor in the university's guidance department. As I sat across from a young man, most likely a graduate student, I told him of my aspiration.

"Why would you want to do that?"

"Well, to help students, to give them good advice on colleges, especially disadvantaged students."

"Are you interested in a doctoral program, in doing research?"

"Not really, not now."

"Then there's a newly funded Ford Foundation program for liberal arts graduates who want to be high school teachers. A good teacher is worth a hundred guidance counselors."

I was accepted into the two-year master of arts in teaching (MAT) program in the fall of 1964. As I sat in the program's orientation sessions, I was ambivalent. I had never wanted to be a teacher because that was considered a traditional "women's job." I took heart in seeing that my cohort preparing to teach was mostly balanced by gender. Planning to be a teacher of disadvantaged children made this choice even more acceptable. For the first time, I found myself among liberal arts graduates from "Protestant" colleges around the country, such as Reed, Wellesley, and Pepperdine. I felt self-conscious and apologetic as the only graduate of a Catholic women's college. The first time I spoke at the program's orientation, I prefaced my remark with "for someone with my background." Before I could make my point, a graduate of Wilberforce, a historically African American college, said, "Get over it. We all have our backgrounds."

Soon, I came to realize that the most shocking thing about my background was the difference between the education I had received at the Mount and the one I was to experience at the University of Chicago. The MAT program was designed to produce teacher scholars or teacher/scholars or teacher-scholars. The first year, we took nine quarter-length courses in our area of specialization. Mine was social studies, so I took mainly history courses. Instead of courses all taught by Sister Juanita, I now attended classes taught by prominent working historians. As my interest shifted from modern Europe to America, I studied with John Hope Franklin, the noted African American historian whose book *Reconstruction after the Civil War* had just been published. I had a course on the American Revolution with the radical Jesse Lemisch. And there were others—Hanna Gray, Hans Morgenthau, Leonard Kreiger, and Walter Johnson, for example. When the syllabus was handed out for Lemisch's course, I took it to the bookstore and purchased more than two dozen paperbacks. How, I wondered, as I walked up and down the aisles of the bookstore, am I ever going to read all of these?

The education component of the MAT program consisted mainly of courses that featured a different star professor from the School of Education, with each class meeting to talk about his research. We also observed a master teacher in the university's Laboratory School one quarter, taught the next, and returned to observe the last quarter. My disdain for teaching began to erode as I observed John Patrick, my master teacher, begin an eighth-grade American history course by using novels such as *Lord of the Flies* to introduce a unit on the formation of American democracy. I came to see textbooks as reference books. The second year of the program, we had sole responsibility for three classes (instead of five, a regular teacher's load); attended an education seminar; and wrote a masters' thesis.[1] My teaching assignment was at the all-black Parker High School on the city's South Side.

Each morning, I and three other teacher interns, all white, drove from the Hyde Park neighborhood to Parker, a thirty-minute ride west through Washington Park, along one of the broad boulevards laid out by Frederick Law Olmsted in the 1870s. Here was Chicago's racial history writ large. As Southern blacks came north for work, Chicago's African American ghetto moved southward; the area rapidly changed from white to black in the 1920s. By 1930, the population was only 7.8 percent white. By 1960, it was 0.5 percent white.

A few weeks after we arrived, I heard a voice shout, "Here they come. Here come the missionaries." The man calling out my arrival and that of a colleague, Debbie Nicholson, was Mr. Duncan, an English teacher rumored to have been a vaudeville tap dancer in the 1930s. Lean, erect, and tall, he moved with a gracefulness that made the rumor plausible. Everything about him suggested performance. His high-fashion suits were set off each day by a flamboyant shirt and tie. I rarely saw him without the English teacher's curse, a stack of student papers stuffed into his attendance book, waiting to be graded.

Debbie and I laughed as we walked into the teachers' lounge, seeing the humor in the joke; the majority of teachers were black. She and I shared a common desire to teach our students the black history they had been denied in school, a history that went beyond the achievements of a few "safe" people like George Washington Carver or Booker T. Washington. A major challenge was finding materials our students could read. Of the three classes I taught each day, two of them were "Essentials," the code name for students who read below grade level.

But not all my students appreciated my efforts. My third assignment was a senior honors class that I introduced to Charles Silberman's *Crisis in Black and White*. His analysis contained valuable learning for me but not the students. After we had been discussing the book for a number of classes, a male student came up to the front of the room, dropped to his knees, and held out his hands, raised upward in a gesture of supplication as he said, "Miss Thompson, Miss Thompson, could we please study something besides race?!" When I heard the students' uproarious laughter, I was reminded that Mr. Duncan had called me a missionary.

The halls at Parker High School, while free of litter, hadn't been painted in years. As I passed classrooms, I could see how sparsely they were furnished. In each room, thirty or so battered students' desks faced a teacher's, all scarred from years of use. A map or two hanging askew and an American flag were the only things that decorated the walls. Rumor had it that the expenditure per student at Parker was four hundred dollars per year, while it was more than one thousand dollars in affluent North Shore neighborhoods. The food in the cafeteria was very good, though; the black female cooks prepared food that tasted like home, serving up lemon meringue pies as good as my mother's.

Parker had the reputation of being a dangerous place; like most "ghetto" high schools, a full-time Chicago policeman was present each day. Officer Howard, a well-built African American man who looked as if he belonged on a recruitment poster for the police department, exuded calm as he walked the halls or sat drinking coffee in the student cafeteria. His demeanor was in sharp contrast to the white policemen who jumped out of squad cars when called, guns drawn. I had never experienced such a threat of violence as the first time I saw six squad cars careen into the concrete yard in front of the school, their sirens blaring. A swarm of white policemen jumped out. "My god, what happened?" I asked. A colleague responded, "Mr. Duncan said the principal called them when someone reported a fight in the boys' gym."

I was called into the principal's office only once during my years at Parker, in 1965. Expecting to meet with a white man I rarely saw, I was instead pointed to a frosted glass door that read, "Vice Principal." There, at a stately desk, was a stern-looking white woman whose face was framed by an upswept pompadour that was beginning to gray. I took the chair opposite her desk. "Students from your third-period class gathered outside your classroom yesterday, a noisy group. What was the reason?"

"I brought in a speaker from the community to talk about the history of Afro-Americans and the civil rights movement. It's part of a unit on the movement. When the bell rang, students followed him out into the hall to continue the conversation," I explained. The assistant principal frowned. "You need to be careful bringing in speakers from the community. The students are immature and often easily swayed. These are dangerous times."

I didn't describe the speaker, a young man most likely from the Nation of Islam, who'd worn a dashiki and the small hat like the one worn by the black Muslim Louis Farrakhan, nor did I relay his message:

> I'm one of the brothers here to talk to you today about how we must undo the type of brainwashing that we have had to undergo for four hundred years at the hands of the white man. You have to have a knowledge of history no matter what you are going to do; anything you undertake. . . . The thing that has made the so-called Negro in America fail, more than any other thing, is your, my, lack of knowledge concerning history. . . . Since the black masses here in America are not in open revolt against the American system of segregation, will these same black masses turn toward integration or will they turn toward complete separation?

It was also too dangerous to tell her about my students' reactions. When the bell rang, they had followed him out of the classroom and into the hall. He continued talking, while students from other classes began to gather. Fearing that things were getting out of hand, I shouted, "You've got to move on, move on, and get to your next class." The speaker and some students headed for the down staircase, and the crowd dispersed.

I believed that my students, including those in Essentials classes, deserved the same education as those at the University of Chicago's Laboratory School, where the dominant pedagogy was the discovery method. Where possible, I used primary source materials that I had learned about while an intern at the Lab School.

For example, one day I decided to teach my fourth-period class about frame of reference. As a way to bring home the lesson of different points of view, I arranged to have several male students from the media center bring in a TV monitor and then get into an argument about where to place the large cart that held the equipment. My plan was to stop the argument after a few minutes and then ask students to write about what they had seen. The differing descriptions and points of view would enable them to understand better how history was a construction stitched together from different perspectives.

No sooner had the media center aides begun the argument I had rehearsed with them than Ben—a tall, broad-shouldered, mature student—jumped out of his seat and began walking quickly to the front of the room, shouting, "You're messing with some of my boys." Several other boys jumped up to follow him. Recognizing that "boys" most likely meant gang members, I tried to restore order.

For days, the students would double over with laughter as one of them described my response to Ben's action: "And then our little white teacher jumped up and down shouting, 'This is an experiment; this is an experiment!'"

Regrettably, I have no way of knowing if my efforts helped my students. I now see deficiencies in my teacher preparation that limited my capacity to know what my students were learning. Formative and summative assessments of student learning beyond traditional course exams were not covered in my university courses, nor was there instruction in how to teach reading to students testing below grade level.

Mr. Duncan was not the only African American teacher who saw us as missionaries. Many of the black teachers had been at Parker for years and, indeed, saw young white teachers as missionaries, overly confident that we could make a difference in our students' lives, believing that education could overcome the hidden and not-so-hidden injuries of racism. "You young zealots will eventually move on," one said to me. I knew she was correct; I did not return in the fall of 1967 because of a trip to France.[2] But I took what I had learned with me. I identified with race oppression as well as African Americans' resistance to it. A combination of factors contributed to this identification: my exposure to Catholic priests in Oklahoma, who had a zeal for social justice; learning African American history at the university; and living and working on Chicago's South Side. My students' laughter at some of my efforts taught me that they were the authorities on being black in America. What was below the surface that I could not see was how these lessons in race awareness would later inform my views on gender oppression and resistance as well.

Even though I was no longer the secretary at Calvert House, I continued to socialize with students there. Prominent among them were several Australians, all male, doctoral students in mathematics and the sciences. One of them, Mick Deakin, a mathematician, was slight—about my height of five feet, four inches—and a chain smoker. He brought together a group of Catholic graduate students in physics, chemistry, political science, and the Committee on Social Thought[3] to figure out what it meant to be a Catholic and an intellectual, particularly in light of the reforms that were being proposed by Vatican II. I was happy to be included in this mostly male group because I too was interested in our central question. Aside from me, the other women were an undergraduate whose father was a philosophy professor at the university and the wives of two of the married students in the group.

At our first weekly meeting of the Wednesday Night Group, sitting on stiff folding chairs in the basement of Calvert House, Deakin said, "I'm seeking an intellectual argument for being a Catholic, a way to accept the teachings of the church on intellectual grounds." He went on to summarize how he was taught that there were four pillars on which Catholic theology stood: the existence of God, the immortality of the human soul, the freedom of human will, and the divinity of Jesus Christ. He finished his raison d'être by saying, "Contrast this with another case. The mathematician Leopold Kronecker is reported to have asked of the mathematical constant ϖ, 'But does ϖ exist?'"

A physicist jumped in. "Well, ϖ certainly doesn't exist in the way that the material world exists. It is a mental construct. But we can say exactly what is meant by ϖ and can use this definition to prove things about it. It can be and has been computed to millions of decimal places, and a unique digit occupies every one of these places. There is no ambiguity about it. In this sense, ϖ exists."

Next, it was the married man from the Committee on Social Thought who spoke: "But this is not at all the way God exists. The various proofs given for 'His' existence either fail or leave us well short of the monotheistic God. We need to expound a version of the 'cosmological argument,' as it is often called. Why is there something, when there could instead be nothing? Well, it is a good question, and I've never seen a satisfactory answer. But simply to answer that God, a necessary rather than a contingent being, wills it so? That strikes me as an intellectual cop-out."

The group's pattern of men talking in highly abstract terms and the women mainly listening continued for a couple of years. Occasionally, a woman would ask, "Doesn't this intellectual argument have to be lived rather than expounded?" Her query was ignored. I felt mostly alienation at each meeting, rarely saying anything, allowing the overactive editor in my head to censure my thoughts even when we adjourned to Jimmy's, a bar frequented by students. But I continued to attend the group with a mixture of emotions: feeling good about my inclusion, always hoping to have something to say, and always feeling marginalized.

In time, I became more accepting of the idea that I would still be able to have a life if I never married. During this period, I had an interesting patchwork of relationships: a platonic relationship with a fellow MAT student whose mustache was full and stiff as a brush and who took me to plays such as Martin Duberman's *In White America*; a brief relationship with a mathematician, a man of German heritage with the body of a football player, who took me to Saturday night meals of Mexican food cooked up by his friend from California where we swilled down margaritas; and a businessman from off campus, who I'd originally met the first time I lived in Chicago and who assuaged my loneliness when I returned.

Someone on the outer periphery of my social circle was the MG man. I had reconciled myself to the idea that he and I were "just friends." One Sunday early in 1965, he sat alone at a table in the basement of Calvert House as students gathered for coffee after Mass. As we said hello, he added, "You look good, but then you always look good." His eyes traveled over my cashmere sweater, rich in colors—avocado and tan and persimmon, a floral theme bold against my matching avocado pleated skirt, a gift from the businessman. His slightly parted lips and inquiring look were a departure from our former exchanges. Flattered by his attention, I thought, *What a tease.*

In March 1965, one of my roommates, Mary Margaret McAlpin, and I decided to spend our spring break in New York City. We purchased tickets to *Funny Girl* and *Fiddler on the Roof* (standing room only), arranged for a "drive away" car from Chicago to New York, and invited the MG man to come along as an extra driver. He declined but dropped a long list of inexpensive, charming French bistros in the East 50s with names such as La Grenouille and Le Cheval Blanc. When Mary Margaret and I returned home, there were three notes for me, each with the same message. Marc Tetreault called; call him as soon as you get home. I thought back to the first time I had seen him, the MG man at Calvert House.

As I got to know Marc, I came to understand that his aloofness was a protective shield. Once, he laughingly told me that when we had first talked, the day he'd made his visit to the chapel at Calvert House, he had slipped through the curtain, touched the holy water font, made the sign of the cross, knelt down, and prayed, "Dear God, don't let that woman get her claws into me. She's dangerous." Eventually, I learned that Marc had narrowly escaped being a priest, leaving the seminary after five years of study. He told me of an occasion that was crucial in his decision to leave. While visiting a friend in the military, the man brought in his son, who crawled on the carpet toward the visitors. At that moment, Marc thought, "I want one of those." When we first met, he had sworn off women. Too many of his relationships had ended badly. His plan now was to get his PhD in French literature and spend summers doing research in France. No entanglements. "But I had a problem," he said. "I loved women. I couldn't swear off them permanently, so I thought it better to have a stable of women for casual relationships."

The day before Thanksgiving 1965, Marc and I lay in front of the fireplace at my parent's home in North Platte. We both knew the purpose of this trip was for him to meet my family and for us to become engaged, even though he had yet to ask me to marry him. I could now admit to myself that accepting the idea that I might never marry had been a defense. With the fire burning brightly, he whispered, "Will you share your life with me?"

"Yes. Do you mean marry you?" At the time, I mostly imagined my life as secondary to his—he, the French professor, and I, the French professor's wife. The turns that our life together would take gradually helped me understand the importance of his choice of words. I now wonder whether, especially after my time in Oklahoma, I was attracted to Marc because he had stopped just short of being a priest (and so still had a lot of the qualities of the priests that I respected and admired) or because he was preparing to be a university professor. More important than those considerations, though, was my attraction to him, knowing deep down that we could make a life together.

When Catholics married, we were expected to attend Pre-Cana conferences, "seminars" in which a celibate priest talked about the responsibilities, tribulations, and joys of marriage.[4] Marc and I missed the session on marital sexuality for reasons I can't recall. Mary Margaret's fiancé, Dennis Brennan, a doctoral student in political theory, was eager to report what he had heard in the lecture. Leaning with his back to the stove in the kitchen where we three Catholic Marys lived—Mary Margaret, Mary Ann, and Mary Kay—Dennis began his summary of the presentation with the three of us, all of whom were to be wed the coming summer, looking on.

The guest speaker, a male physician, had critiqued misinformation about the female orgasm, a "psychological" problem for many women. He argued that for some, the failure to have an orgasm was because they were unable to adjust to their role as women. For others, it was because they failed to transfer the center of orgasm from the clitoris, which produced an "adolescent and incomplete" orgasm, to the vagina. The answer to this perplexing situation was not what some radical women were proposing—that the source of female satisfaction is in the clitoris, not the vagina. Instead, he insisted that the ideal sexual climax was when a wife had a vaginal orgasm at exactly the same time as her husband.

The problem with the clitoral orgasm, the speaker had said, was that it was often separate from the man's and thus took away from the couple's pleasure and commitment to one another. We three Marys lacked the consciousness of the workings of patriarchy to question a male physician as an authority on female orgasms.

The seminar on reproduction that Marc and I did attend was packed. We knew we wanted to have children. A childless marriage wasn't something we could even imagine, but we didn't want a baby immediately. Marc was still in graduate school, and my teacher's income was vital. Besides, we relished our time alone together.

"Well," Father McDonough began, smiling and rubbing his hands together, "I'm here to talk to you about birth control." A ripple of self-conscious laughter moved throughout the room. "There is presently a papal commission on birth control. It is rumored that an encyclical, *Humanae vitae*, will be released soon. But until that is issued, I can justify a new and modern form of controlling reproduction, the pill, on the grounds of a prior ethically settled precedent. There are a variety of precedents in Catholic moral theology for avoiding conception—for example, the beloved rhythm method."

I leaned over and whispered to Marc, "Am I hearing what I think I am hearing?" He squeezed my upper arm.

McDonough then wove an argument that held that humans are the one kind of created being that God intended to be allowed to discover and shape their reproduction in the freedom of their own nature rather than be biologically determined to procreate like other animals. "This controversial question, something those at the Vatican are excited about, is of no particular theological urgency. Common sense should guide each of you to a workable solution to this overhyped issue. It is still a matter of discussion whether the expected encyclical will have the force of an ex cathedra decree, and until the matter is resolved, Catholics are at liberty to follow their own consciences."

Therefore, a circle of variously colored pills, programmed for a woman's reproductive cycle, lay secure in a drawer near my bed a month before our wedding on July 9, 1966. One of the blessings of my life has been timing: marrying just as the pill became widely available, having a liberal priest make a case for practicing birth control, reading soon after we were married about the myth of the vaginal orgasm, and having a husband who listened to the radio program of a British philosopher, Alan Watts, who held that a man's greatest pleasure was giving a woman an orgasm.

⋘

Mary Ann Killilea and I settled into the back pew of University Church in Hyde Park. Only a wooden cross, without the body of Christ, hung on the front wall above a barren altar. Three colorful banners, contrasting the gray pillars that marched alongside the outer aisles, dominated. The weak overhead lights only served to darken the unadorned windows. It was January 1969; we were attending a lecture with a title something like "The University of Chicago: No Place for Women." Mary Ann was always the first to sense that something important might be beginning and know where to go to check it out. The vestibule was full of clusters of young undergraduate women passing out mimeographed sheets listing their demands and calling for the cancellation of classes. They wore heavy

Figure 9. Bridal photography, July 9, 1966

peacoats and thrift shop wear to protect them from the Chicago winter. In those days, paying attention to what you wore, especially among undergraduates, was the sign of an inferior mind. The only thing that you really wore was your intelligence.

In contrast, my teal-blue maternity dress, poking out of my coat and tented as it stretched out over my stomach, was the least glamorous outfit I had used to conceal my pregnancy as I continued to teach in the Chicago public schools, in defiance of the policy that dictated that pregnant teachers resign at the beginning of their fifth month. As I assembled my maternity clothes during that period, I felt like an unmarried teenager attempting to conceal the inevitable. My mother helped, transforming an outfit I had seen in the *New York Times* from hip fashion into subtle maternity wear: a brown leather sheath, worn over a midthigh herringbone wool skirt and white sweater with brown leather buttons on the arms. I seemed to have fooled the principal but not one of the African American teachers, who in late October raised her eyebrows and said, "Honey, are you going to have that baby here?" I held out until Christmas vacation—the baby's due date was February 14.

My attention was brought back to University Church. A tall woman dressed in jeans and a bright-red sweater shouted into a microphone: "Hi! I'm Marlene Dixon, a Marxist sociologist." (This was followed by loud clapping and cheering.) "My department, in its paternalistic wisdom, has voted not to renew my contract, effectively firing me. This is their signal that I will not succeed, not get tenure in three more years, that I am not fit to join their procession of educated men." (Loud and sustained boos rose up throughout the church.) "But it is also a signal that women are not welcome at this university. It's time that we engage in what the Chinese Communists call"—she raised her fingers to denote quotation marks—"'speaking bitterness.'" Her voice rising, she continued: "Recognizing our own oppression and the sisterhood of all women—these are the first steps on the road from sisterhood to radical politics, from radical politics to revolution." Clapping and a shout of "Revolution now!" ricocheted off the walls of the church. Uncomfortable with her revolutionary rhetoric, I put my hands on my stomach as I felt the baby kick.

On our earlier walk to University Church, Mary Ann had filled me in on recent undergraduate student protests: a group of students, preceded by a guerrilla band, had marched through campus tooting horns and whistles, shooting cap pistols, and carrying a bright-orange flag to protest Dixon's firing. A thousand students had shown up at a meeting the day before to decide whether to hold a sit-in aimed at earning students the chance to have input into tenure cases. One of their main gripes was that there were almost no women on the faculty. "A student group, calling themselves something like the Women's Liberation Front," Mary Ann said, "is angry about the attitude of professors toward women students."

My attention shifted back to Dixon. "Here to speak about oppression, because this isn't only about me, is Naomi Weisstein, a psychologist and neuroscientist, a Phi Beta Kappa graduate of Wellesley College, and a recipient of a PhD from Harvard, which she obtained—get this, girls—in a mere two and a half years. And she has a job! She is an assistant professor at Loyola University of Chicago."[5]

Weisstein walked to the podium, looking diminutive next to Dixon. There was nothing about her appearance—glasses, long dark hair, casual pants and shirt—to distinguish her from the young women in the church pews. "Greetings, sisters," she shouted. "I'm a stand-up comic." Clapping and cheers rose up into the church's rafters. "And what I have to tell you is no joking matter." She began to pace as she wove a tale of how she had remained ignorant about women's lot in universities until she was accepted into graduate school at Harvard. She told the audience that when she shared her news of getting into the nation's top-ranked program in psychology with her brilliant, overworked professor at Wellesley, her professor said, "Watch out once you are there. Men won't like competing with you."

"I wanted to say to her, 'That might have been true of the nineteenth century but certainly not the late fifties.' Was I ever wrong."

The stand-up comic in Weisstein came through as she described a luncheon she attended for entering doctoral students on her first day of classes. Eager to meet one of her star professors, she described him: ". . . He was dressed in the uniform of Ivy League professors: tweed jacket, bow tie, dark horned-rim glasses, and oh yes, a balding head." She paused until the laughter subsided. "Everything about his persona, including his condescending smile, signaled unacknowledged privilege. After lunch, he leaned back in his chair, lit his pipe, and announced: 'Women don't belong in graduate school.' Did I hear him correctly? My fellow male graduate students reached into their jackets, pulled out their newly purchased pipes, and lit them. I saw that they would never be told they didn't belong." The crowd was silent. She continued pacing back and forth. "I was shown in multiple ways that I didn't belong. Even though I was first in my class, I couldn't get access to the necessary equipment to do my research. I had to go to Yale, where they allowed me to collect my data."

I looked up at the ceiling, unable to take in what Weisstein was saying. I had never heard of such things. Was it a coincidence that most graduate students at Chicago were male? I thought of my attempt to be admitted to the university's doctoral program in history. A fellow student in the MAT program, a graduate of the college and a woman, had said to me, "I got into the doctoral program in history on the basis of my record in the master's program. You can do the same. Just write a letter saying you want to be admitted."

I had sent the letter, hoping they'd overlook the fact that not all my grades had been As. Months later, an envelope had arrived in the mail, battered, bearing all the marks of landing in the wrong mailbox, thrown out, and trampled underfoot by snowy boots. It was a miracle that the letter had found me at my new apartment to deliver its message of rejection. Pushing aside my remembered disappointment, I knew that beginning a doctoral program would be out of sync with Marc's doctoral work, now in its fifth year. I told myself that I didn't need to be a professor, that life was less complicated as a professor's wife. I brought my thoughts back to the podium where Dixon was beginning to detail her treatment at the University of Chicago.

꧁꧂

By the time Chantal was born on February 15, 1969, Marc and I had effectively talked our way out of the church. Following family tradition, Marc's brother Jean, the monsignor who had married us, offered to come to Chicago to baptize the baby. Marc was adamant that she not be baptized. I saw no harm in doing so. "Why can't you see it as a ritual, as a way to welcome her into our community? We both agree that we won't raise her Catholic."

Marc did not agree. "Baptism has to mean something. It's setting her up to be a Catholic in a way that I don't want. Besides, I told Jean that she was already baptized."

If someone had predicted our easy "falling away"—Marc once a seminarian and I a lay volunteer in Oklahoma—I would have said, "You don't know who I am as a person." What I failed to perceive was the influence of the University of Chicago and Pope John XXIII (1958–1963). The pope's openness to change and his efforts to bring the church up to date gave us permission to think in new ways. For instance, in late 1964, our central question in the Wednesday Night Group shifted from what it meant to be an intellectual and a Catholic to what it meant to be an intellectual and a Christian and, by 1966, what it meant to be an intellectual and a humanist. Although we were not conscious of this evolution, we were collectively talking our way out of the church with no guilt.

A proximate cause may also have been the freedom Father McDonough gave us to decide for ourselves about the pill and contraception. Sexuality was an obsession for Catholics from the time we were elementary-school children until we married. Being told that common sense should guide each of us to a workable solution on birth control suddenly took away the authority of the church over that and other aspects of our lives.

And leave Marc and I did. When we moved from Chicago in August 1969, we would never be members of a Catholic congregation again and would only enter a Catholic church for weddings, funerals, and occasionally to attend Mass when we visited Marc's mother. In one generation, Marc and I erased the beliefs of all our Catholic forbearers—Louie Tetreault, who immigrated to Quebec from France in 1687, an indentured servant to the Jesuits, and the Boyles, who immigrated in 1857 to Nebraska in Father Trecy's colony. Erased was our belief that being Catholic made us special. Also erased were fears of unwanted pregnancies, of families too large to sustain. The difference a generation can make was brought home to me one Christmas Day in the early 2000s, when Chantal was in her thirties, a doctoral student in anthropology. We were on our way from Portland to Seattle to have Christmas dinner with my sister Peggy and her family. As we passed a Catholic church in our neighborhood, a priest was standing outside, welcoming parishioners, who were streaming in for Christmas Mass. "What happened?" Chantal asked. "Did somebody die?"

Other "truths" became our religion—the life of the mind we came to embrace at the university, the civil rights movement, later the women's movement, and eventually the visual arts. When *Humanae vitae* was later issued condemning birth control, we fortunately were no longer paying attention to anything the church proclaimed.

CHAPTER 6

BECOMING THE MEN
WE WANTED TO MARRY[1]

Shortly after Chantal was born in 1969, Marc learned he had not passed his quali-fying exams and would be prevented from continuing his graduate education from his coursework to the dissertation phase. Our joy at having a newborn was clouded by his feelings of failure and rejection. He was prevented from doing what he thought he wanted to do. Not one to sink into a hopeless depression of inaction, he went to work at the U.S. steel mill in Gary, Indiana, driving the twenty-five miles from Hyde Park; enrolled in a ceramics course; and decided to return to high school teaching. The University of Chicago's job placement office listed a position for a teacher prepared to teach advanced placement courses in French at Framingham North High School, a town about twenty miles west of Boston, so Marc applied. Moving to Massachusetts appealed to us—the city offered an endless variety of music, art, and culture; New England was a cornu-copia of natural beauty. We would be close enough to Marc's family in Connecti-cut to celebrate holidays but far enough away that his family could not meddle in our daily affairs. Relocating to Nebraska was never a consideration because we believed the East Coast offered us much more. Equally important, my father was in Vietnam in 1969, and my mother was living in California.

Yet this turn of events left me numb and disappointed. I also worried about the effect on Marc. He was certainly more important to me as a lover, a hus-band, a friend, and now a father than as a French professor, but my status had changed as well. I would not be the professor's wife, smiling through dinner par-ties where I was the only non-French speaker. Little did I understand how much and in what ways this derailing of our expectations for him would actually affect my future.

Several days before we left Chicago, I sat in a chair on the wooden porch at the back of our third-floor apartment overlooking the Bixler playground, with children's shouts and laughter rising up, and began to throw away folders that held teaching materials. I reasoned that I wouldn't be teaching for at least

87

ten years while I mothered several children, but I couldn't bring myself to discard the units in U.S. history that John Patrick had developed at the Laboratory School. I remembered how my third-period Essentials class at Parker High School had risen to a discussion of Nat Turner and how my honors class had brilliant insights as we discussed *Animal Farm*. These lessons were a part of me. I couldn't throw them away.

We thought we wanted to live in Cambridge, Massachusetts, but we soon gave up that desire after seeing one too many grim third-floor walkups, and instead we rented a turn-of-the-century house on Concord Street in Framingham. Worn out from our move and the change in our lives, I had little interest in venturing out the front door except for trips to the local library and hardware store, which drew me in with its coupons, pushing Chantal in her stroller. I marveled at the baby's life unfolding before me and felt a love unlike any other, yet I moved in a fog of nursing, depositing diapers in a pail, and descending into the basement to wash baby clothes. One morning in March, I asked myself, *Is this how you're going to lead your life for the next ten years?*

What finally brought me out of the house was an announcement of a six-week course, Women in Society, at the Cambridge Adult Education Center, on Wednesday mornings from ten to eleven thirty. Marc would be teaching at that time. What could I do with Chantal? I decided I'd take her with me. Surely a course on women would make some accommodation for children! The first day of class, I walked into the center with Chantal on my hip. A thin woman at the reception desk, some years over sixty, stood up and said, "We don't allow children in the center."

"Could you make an exception just this once? I've come all the way from Framingham; she's a very quiet baby. I'll put her here in her portable seat. If she fusses, I'll leave."

"Sorry. No children. Put her outside in the front yard. She'll be fine."

From the center's porch, a grassy area stretched out to the sidewalk interrupted by a low hedge. I put Chantal in her seat and looked around. She was a beautiful baby—dark-brown eyes, olive skin, and fluffy blonde hair. She looked up at me, smiling. Suddenly, my mother's instincts kicked in. What if someone took her? *No, no, no*, I thought and headed toward our Volkswagen Beetle.

Successfully locating a babysitter, Chantal's first, I traveled weekly into Cambridge, exhilarated by much of what I was learning about cross-cultural studies of sex-role socialization. But it was some unanticipated connections that set me on a new course. On one of my trips to the local library with Chantal, I saw a notice for a community forum, a series of public lectures that covered timely topics such as the war in Vietnam and new paradigms for public education. Margaret Mead would finish off the series with a lecture, "Marriage in an Age of Social Change." An extensive bibliography, surely the work of a scholar, accompanied the notice. After the first forum, I stood in line to talk with one of the organizers, Liz Fideler.

"I'm new in town," I said somewhat breathlessly, "and would like to know how I can be involved in this community."

"Well, welcome," she said, smiling broadly. "I suggest you join me and some other women at a weekly gathering at the Unitarian church. It's called 'Mothers and Others,' Thursdays at ten thirty."

The next Thursday morning, I walked into a large function room adjacent to the Unitarian church on the Framingham Common. I had learned that the minister and the congregation were active in the anti–Vietnam War movement; for instance, they had organized a large march and demonstration in downtown as part of National Peace Action Day in October 1969. A solemn-faced young man with hair of a length fashionable at the time, clearly the minister, sat at the head of the table. I took a chair alongside Liz. The others around the table were older women. "Welcome," the minister said to me. "Here at Mothers and Others, I have one rule, and that is that you are encouraged to open up and say what is on your mind."

But it was a suggestion by Liz's husband, Paul, a historian at Lesley College and her coauthor of the community forum's reading list, that shook my intellectual foundations. He thought I might benefit from a book he was using in his U.S. history course, *A Century of Struggle* by Eleanor Flexner, which had been published in 1958. My strongest feeling while reading the book was disbelief. How could I have majored in history as an undergraduate and taken graduate courses at the University of Chicago and learned so little of this? Thinking about history led to questions about the nature of knowledge. If all of this history had been lost or suppressed, what did it say about what counted as legitimate knowledge?

When I finished Flexner's book, I couldn't wait to get to the next meeting of Mothers and Others to tell them of my discovery. "I found the most wonderful book in American women's history. It's all about the knowledge we've been denied. I can't believe I learned none of this in my history courses." Before any of the women could respond, the minister, who facilitated our discussions, glared at me and said in a firm voice, "I don't want you talking about that. I don't want you ruining our group." *Weren't we to talk about what mattered to us?* I thought. I wonder now if he saw feminism as threatening his dominant position in the group. In that instant, I knew that I could no longer stay with that group.

Suddenly, I saw that the future I had expected—staying home for ten years while I raised my children—was not for me. I left the meeting resolved to get a part-time teaching job. I would have to move fast. It was already late August. After talking with Marc about how we'd manage Chantal's care, I drew a fifteen-mile circumference on a map, with our home at the center. My plan was to contact school districts within that area until I found a part-time job. I used the telephone near our bed, propping my feet up into the most comfortable position possible, knowing this might take a while. With a list of the telephone numbers of school districts nearby, I dialed the number for the Framingham School District. A woman in the personnel office quickly informed me that the district had no part-time openings this year, emphasizing that they rarely did. My heart sank. What would I do if I heard a similar response in each district?

I dialed the number for the next town over, Wayland, panicked that I might never teach again. When I inquired about part-time openings in high school social studies, the voice on the other end said, "As a matter of fact, we do. Just this morning, two courses opened up. We expected two MAT students from Harvard, but they can't be here until early November. We need to fill the classes now."[2]

In the first half hour of my interview, the chair offered me two classes back-to-back, one in American history and the other in freshman social studies. This was perfect. I would only need childcare for two and a half hours each day. A friend, Joan Chasan, an early childhood teacher, recommended a woman who provided day care in her home. One evening nearly a year later, as Marc searched for WGBH, the local PBS station, which played our usual fare of classical music,

Figure 10. Marc and me at a fund-raiser for Congressman Robert Drinan, 1971

Chantal, on hearing "elevator" music as Marc changed the dials on the radio, said, "Mrs. Stybe's music." We laughed at her distinction and knew we needed more professional day care. About the same time, I learned of a meeting that the League of Women Voters was holding to discuss childcare. Sitting in the overstuffed chair in her living room, the president of the group laid out a plan to study the issue. I couldn't restrain myself: "Study the issue? If we take a couple of years to study the issue, our children will be in kindergarten."

"Childcare is too important to jump into. It needs to be studied. Not everyone believes women should leave their children to work."

When the meeting concluded, a law student, Margaret Sofio, and my friend Joan agreed with my observation. "Let's meet to see what we can do," Joan proposed. We three, along with others, knew it was up to us if we were to have day care in our community, so we dove in, learning as we went along. Our discussions of educational philosophy soon revealed that we wanted a child-centered environment, one that was nurturing but educational. The luxury of such discussions soon gave way to other realities: incorporating as a nonprofit, meeting Massachusetts's laws regarding day care such as child/teacher ratios, and even the number of cots for nap time. We delegated responsibilities among us for hiring a director, developing a budget that included a sliding scale for tuition, and fundraising. One member of our group, Arlene Bernstein, took on the challenge of locating a space, which turned up one dank basement after another. It eventually came to her attention that an old colonial house on the town common belonging to the Congregational Church was empty. When she met with the minister, he was sympathetic to her request; Arlene had a verbal rental agreement by the time she left.

By November 1972, when Chantal was 2.9 years old, exactly the age when Massachusetts's law permitted a child's attendance in day care, the Framingham Children's Center opened.

⚜︎

Other things spurred me beyond the house, including the emerging women's movement and the friendships forming among those of us working on day care. In August 1970, to commemorate the fiftieth anniversary of the passage of the Nineteenth Amendment, which gave women the right to vote, marches were held in several cities, including Boston. The call to action, "Don't iron while the strike is hot," was nationwide. Three of my friends and I carpooled into "town," babies held on our laps, their strollers ready in the trunk. Once we were on the Massachusetts Turnpike, our consciousness-raising session began. "Why should women wear makeup?" Ellie Leavitt asked. "Men don't wear it. It's our way of hiding behind our oppression. It's a mask."

"What really pisses me off," I said, "is that they make more money than we do. We only make 59 cents for every dollar a man makes for similar work."

Figure 11. Women's strike, Boston, August 1970

"Well, what do you expect? We're excluded from the high-paying jobs. Did you see the statistics on the number of women in medical school and law school? It's at 2, maybe 3 percent. I'm one of ten female law students in my class at Boston College, ten out of a class of a hundred," Margaret said. "You should hear the laughter and scoffing of my male classmates when one of the women brings up the restrictions we face in some states—laws against women obtaining credit cards, making wills, or owning property without a husband."

"I don't have to go outside my house to feel oppression," Ellie said. "My husband thinks my son is my responsibility. 'You were the one who wanted a baby,' he'll say to me. Once in a while, he'll deign to pick up the vacuum cleaner and clean a little. And he expects me to thank him for that. What does it imply about whose job it is when I'm expected to thank him for doing a tiny fraction of the housework?"

Once the laughter subsided, I said, "I found this amazing article, 'The Politics of Housework.' That's what this is about, the politics of housework." On that drive to Boston, I didn't share the facts about the politics of housework in my home. When we married, Marc and I slid into the traditional gender roles of our parents' generation. Maintaining the household was my responsibility, and supporting us was his—except he was a graduate student who sometimes taught a class, and I supported us by teaching full time in the Chicago public schools.

One Friday evening in our first year of marriage, exhausted after teaching five classes a day, four of them to lower-level students, I decided to serve the week's leftovers. "This looks like all the food you served this past week," Marc said. "There's nothing worse than a plateful of dried-out meat loaf next to overcooked beans. I wish you wouldn't serve leftovers all on one night. Portion them out; let's eat them during the week. I don't enjoy seeing the week that was." Feeling that I needed to do better, needed to make him happy, I said, "Sure. I can do that."

Now the politics of housework were under scrutiny. One of my feminist friends thought we might gain some ground by bringing the men more formally into our discussions and asked me to speak to a group drawn largely from couples known for their liberal political views. The topic was a question circulating at the time: What is it that women want? When I walked into the host's basement "rec" room, I saw that nearly all the chairs, more than twenty-five of them, were filled with couples, mostly in their thirties and forties. I don't remember the details of my talk, but the message was simple. Women want what Freud said men want—love and work. When I finished, I asked if there were any questions, and one of the men said, "Marc, what is it like to be married to a woman who wants it all? Isn't love, your love, enough for her?"

Marc laughed, moved forward in his chair, and said, "It isn't easy. There's a lot to negotiate. There are lots of expectations, expectations I didn't, well, expect. I take care of our daughter afternoons when I pick her up from the day care center. I sometimes vacuum." His voice trailed off. The men turned away from

Marc in silence. The women continued to look down. Our host asked, "Any other questions?" Silence. I got up from the table where I had been sitting and moved toward the back of the room. No one spoke to me or looked me in the eye. Now I wonder if they saw attention to the politics of housework as a threat to their own domestic arrangements.

But changes, slow glacial changes, are often so subtle they are hard to perceive. On the special occasions when Marc did cook before we were married, his signature dish was beef chuck smothered in Lipton's onion soup. But once he opened Julia Child's *Mastering the Art of French Cooking*, a wedding gift, he began to prepare meals for our guests. A photo of a dinner party in the fall after we married shows the three "Virgin Marys" that Dennis had spoken to earlier about vaginal orgasms and our husbands, smiling over Marc's lobster thermidor. The pages of the recipes for kidneys in red wine sauce with marrow and coq au vin are stained from preparations for multiple dinner parties that followed.

The 1970s were a time of anger for me: anger at women's secondary position, anger at Marc because our domestic arrangements hadn't kept up with the feminist rhetoric about the politics of housework. Marc's reaction to my hostility was sometimes noncommittal and sometimes angry as arguments escalated: crashing a stack of our favorite Dansk plates to the floor after a dinner party, putting a fist through the wall in our entry hallway. "Do you remember what you were angry about?" I asked him more than forty-five years later. "Everything," he said. We both laughed.

Some of my anger, and Marc's, was directed toward the idea of the nuclear family. At dinner parties, our conversations had a ring of repetition: "It's isolated, it's inefficient, and it may not be good for the children."

"R. D. Laing had it right when he said the nuclear family is at the root of our problems."

"Ah, and the sociologist Jessie Bernard says marriage makes women sick."

When morning dawned, we mostly tried to creatively and collectively meet the needs of our young families. We had friends in Cambridge who lived in a commune. That was too experimental for us—better to move cautiously. To ease the burden of preparing dinner each day, we decided to share a weekly meal, alternating between houses, with our friends the *Warrens, who had three children. When this arrangement was successful, Joe Warren proposed that we also share weekly grocery shopping. One couple took responsibility for shopping every other week, filling a second grocery cart with items from the other family's list. As the months went by, Joe began doing the shopping when it was their turn and returned later and later, picking up our list at nine thirty and not returning until four thirty in the afternoon.

"He's having an affair," Marc said.

"That's ridiculous," I said. "He's got a wife and three children."

"As if that matters," Marc said. Joe and Nancy were the first among our friends to divorce in the 1970s.

The practice of my doing the daily cooking and cleaning up for our family continued until the summer of 1973, when Chantal and I took a trip to New Mexico to visit my sister Trish. Marc stayed behind to take art classes. When Chantal ran from the plane to hug Marc shouting, "Daddy, Daddy," and we kissed over her, he said, "I'm going to start doing the dishes. It's only fair."

Neither Marc nor I could recall exactly when he started cooking half of the time. Since our memories failed us, I asked Chantal about her recollections of her parents sharing household work. Her answer came in this email:

> I'm trying to think about this—one thing that does come to mind [from that time] is the collective spirit of a lot of our close family friendships. My great memories of that time have to do with dinners with the Warrens and others, not to mention the day care center that you set up. Lots of shared, collective experiences of community. And our cross-country skiing and shared family vacations as well are another example. In a sense, it seemed like people (our friends and us) believed that you could change the world and human experience by building new communities and family structures. There was a dark side, of course, as with the shared family grocery shopping being a front for Joe's affair.

A poem, written by my friend Alan Feldman, captures that time by recalling one of our cross-country skiing family vacations in New Hampshire. In the fourth and fifth stanzas, he writes:

> Or skiing with Marc, Mary Kay and Chantal, with Daniel on my back
> And Chantal goes downhill into a tree, and starts to wail
> And nobody's impatient. She keeps asking for more tissues. She's eleven.
> She's never been so weepy. They think it's hormonal.
> I see them standing still on their skis. Their tall daughter calming down.
> And they look like a new, wise race of snow people.
>
> And suddenly I see that I'm happier right now than when I was eleven
> Something I never thought would happen . . . in a safe place among my friends.[3]

When I first read Alan's poem, I saw Marc, Chantal, and me in the bright sun of that day, warmed by the poet's image of us. However, my assumption that "it's hormonal" was destroyed years later when we got out the skis Chantal had been wearing that day and discovered that they were the slickest we owned. It was nearly impossible to stand on them, let alone stay upright on a trail made difficult by melting snow and moguls. It surprises me now that we wouldn't have been suspicious about the skis rather than the hormones of an eleven-year-old.

I didn't see it at the time, but falling back on clichés about Chantal's maturity was a harbinger of my later inability to engage constructively with her adolescent sexuality, one of the greatest costs of having been a Catholic virgin in the 1950s. I did not know how to tell a sixteen-year-old of the pleasures and dangers of sex.

✦

After a few meetings in my consciousness-raising group, I found that being angry was boring and hard to sustain. It was better to move on, to direct that energy to something more positive. It was time I got over feeling resentful that I wasn't a professor's wife. Learning women's history and thinking about how to integrate it into my courses at Wayland High School became the channel for that energy. Wayland was one of the ten richest towns in Massachusetts. Many of the students' fathers worked as engineers in companies along Route 128. Most of their mothers were housewives. They lived in a predominately white suburban cocoon of ranch houses nestled in the woods; the busing controversy that was tearing Boston apart was of another world. Most students had internalized their parents' belief in a system of meritocracy and so were motivated to do well in high school in order to achieve the dream of being admitted to one of the Ivies or the seven sisters. Most of the female students also carried within them the monolithic expectations imposed on them—to be beautiful and to be popular.

The curriculum in the social studies department reflected the latest thinking in the world of education. Works of fiction and film and primary sources were our main texts; textbooks were used only as a reference. A key feature of our innovative curriculum was a series of topical electives for junior and senior courses. During the spring of my second year, the department chair called a meeting to discuss proposals for new ones. The dominant members of the department were young, bright, articulate males, graduates of prestigious colleges—Yale, Amherst, Oberlin, and Princeton—with MAT degrees from Harvard. They had gone into high school teaching to bring about a better world, to move beyond racism to a more equitable multicultural world. The one exception to the boys' club was Lucille Champagne, a woman in her sixties who taught freshman and sophomore social studies classes.

*Tom Schlageter, a brilliant Oberlin graduate who would later get a PhD in the history of American civilization at Harvard, was the smart one who always spoke first. I often imagined him as one of Groucho Marx's sons. He had the same dark bushy mustache and a comical gait. "How about one on the Depression? Many of my students are worried that their fathers may be laid off as part of the slump in engineering that's been happening along Route 128."

The men in the department knocked Tom's idea around. I waited my turn. "I've found my students have a high interest in learning women's history. I'd like to offer an elective on women in American society."

"Humph," said Lucille. "I'm not sure women's lib belongs in the classroom."

"Well, if we're going to consider that elective, we'll have to assess students' interest," the chair said. Several months later, I walked into our department office, a cramped room housing all eight faculty in desks separated by chest-high cubicles. Several colleagues were listening to the chair read numbers from a sheet. Suddenly, I felt the climate turn chilly. He continued, "So the biggest draws for students are the Great Depression and Revolution and Reform. They look like the two new offerings for this year."

"What happened with women's history?" I asked.

The chair gave Lucille a sideward glance. "The forms for that topic can't be found."

"Can't be found? How can that be?"

"I don't know. They can't be found. Somehow they got lost. You'll have to wait until next year when we do the assessment again." Lucille gave me a bone-chilling look. I ignored her and said, "I can't believe this. Can't be found. You can bet I'll be back next year."

During the ensuing year, Schlageter would come into the office many mornings with an article from the *Boston Globe* about some feminist demonstration or effort promoting women's rights. He particularly relished those that described outrageous acts; descriptions of bra burnings were his favorite. He insisted on reading each article, precisely cut out, in its entirety. He would pause in his reading to laugh uproariously, often to Lucille's delight, at any inflammatory statement, hitting his fist against his knee. I tried to ignore them.

I suppressed my anger until I got home, exploding as I related the latest outrage to Marc. "You won't believe what happened today at our department meeting when I brought up the question of the elective in women's history. That sexist pig Schlageter said, 'As I say to my students: "Women's history? There isn't anything to teach is there?"'" Marc frowned and said to me, "The next time he says that just look at him and say, 'Oink, oink.'"

"Oink, oink," I said, laughing, practicing my newfound mantra. A week or so later, Schlageter pulled out one of his newspaper clippings and said, "Do I have something for you 'women's libbers.'" I had been lying in wait for him, a chorus of oink, oinks darting through my head. I squinted my eyes and gave him the most intense stare I could muster. The words "oink, oink" were forming on my lips. Tom returned my gaze and then looked away, saying nothing. I never had to utter my mantra. His goading stopped; the course was approved and so popular among students (all female with one exception) that two sections were scheduled for the next year. Panic set in. Where was I ever going to find enough materials for a ten-week course? There were no texts for high school students.

I knew from reading *A Century of Struggle* that the Schlesinger Library was a place to start. When I located the library and pulled back its heavy front door, full of anticipation, an attendant sitting alone at a desk looked up at me and said, "You must check all of your pens. We only allow pencils in the library because we need to protect our valuable collection—unpublished diaries, unpublished papers, historic copies of books out of print." I gave her my pens and sat down at a table not even knowing what to look for, feeling inadequate. I took out my copy of Flexner's book and studied my jottings: Edmund Morgan, *The Puritan Family*; Elizabeth Dexter, *Colonial Women of Affairs*. I went back to the woman at the desk and inquired where I could find Morgan's and Dexter's books. "You won't find them here. You'll have to go to Weidner, the main library at Harvard, and I doubt if you have a card there. You can't get into the stacks unless you have one. Do you have a card?"

"Well, no," I said.

"You can probably find what you're looking for at the Wellesley College Library. And they might let you into their stacks." The Wellesley Library did let me into their stacks, although I couldn't check out books because there were no circulation privileges for people outside the college. The "must find" books from Flexner's footnotes were all there, primary sources and long forgotten narrative histories that I could use in my course. I spent hours digging out materials, Xeroxing some, and laboriously copying text on three-by-five index cards, letting out my breath occasionally and thinking, "Thank you, sweet Jesus." I didn't know at the time that this research would have other uses.

But I didn't dig up only historical materials. I had learned earlier—learned the hard way—about student resistance to some lessons while I was teaching a two-week unit on sex roles in a colleague's senior social studies class. Heterosexual relationships, fear of success, and sex-appropriate behavior in adulthood, all hot topics among feminists at the time, were issues that high school seniors were endeavoring to resolve for themselves and felt ambivalent and anxious about in general. To teach them, it was better to start with a stage in the life cycle where adolescents are the experts: childhood. I used *X: A Fabulous Child's Story*, in which Lois Gould humorously describes an experiment in nonsexist childrearing. With that beginning, they would be able to move on to a historical examination of childhood and adolescence by asking, "What was it like to be a girl (or boy) at various times in our history?"

It was too dangerous to talk about what I was learning with my departmental colleagues for fear it would set off their worst fantasies of a women's libber among them. I turned to a friend, Sheila Stanley, a psychologist who worked in the Family Counseling Program. When I talked to her about what I was learning and showed her my materials, she said, "You should get these published."

"Me, publish something? No one in my family has ever published anything."

"Doesn't matter," Sheila said, "and you should be department chair."

"You know I can't be department chair. I'm a woman."

At the time, in 1973, there was an author in my department, Marty Sandler, teaching one class in American history to gauge students' reactions to his recently published textbook, *The People Make a Nation*. A collection of primary sources in American history, the book was an exciting innovation—he threw aside the traditional pattern of organizing documents chronologically and instead had a thematic organization that mixed historical and contemporary materials. For example, he began with an account of young volunteers working for the McCarthy campaign in New Hampshire in 1972. The book was rich with visuals—photographs, paintings, and scenes from films—that illustrated the complexity of American history. What Marty had done was the exact model for what I wanted to do with American women's history.

The next time I saw him in the department office, I summoned up my courage and said, "I absolutely love your new textbook. It's so innovative. I love the mix of contemporary and historical materials. And the photographs! I especially like what you've done because I'm beginning to gather primary sources in American women's history, and your book inspires me to do that in an equally creative way. In fact"—I gulped—"is there any chance you'd be interested in doing a textbook with me?"

"Promising idea. I would be. Show me what you've got."

I went home and worked frantically to add more readings, polish up the introductory text, and refine students' activities and questions. I put a package in Sandler's mailbox about a month later and gave a sigh of relief when I saw it was gone the next morning. A couple of days later, Marty handed the manuscript back to me and said, "You don't need me. You'll get these published. I'm currently doing another textbook for Ginn, and they might be interested in this. I'll show it to my editor."

Months went by, and I heard nothing from Marty. When I eventually saw him, he turned to me and said, "I'm sorry this has taken so long. I've had a lot of personal challenges lately. My ex-wife's boyfriend was stabbed in the stomach, and . . ." His voice trailed off. He finally continued, "Ginn is not interested. But I know that Rand McNally is doing some very innovative textbooks these days. I'll show it to an editor there."

Again, there was a long period with no word from Marty or from Rand McNally. In the spring, I went to the regional National Council for the Social Studies meeting in Boston. Seeing the publishers' displays of new textbooks, I was reminded of the quote my high school friend Kathryn Swanson had written in a graduation gift to me, *The Best Loved Poems of the American People*: "For of all sad words of tongue or pen, the saddest are these: 'It might have been!'" I didn't want to be saying, "It might have been" on my deathbed. I wandered through the aisles of displays until I saw Rand McNally's banner. I walked up to a meek-looking young man arranging books on one of the tables and said, "Did a guy named Marty Sandler ever give you a set of materials in American women's history called *Women in American Society*?"

"It doesn't sound familiar. The person you need to contact is Phyllis Goldstein. She's the social studies editor, but she's not here." I got together yet another copy of the manuscript and sent it to Goldstein. Two weeks later, she called to say she would be in Cambridge the following Friday and asked if I was available for lunch.

The elegance of the dining room in the Commander Hotel in Cambridge was a surprise. It was nearly empty as I approached the thirtysomething woman sitting alone. "You must be Phyllis," I said as I extended my hand. The "yes" that she spoke in a high, little girl voice took me aback. Her voice, I would soon learn, masked her brilliance.

We made small talk during lunch, mostly about the University of Chicago, where she had been an undergraduate. Once the dishes were cleared, she said, "We're very interested in publishing your textbook. There is a freshness about it, beginning with the choice of materials, that we think will have great appeal. In fact, our editor of high school textbooks thinks this could be a prototype for a twelve-volume paperback series. Depending on how things go, you could be the editor of the series." I was beside myself with joy. I couldn't believe this was happening to me, and happening so effortlessly, with no need to make a case for publication.

It took more than a year for a contract to arrive and a date of publication to be set. It was as though my manuscript were one of the planes that circled airports waiting for its turn to land. Once I had a contract, summer vacations from school gave me the time to work on my book. I had a feeling of unbelievable harmony as I sat in the sunshine in a low sand chair, books in American women's history surrounding me on the grass in our backyard. I could hear Chantal and her teenage babysitter's muted voices as they played nearby.

As I continued work on this project, our lives took other twists and turns. We bought our first house, set on the winding and wooded Belknap Road, where the first house built in Framingham (ca. 1630) still stood. Stately colonial and eighteenth-century houses with open fields fanned out in either direction. Cannons had rumbled by during the Revolutionary War as they made their way from Fort Ticonderoga to Boston. Our house, one of several more modest ones built in the 1950s, sat above a brook with woodlands to the west and a backyard that gradually rolled down to wetlands.

In the early 1970s, Marc and I both rejoiced in our domesticity but were surprised at our differing expectations. When Chantal was barely two, before we moved to the house on Belknap Road, I decided it was time to have another baby. When I told Marc, he said, "Why? I see no reason for a second child. There are too many children in the world as it is." I was stunned. This bone of contention hovered over us for several months. It was resolved when he finally said, "If someone has a positive reason for doing something, it should carry more weight than a negative one," giving in to my desire.

When I was five-and-half-months pregnant, there was an evening when I didn't feel well, so I lay down after dinner, worried that the "spotting" of the past few weeks threatened a miscarriage. Marc and Chantal were out in the garage fixing our 1964 Ford Falcon, one Joe Warren had found for us, a quick sale from an engineer being sent abroad by his company. "Fifty dollars in cash and it's yours," he'd said. Just as I dozed off, I felt a gush and looked down; there was blood all over the sheets. Marc rushed me to the hospital in Newton, where my gynecologist practiced. He took one look at me and said, "You're having a miscarriage." I was taken into the operating room immediately, and my strongest memory is of looking up when the fetus emerged. My doctor's only words were, "These things happen." When Marc walked into the recovery room, I said, "It was a boy." He touched my cheek, tears welling up in his eyes, and said, "I'm sorry, so sorry. The loss must be harder for you because you carried the child for so long."

Once I returned home, I spent nearly a week recovering on the living room couch, looking out our picture window, feeling numb. My departmental colleague Lucille came by and, despite our differences about feminism, comforted me, saying, "Life takes many turns and somehow we get by." *These things happen,* I thought. *We'll try again.*

And we did try again, but I miscarried even sooner. After my second miscarriage, we decided one child was enough. Chantal was a dream of a child. How fortunate we were that there were no complications with her birth. Now we were ready to live our lives together as a threesome.

⋘⋙

Marc coped with teaching high school ten months of the year by taking ceramic classes at the Worcester Arts and Crafts Center, beginning in the summer of 1970. Soon he bought a handmade potter's wheel: the rear axle of a ten-ton truck with the tire filled with cement, perfectly balanced so it would turn the smaller wheel on which he placed wet clay. The rhythmic sounds of that heavy wheel turning soon became a part of our household's noises. Pots and ceramic sculptures lined the shelves in his studio, including one called Richard Nixon, a cuboid with a crown-like projection on one end that had been glazed red, white, and blue, which Marc dubbed, "A blockhead, who thinks he's a king."

Increasingly, he came to see himself as an artist; the courses that the center offered didn't satisfy his desire to do ceramic sculpture. In the fall of 1973, he took a one-year leave of absence from teaching and enrolled in the Museum School, associated with the Museum of Fine Arts and Tufts University in Boston. Criticism about the extent to which Marc was going against expectations for men at the time came not from our families but from a friend we had known at the University of Chicago: "My brother doesn't think you should leave a secure teaching job to go to art school. He wonders where you think an art school degree will lead. He wonders how in the hell you're going to support your family."

Marc and I ignored his remarks. Marc returned to teaching in 1974, a required "payback" for his leave, but he couldn't wait to return to the Museum School full time once that obligation was met. Courses in art history, drawing, and painting broadened his work beyond ceramics, and by the end of his first year, he declared painting as his major and was committed to completing the school's four-year studio program. By then, Chantal was ready for kindergarten. "What," I asked myself, "can I possibly do when she is in school for only two and a half hours a day, from nine to eleven thirty?" Wayland High School made no accommodations for a mother (or father) whose child had such a schedule. There was no transportation system to get her from day care to school and back. Another reason to pursue other options was that I was tired of high school teaching, thinking to myself, *If I have to teach the American Revolution one more time, I'll go crazy.* An attractive option was to consider work on a doctorate.

There were other motivations for doing graduate work. I was deep into doing research for my textbook and wanted to understand if learning about women's history made a difference in students' lives. The overriding paradigm of feminism at that time was sex role socialization, how children learn to behave as males and females and how they carry those attitudes into adulthood. If we could understand the workings of this socialization at home, on the playground, and in school, we could alter the way an individual perceived those roles and imagine a "sex fair" world. I wanted an academic mooring for these ideas and also to know if the materials I was compiling squared with current curriculum theory.

I decided to look around for graduate programs in education. There weren't too many choices in the Boston/Worcester area for someone with my interests. The Harvard School of Education wasn't interested in accepting midcareer professionals into its doctoral programs, and Boston University had the reputation of being a degree mill. Clark University in Worcester had a good reputation—hadn't Freud taught there? I made an appointment with a professor in social studies education, my specialty, and was surprised when he turned out to be an assistant professor, younger than I.

"So what is it you came to see me about?" he asked.

"I've been compiling primary source materials in American women's history for high school students; in fact, I have a publisher for them. So I'm interested in seeing how what I'm doing coincides with the latest thinking." I laughed. "Or doesn't."

"Well," he said, drawing his shoulders in tighter, "I'm not aware of any interest in women's history in social studies curriculum circles."

Taken aback, I said, "I just thought it might be worth asking." He went on to explain that the emphasis at Clark was on political theory because education professors believed that students in their doctoral program needed to have that emphasis in order to be more marketable in the academy.

"Are you married?" he asked suddenly.

"Yes," I said, touching the wedding band on my left hand.

"The reason I ask is that I'm sorry you don't have the life my wife has. She's not at all concerned about women's lib. In fact, she's out playing tennis right now.

Plays most every day when she isn't looking after our two children. It's too bad you have only this to be concerned about." Stunned, I felt my face flush, so taken aback that I was speechless.

Afterward, I sat in my car, not quite believing our conversation. *Screw him*, I thought. *I'm going to see what Boston University has to offer.* After being bounced around from department to department, I was directed to Steve Ellenwood, chair of the department of social education. I learned that the program, which led to a doctorate in education, an EdD, had course requirements in education, the humanities, and social sciences. "Harvard, which offers the same degree, wouldn't stand for our offering a PhD," Ellenwood said. While I had fantasized about earning a PhD since my days at the University of Chicago, this would have to be good enough. I liked the idea of being able to take courses in women's studies—women's history, the sociology of women, the psychology of women—along with courses in curriculum theory.

I was one of three students admitted into the program, along with a Radcliffe graduate with a MAT from Harvard and a Wellesley graduate. At least I'd be in the company of smart, well-educated women. I first met my two colleagues during a meeting Ellenwood held to introduce us to one another. As I sat down, one of them pointed to the ceramic beads I was wearing and said, "Where did you get those beads? I want some."

"My husband—he's an artist—made them." The combination of her dress, a shift that I had seen in the window of the Marimekko store in Cambridge; dangling earrings; skin unadorned by makeup; her nearly white hair; and a confident smile gave her an aura of being totally at ease with herself.

"Hi, Frinde Maher."

"Frinde?" I asked tentatively.

"My name is actually Frances, as is my mother's, who was called 'Frin' when she was little. My middle name is Dorothea, so 'Frin' plus *D* makes it 'Frinde.'"

The other woman, a blonde, said, "I'm Barbara Oder; that's my married name. I was quite happy to leave my Polish family name behind." Barbara was quick to note that she was a physician's wife, "a true curse." When my turn came to talk a bit about myself, I didn't mention Mount St. Scholastica College but emphasized that I had a MAT from the University of Chicago. We soon learned that we had a lot in common—we were all married with small children. Barbara and Frinde had two each. Now we were ready to move beyond being wives and mothers and teachers, uncertain of what we were preparing ourselves for. I didn't think it was appropriate to say, "What's a woman to do if her child's in kindergarten from nine to eleven thirty each morning but begin a doctoral program?" They would have laughed and understood, though. When Barbara left to go have lunch with Steve, Frinde and I exchanged information about our children.

"How old are your children?" I asked.

"Sarah was five last February, and Matthew is soon to be three."

"February! Chantal was also five last February. When is Sarah's birthday?"

"February 15."

"I can't believe it. That is Chantal's birthday as well." We laughed over the coincidence. Neither of us could have imagined how our lives would grow together over time.

But that promise wasn't present when we had coffee some weeks later in a small café in Brookline, the only two people there, sitting at a small, round ice cream table. I began the conversation by telling Frinde how women's studies was one of my intellectual interests, my passion really, particularly women's history. I was surprised when she said, "I think the women's movement, with its focus on male chauvinism, is a vicious tool to divide the working class. Class. That's what really matters."

"But how can you say that when American women in the nineteenth century had few if any rights, couldn't vote, and had no right to their children in case of a divorce? In fact, we couldn't get credit in our own name until recently and had to take our husband's name when we married in most states."

"Women, as such, aren't oppressed. It is only women of certain classes who are oppressed."

Despite our different views on feminism, Frinde and I became friends. As Marc and I got to know her and her first husband, John, and their close friends, we agreed that we had never known people like them. Frinde and John (a Harvard graduate) had been leaders in one of the factions of SDS (Students for a Democratic Society) called the Worker Student Alliance. It was sponsored by the Progressive Labor Party, a "revolutionary communist organization" committed to creating a socialist society through a workers' revolution. Their vision was that intellectuals and former members of the bourgeoisie would inspire and lead the working class.

Notwithstanding all their interest in social class, I believed that to fit in I had to keep silent about mine. The Stanford psychologist Hazel Markus contends that social class is not something that people have; rather it is something they "do, something they perform."[4] My mother, a perfectionist, worked tirelessly at performing the role of a post–World War II middle-class housewife, worrying about her children's psychological health, clipping nutritious recipes from *Family Circle*, and sewing beautifully tailored Vogue patterns. Working class was not a concept we used or understood in Nebraska. Despite our class differences, it came to feel natural that Frinde and I were friends, young and variously privileged, appreciating one another as individuals.

⋘⋙

I returned to Wayland High School in the fall of 1975, my enthusiasm for high school teaching diminished. An intriguing alternative came by way of the wife of one of Marc's colleagues at Framingham North High School, Cathy Minicucci.

She was the chief of staff for the head of the Education Commission in Massachusetts, which was responsible for desegregating schools in Boston and sixteen other cities. One evening, she and I were in my kitchen in Framingham, waiting to go to dinner while Marc showed his new gas-fired kiln to her husband, Paul Minicucci. I leaned against the refrigerator as Cathy said, "You know that new law, Chapter 622? It is ready for the implementation stage, and the Department of Education has funded six coordinator positions."

"Isn't that the state law prohibiting discrimination in the schools?" Ambition and insecurities welled up inside me. What an opportunity she was suggesting! But would I ever be able to compete with women such as Cathy?

"Yes, and it is fabulously comprehensive, prohibiting discrimination on the basis of race, color, sex, religion, and national origin. It is a good companion to Title IX, which focuses only on gender, but this new law goes much further."

"So what do you think those coordinators will do?"

"Lots, since the law applies to school admissions, admission to courses of study.... Let me see," she said, beginning to tick things off on her fingers, "guidance, course content, and extracurricular and athletic activities. For example, there's a girl in Somerville who wants to play football, and she's brought a discrimination case against the district. You should apply for one of the positions."

"Do you think I'd have a chance?"

"Of course! Haven't you done a lot of curriculum work in women's history? And the fact that you taught in all-black high schools in Chicago will help. There's just one downside, though. The position is half time, but there are hopes that it will become full time in a year or two."

When I told Marc what Cathy had conveyed, he surprised me with his response: "You agreed to support us until I finished at the Museum School, which is three more years. When I resigned from high school teaching, we went from two incomes to one. How can we possibly live on half a salary?" Suddenly, the reality of our financial situation sank in. Yet, reluctant to give in, I said, "Just let me find out about the position."

I applied to be the Chapter 622/Title IX coordinator for the Greater Boston Region, which served forty school districts within the Route 128 belt west of Boston, including Boston and Cambridge. When I met the statewide director, Sally Dias, and coordinators from the other five regional centers, I knew I couldn't turn down the opportunity to work with this all-female team. They were, to a person, smart, tough, and strategic thinkers. They expressed no doubt about the power and value of the law and their capacity to implement the legislation's intent: to improve the education of girls, especially girls (and boys) of color, and to change the public schools in the state in the process. What a contrast to my mostly male colleagues at Wayland High School!

When Dias offered me the position, I had to decide how best to tell Marc. That evening when I came home from work, I walked in the front door and peered

into the living room. He was sitting on the couch, smoking a cigarette and holding our Mastermind board. Chantal snuggled next to him.

"Well, she offered me the job."

"I've never been one to tell you what to do," he said.

"Are you sure? It's such a wonderful opportunity for me."

I resigned from Wayland High School in November 1975; by doing the math,
Marc and I knew we could keep our heads above water financially if I cashed in
my teacher's pension. Hazy as our futures were, the uncertainty was preferable to
teaching secondary school for the next twenty-five years.

～～～

The next five years, from 1975 to 1980, were a time when I wove together various strands of my work life and intellectual interests into a tapestry, and I was
being paid to do it. It was a time when the second women's movement was at
its most powerful. For example, the movement addressed the politics of housework, sought to change sex role socialization, and returned offensive magazine
ads to publishers with a note attached—"This Ad Insults Women." Publications
proliferated—bibliographies, research studies, books, filmstrips, periodicals,
handbooks, and films such as *Girls at 12*, *Men's Lives*, and *Free to Be You and Me*.
I had a new religion.

Now that I was a Chapter 622/Title IX coordinator, my feminist work took me
beyond classrooms at Wayland High School to school districts in my far-flung
region that included poor communities such as Chelsea, Revere, and neighborhoods in Boston, whose school buildings resembled nineteenth-century facto-
ries. In rich towns such as Weston and Wayland, the schools' buildings and grounds
looked like the campus of a think tank.

Early on, the 622 team understood that implementation of the state and
federal laws would require staff development programs targeted to both male
administrators and faculty, most often women, who understood the workings
of sex role stereotyping, were committed to addressing school policies that
discriminated, and were open to taking the lead to bring about change among
their colleagues. Male administrators were a harder sell than the faculty teams
participating districts appointed. Once in a meeting with department chairs in
Waltham, all men, arms folded across their chests, I began to review the laws'
requirements. My thoughts were interrupted by a faint sound: clip, clip, clip. I
looked into the men's hostile faces and saw the football coach, openly and slowly
clipping his fingernails as I spoke, timing each clip to follow a point I made.

My intellectual interests were fed not only by this staff development work but
also by my continuing work on *Women in America*, which was published in 1978.
When it came time to select a dissertation topic, I wanted to know if high school
students' attitudes toward sex-appropriate behavior would change if they studied women's history materials. And would those attitudes change more if their

teacher participated in thirty hours of training in how to use the curriculum? I met with my dissertation advisor, an empiricist if ever there was one, who told me that for my study to have validity, I would need sixteen teachers in each of four cells I had identified:

Cell One: Teachers who received the curriculum and the in-service training
Cell Two: Teachers who received the curriculum only
Cell Three: Teachers who received in-service training only
Cell Four: Teachers who received neither the curriculum nor the training

My brain went numb. Sixteen times four is sixty-four.

My position at the State Department of Education would enable me to recruit the teachers. The curriculum was there in the readings and activities in *Women in America*. I was able to convince the director of student affairs that supporting me half time to work on my dissertation in 1977 was consistent with the purposes of a recently funded federal grant, Project SCEE (Student Commitment to Equal Education). Despite the title of my dissertation, "The Inclusion of Women in the United States History Curriculum and Adolescents' Attitudes toward Sex-Appropriate Behavior," when the findings came back, there were no statistically significant differences among the four groups. My heart sank the first time I saw an unopened box in the corner of a teacher's classroom. In more cases than I cared to acknowledge, teachers, many of them female, told me that the pressing need to "cover the traditional material" kept them from getting to my women's studies materials. The one positive finding was that teachers' participation in the in-service training program resulted in greater inclusion of women in the regular U.S. history curriculum and liberalized attitudes toward sex-appropriate behavior for both female and male students. I received my doctorate in 1979 and didn't care enough about my dissertation to order a copy. I never wrote a word about that research, too disheartened to report my disappointing findings.

It was about this time that I learned of an organization with the innocuous name of the New England Coalition of Educational Leaders (NECEL), which had been formed to help women break through the thick layer of men that dominated the highest levels of public school administration. I decided to attend its next meeting. Excitement at doing something dangerous ricocheted off the beige walls at the Boston Holiday Inn. I looked around and saw other good girls, teachers mostly, who looked ambitious and dressed for success, many wearing brightly colored scarves at their necks that simulated a man's tie. Just as I sat down, the organization's president began: "We've scoured all the school directories in New England, and surprise, surprise, we are being discriminated against. Women constitute less than 1 percent of New England's superintendents, 5 percent of its assistant superintendents, 1 percent of its high school principals, 2 percent of the junior high school principals, and 20 percent of the elementary principals. We are going to change that."

There was loud clapping. "Now let me introduce Shirley Jabowski, our first success story. She was just hired as an assistant principal at Watertown High School." Jabowski went to the podium amid more clapping and a shout of "Right on, sister!" She held up her hands to quiet the clapping and said, "Let me tell you what it takes. Be prepared." The scarf tied in a bow at her neck jiggled. "Learn everything you can about the district and the position. Use any informants you might have. And overlook any insults that might come your way; let the jock jokes slide right off your back." Some heads in the audience were nodding in the affirmative. "But," she said, "the most important asset I have is a group of women friends I can rely on to pick me up off the floor after each rejection. Only that has made it possible for me to persist. I would never have gotten there without them. I've taken the first step on the ladder to becoming a superintendent, and I'm doing it in high heels."

I left the room thinking, *I can be an administrator now that I have a newly minted doctorate in social education.* The first position I applied for was to be the assistant superintendent for curriculum and instruction in the Newton public schools. I was terrified once I learned I had an interview. With Jabowski's words ringing in my ears—"Be prepared. Learn everything"—I still couldn't get beyond the things friends said to me: this was the best school district in Massachusetts; it sent many students to Harvard; and this was a very liberal community of doctors, university professors, and lawyers and had lots of inherited wealth.

When I walked into the district administrative offices, down a long hallway to the room for my interview, my heart sank. Every chair save one was taken around the interview table. Except for a lone white woman and a single black man, the others at the table were white males, all seemingly successful. When the search committee introduced themselves, I tried to keep track of who was a school board member, a teacher, or a parent. The portable blackboard at the front of the room loomed large, reminding me that I might be straying too far from the safety of classroom teaching. I was not surprised when later the head of personnel called and said in a solemn tone, "The pool of candidates was very rich, very experienced. We selected another applicant."

Still, I was disappointed at not getting the job, and my disappointment turned inward. I could have been better prepared for the interview. I should have taken NECEL's advice and done mock interviews with friends. Eventually, replaying that script in my head became boring. I had learned to keep the devil from the door by "doing" something. I had turned my anger at women's oppression into the project of learning women's history. But what could I possibly do now? I left my office at the regional center and headed for Gutman, the education library at Harvard.

CHAPTER 7

MY LEWIS AND CLARK
CHAPTER CONCLUDES

When I was told in my pretenure review in 1982 at Lewis and Clark that I hadn't done enough, the message was clear: if I continued going into the office from nine to five, leaving my door open, accepting every "service" assignment that came my way, I would not get tenure. But I was torn, drawn to the life of both a teacher and a scholar but also that of an administrator. Yet I knew that my future depended first on my success or failure as an academic. I hadn't uprooted Marc and Chantal to be denied tenure in my sixth year.

Learning What Being a Professor Entails

Once my initial fear and confusion lifted, I wondered if the example of anyone on campus could help me learn what to do. The two most productive people were men who made research a priority, a senior professor in the liberal arts and Dan Duke. Neither of them came to campus until afternoon, staying home in the morning to write. Holding up their practices to mine, I saw one thing I could change. I needed to carve out a specific time to "do my work." I set goals for how many hours a week I would devote to research, strategizing to reach fifteen. Fearful that staying home each morning was too radical a deviation from the program's culture, I chose Friday as the safest day because the office was mostly quiet then and set aside a couple of hours the other days of the week for research. I felt a deep sense of satisfaction on those Friday mornings as I stretched out on the floor in my bathrobe, a cup of coffee in hand, leaning against a soft backrest, books spread about me, electric typewriter warm against my thighs, our Yodel stove emitting a satisfying heat that permeated my bones.

It wasn't only my resolve that mattered; I needed to figure out how to pursue a research question that had captured my interest: How had the new scholarship on women changed the way professors and textbook publishers thought about their disciplines? This interest stemmed from the time when my editors at Rand

McNally and I struggled to break away from a public and political framework for organizing the readings for *Women in America: Half of History.* What had finally helped us break free of a traditional organization was historian Gerda Lerner's 1975 essay tracing the stages of conceptualization that historians had proposed during the five years that women's history developed as an independent field. Lerner argued that the central concern of women's history should not be activities in the public sphere, where women were often excluded, but what the majority of women were actually doing and experiencing during a particular time. As I read her essay, I saw my own thinking in the evolution she chronicled.

What better place to pursue this question than in the four-week women's studies seminar, scheduled for the summer of 1981, which was designed to prepare faculty teaching Freshman Inquiry to incorporate topics and materials on gender into their courses. Susan Kirschner, who was coordinating the seminar, had encouraged me to consider participating, but she hit a roadblock when she mentioned the idea to David Savage, the project director. A dark expression crossed David's face. "But the seminar was funded for undergraduate faculty. And Mary Kay teaches in a graduate program."

I felt stopped in my tracks. "Oh, but I'd love to teach Freshman Inquiry." David shook his head slowly in the negative. "Let me think about it." Would I be able to assess the seminar if I weren't able to be a faculty participant? I walked back to my office and dropped my briefcase on my desk just as the phone rang. "I convinced him that because of your book, you are essential to the seminar," Susan shouted.

Feeling confident, I sought out a seminar participant, *Jane Hansen, and told her about my research question. Quickly, she said, "I was thinking of doing the same thing." I proposed we team up, my heart swelling at my good fortune. My elation was tempered when she proposed including her friend. When we three met, I attempted to explain my idea. "I want to document some of the subtle conceptual changes in the way seminar participants think about including women in their disciplines. And then to see if they do things differently in one of their courses." It soon became clear that we were not in agreement about how to evaluate the seminar.

We continued to talk past one another about the value of measuring biases, measuring attitudes, and my questions about participants' disciplines and courses. Jane broke our stalemate by pointing out the things we could do: design questions, interview participants before and after the seminar, and collect syllabi. As I walked away from our meeting, I wondered if we would ever be able to work together.

In the summer of 1982, we three traveled to the National Women's Studies Associate (NWSA) meeting at Humboldt State University in Arcata, California. On the long drive from Portland to Northern California, lying in the back seat of the college's station wagon, I looked up at the sun dappled through giant red-woods. Anger at the two in the front seat welled up with each breath. I blamed them unfairly for having nothing specific to report about the effect of the seminar on participating faculty.

Recalling the previous summer, I felt a knot of disappointment in my chest that my expectations for the seminar, which had occurred each week with a feminist scholar of national reputation, hadn't measured up. The scholars were an impressive lot: Carolyn Lougee, the first woman hired in the history department at Stanford in 1973; Florence Howe, the founder of the Feminist Press; Michelle (Shelly) Rosaldo, an anthropologist at Stanford whose theoretical work about the workings of gender in the productive and reproductive processes of societies across cultures was pathbreaking; and Susan Contratto, a doctoral student in psychology at the University of Michigan who had recently published an article on maternal sexuality in *Signs*, the premier feminist journal.

Each day was much like the others: discussions of assigned readings and lectures by each scholar about her research—for instance, Lougee's on the declining health and frequent deaths of girls in French boarding schools in early modern France. When some participants complained about Florence Howe because she failed to present the latest feminist literary theory, I said, "Ah, but she is the mother of us all; she was there from the beginning. She sent out mimeographed copies of women's studies syllabi—Feminist Studies I and Feminist Studies II—helping us see we were part of a larger movement."

By the end of the seminar, my greatest frustration was that I didn't experience moments of intellectual insight or "clicks," those aha moments that sent a jolt through me in the early days of the women's movement.

My path to answering my research question was not as smooth as I would have liked. With no "findings" to report about changes in faculty members' courses following the seminar, and further hobbled by my inexperience with academic writing, I read a paper at the NWSA conference proposing stages of thinking about the incorporation of women into course syllabi, ranging from male-only scholarship on one end to a bifocal, two-sex perspective that fuses women's and men's experiences into a holistic view of human experience. My two colleagues and I invited Peggy McIntosh, then the director of faculty development at the Wellesley College Center for Research on Women, to critique our papers because she was talking about similar stages that might capture the changes that feminism was bringing to the disciplines. I imagined that my thinking would advance when McIntosh critiqued my paper during the session. When she made no public comments, I worried that her silence meant that she thought my paper was of no value or conceptually flawed. It is likely that she did not want to be seen arguing with me. After everyone had left the room, she said, "You should think of these stages more as concentric circles rather than advancing from one to the other. What you have is too sequential, too hierarchical." I slowly began to see that her critique had value as I evaluated the Lewis and Clark women's studies seminar and published related articles over the next several years.

Feeling most secure in my knowledge of women's history, I decided to see what changes, if any, had occurred in U.S. history high school textbooks. A journalist, Janice Law Trecker, had published an article in 1971 on the topic, and I was inspired to update her findings.[1] However, to do that would take months. Feeling pressure to publish, I wrote an article reexamining Trecker's analysis, reviewing the progress that had been made in the past decade, and considering what needed to be done in the next. Yet the publication of the initial article I sent off to *Women's Studies Quarterly* was uncertain. The editor, Nancy Porter, who was on the faculty of Portland State University, called and said, "I received your article, and while it is hard to follow your argument at times, I think there is something there. I'd like to work with you on revisions to see what we can make of the article." Porter, as promised, did work with me, and the article appeared in the fall 1982 issue.[2]

Happy as I was to finally get my first academic publication in a credible journal, I decided I was ready to undertake a comprehensive look at the changes, if any, in high school textbooks. I wrote to a dozen publishers of the most widely used U.S. history textbooks published in the 1970s and 1980s, requesting copies and telling them what I needed them for. Once the tomes showed up, I examined all of the text and the visuals for their treatment of women and then categorized each sentence or visual according to categories I named male history, compensatory history, bifocal history, feminist history, and multifocal relational history. In the end, I referenced each entry, believing that such attention to detail would strengthen my findings. Since there was no way I could transport these backbreaking textbooks from home to campus, I spread them out on the floor of my study, where they rested in various positions as I worked on the project over the next two years.

I was coming to realize that it took a community to develop and nurture a scholar. Central to this awareness was a national group of like-minded feminist friends such as Frinde Maher, who accepted an appointment in teacher education at Wheaton College in Massachusetts in 1981. The previous year, Wheaton had received federal funding for the Balanced Curriculum Project, launched to integrate the new scholarship on women into introductory courses. Soon Frinde was not only a part of the feminist culture but one of its leaders, eventually directing the project. With her newfound consciousness about women and gender, we became one another's most important critics of our research and writing, sharing hotel rooms at several national conferences each year. We would run from session to session, talking rapidly all the way about the ideas presented. In the spring of 1983, I returned to campus after a conference, knowing that I needed a comparable community at Lewis and Clark.

Seeking out Dorothy Berkson in the English department, I told her of my heartfelt realization. Together, we decided to gather feminist faculty members to critique one another's writing. The first paper discussed was mine: "Stages of Thinking about Women in U.S. History Textbooks." That evening, six feminist scholars, all Americanists in history or English literature except for me, assembled in one of the seminar rooms in the student union. The overhead lights were sharp, accentuating the circles under most eyes. Everyone had read my paper beforehand. Looking out from the head of the table, I had no idea of what to expect. This was the first time a group had critiqued my work. Questions and critical commentaries spewed forth for the next hour: "Who is the audience? Is it for publishers? Teachers? Professors?" "The article is too long." "The stages are significant and helpful, but I have some suggestions relative to women in the discipline." "Try to organize the paper around something other than the stages." "It seems your central thesis is that the publishers have done a lot in the past ten years, but it is at the level of compensatory and contribution history. If that is so, you should cluster examples around the thesis to make your point." "Your use of so many examples distorts what is actually there."

Their suggestions made me think of Saint Sebastian, each criticism like an arrow that pierced another part of my body. What had ever led me to think this was a good idea? I was in a daze driving home, not knowing where to turn. I felt small and inferior, suppressing the thought that I had wasted more than a year of my life on a fool's errand.

When I walked in the door at home, Marc asked, "Well, how did it go?" Before I could answer, I began crying. "Awful, awful."

The next morning, I called Frinde, who listened quietly to all I reported, and with her usual confidence said, "Well, they're right about this point, but they're wrong about that."

When I hung up the phone, I forced myself to go back into my study, the gloom lifting a bit when I recalled a scene from the movie *Butley,* in which the actor Alan Bates plays a professor who vomits at the thought of reading his students' papers. I couldn't quit; I had to get tenure. As I began to work, I felt a hardening around my researcher's heart, scar tissue forming with each revision. I would never cry again over a critique of my work. I now knew that they would only make my work better.

When I finally finished the grueling study in 1984, I sent the manuscript off for consideration for the American Educational Research Association's (AERA) Women Educators' Research Award. Surprised when I was notified that I was the recipient, I knew the true value of the award would be to strengthen my tenure application. The one-hundred-dollar check would buy dinner out for Marc and me, and the wooden plaque would fit nicely under Chantal's 1975 portrait of me at the typewriter working on *Women in America.* Shortly after that, I received notice of the article's acceptance by *The History Teacher*, a well-respected journal concerned with historiography and teaching at primarily the undergraduate level.

I had yet to use the pre- and postinterviews and the syllabi from participants of the women's studies seminar in 1981, and I was determined not to let all that work go to waste. My two collaborators had gone on to other research. In order to use that data, I needed to capture changes in the disciplines represented in the seminar that had occurred since 1981. I knew there were similarities across the disciplines, but I wasn't sure how to systematize or classify them. Beginning with what I had learned about how women's history was reshaping that discipline, I went into my office at the college, and for months, I used my research time to read articles in *Signs*. The articles that I targeted from anthropology, literature, and psychology led me to see a remarkably similar evolution regarding what people emphasized in their research and teaching about women and gender. I would later name these patterns "feminist phase theory." That period of taxonomic work gave me a schema to see if there were any changes in the work of my colleagues at Lewis and Clark.

My research was advanced enough for me to present a paper on it at AERA in 1984. Robert Silverman chaired the panel. When I finished presenting my paper, he turned to me and said, "I'd like you to consider publishing your paper in the journal I edit." He went on to add that the first step would be to submit it to peer review.

Feeling coy and powerful, as the paper presentation had gone well, I said, "And what is the name of your journal?"

"*The Journal of Higher Education*."

"I'm sorry, but I don't know that journal. Let me give your offer some thought and get back to you."

When I called my friend Betty Schmitz, who was working on integrating women and gender into the curriculum at the University of Maryland, and told her of the offer, she said, "The *Journal of Higher Education*! Do you realize that its acceptance rate is only 3 percent?"

I called Silverman, less arrogant, and said I'd be happy to have him start the process toward publishing the article.

My research interests changed around 1985. At a conference in Boston that brought feminist professors together to address the subject "Change in Education: Women as Radicals and Conservatives," the possibility of a new direction of inquiry presented itself. As Frinde and I attended various sessions, it became clear that the newest buzz from the attendees was something called feminist pedagogy. Frinde had been interested in pedagogy since writing her dissertation at Boston University and had published several theoretical articles on pedagogies for the gender-balanced classroom. My work on feminist phase theory led to questions for me about the interaction between course content and pedagogy and, eventually, along with Frinde, how the two combined to construct knowledge in undergraduate classrooms.

Midway through the conference, walking along a wide hallway that inclined upward in one of Simmons College's nineteenth-century buildings, sun shining in through high windows, we began to talk about pedagogy. "You know what the problem is," I said. "Almost all of the talk we're hearing about feminist pedagogy is a narrative about what I already do in my own classroom."

"Yes," Frinde said, "somebody should study what feminists are actually doing in their classrooms."

"That somebody is us, Frinde."

"Let's not talk about it now. Let's think about it and talk next time we meet."

At the annual AERA meeting in the spring, we danced around the idea of doing a book on feminist pedagogy together and agreed that we'd have a conversation about it before we went back to our jobs and homes at opposite ends of the country. The day before we left the conference, we agreed we couldn't put off the conversation any longer. We circled around whether we would address both curriculum and pedagogy, coming to the conclusion that the two were intertwined; whether we should go to multiple campuses or just study classrooms at our own institutions; where we might find funding for multiple campuses; and how to find practitioners who best exemplified these new teaching methods in their classrooms.

We eventually decided to visit college classrooms around the country and document what professors who described themselves as feminists were actually doing in their classrooms. We knew feminist pedagogy had some of the same characteristics of the consciousness-raising practices of the women's movement, the progressive tradition in American education of John Dewey, and the more general forms of "liberatory teaching" espoused by Paulo Freire and others. What made feminist pedagogy unique was its attention to the particular needs of women students and its grounding in feminist theory.

Generous colleagues helped us move beyond the realization of how much we didn't know about this kind of research. For instance, Patricia Schmuck, who was hired in the educational administration program in 1982, gave a dinner party at her home in Eugene. Pat, always the generous social engineer, sat me next to anthropologist Harry Wolcott, the author of *The Man in the Principal's Office*. Halfway into the dinner, with me squeezed up against Harry, careful not to bump his arm as I cut my meat, he said, "Pat tells me you are planning to do an ethnography of feminist teaching."

"Oh, yes," I said, feeling courageous after a few glasses of wine.

"Have you decided what you are going to focus on? Will it be the teachers or the students? Are you interested in the formal or the hidden curriculum? In their meaning or yours? It is very important to let the person come through—for example, follow a student, follow a professor."

"Good questions and good advice," I said. "If truth be told, I'm very nervous about doing this work because I'm not an anthropologist and not trained in ethnography."

He looked at me, very much the professor in a jacket and bow tie, the candles reflecting on his glasses, and said, "Isn't it interesting how we've convinced ourselves that we can't learn anything new?"

Jane White, a professor of education and anthropology at the University of Maryland, introduced Frinde and me to Shirley Bryce Heath's *Ways with Words*. Heath's study of language acquisition in two communities in the South, one black and the other white, became a model for me of the ethnographer as a careful observer, never judgmental or condescending. This neutrality of observation was counter to my authoritarian Catholic upbringing, especially the notion that there is a "truth" out there. Frinde and I would need to be careful not to look for the "one true feminist pedagogy."

Another tutor was anthropologist Sylvia Hart Landsberg, who taught at Lewis and Clark and critiqued a grant application Frinde and I submitted to the Spencer Foundation. Her questions were all about how we planned to do our ethnography. After I answered a few of her queries clumsily, she said, sighing deeply,

Figure 12. Teaching at Lewis and Clark, 1985

"You need to read some actual ethnographies, and you need to read some theory. I'll look through my bookshelf for some classics in the field." The next morning at nine sharp, Sylvia handed me a cardboard box weighted down with books. As I struggled to hold it, she said, "This should get you started."

The Saga of My Tenure Case

When the fall of 1985 rolled around, I began to think of going up for tenure. This was a year earlier than the customary six, but I felt my record warranted such action. But I had also believed that was the case at the time of my second-year review, the review when I had been told I hadn't done enough research.

Yet I knew that early tenure required extraordinary publications. That worry was offset by an offhand remark that Paul Magnusson made one night over drinks, citing a study that concluded people get tenure more often for quality publications in top journals rather than quantity. My actual publications were few, but I could argue that some were "groundbreaking ideas in top journals." And I had several soon to be published.

In the weeks before I was to submit my tenure file, Chantal, then a junior in high school, announced that she wanted to have a dinner party at the house for more than a dozen friends. Marc and I were enthusiastic because we wanted her to feel comfortable inviting her friend group of bright, high-energy honors students to our home. Until then, parties had been at their homes in Dunthorpe, Portland's most exclusive neighborhood, a sharp contrast to our architect's spec house in Multnomah, a neighborhood with antique shops and the Fat City Café. I suppressed the thought of a conversation about drinking. To propose that no wine or beer be served would set off a major battle and likely torpedo the party.

The day of the party, Chantal and her friends spent all day cooking, making pasta. In fact, they spent so much time at the pasta machine that one of the girls, moving her foot back and forth with each crank of the machine, a rhythm that reminded me of the 1960s Mashed Potato dance, wore a hole in the grass rug that covered the kitchen floor. Some of the girls spent hours setting our long oak table, deciding where to place popular boys.

Marc and I decided that we wouldn't leave the house once the guests arrived but that we'd "do our work," he painting in his studio in the garage and I upstairs in my study. Doing my work had always calmed my nerves. When the doorbell rang, announcing the arrival of the first guest, and I heard a male voice, I shut the door to my study and brought up a draft of my tenure statement, which documented how my teaching, publications, and record of service warranted early tenure and promotion. After listening to the doorbell ring almost continuously for the next hour, I couldn't resist strolling through the downstairs to Marc's studio. As I turned the corner into the dining room and looked through the opening into the kitchen, I was taken aback at seeing Chantal and her friends standing together in conversational groups, drinking beer and wine, in exactly the postures adults assumed at a cocktail party. How did our children learn to reproduce our behaviors so precisely? I walked through them, making no eye contact. When I got through the kitchen to Marc, I said, "You won't believe that scene in there. It's like an adult cocktail party. Do you think this could cause us some trouble?"

"Come near the door here," he said, "and smell the marijuana coming from that truck parked in the driveway. There's been a steady stream of kids in and out of that truck."

"What do you think we should do?" Marc raised his shoulders and shrugged. I crept back through the house and went back to work, my hands shaking above the keyboard, the glare from the computer screen the only light in the room.

Minutes later, Chantal burst into my study and said, "I need your help. *Eric Petersen just puked all over the living room couch! *Jessica Taylor challenged him to a drinking contest—they must have had five shots each. She's fine, but he's a mess. *Josh Stuart needs help in cleaning it up."

"Did you tell Dad?"

"He's already in the living room helping." I peered over the landing on the second floor and saw that things were under control. *Thank God such cleanups are a man's work in our household*, I thought as I walked back to my computer.

The stress I felt the night of Chantal's party would pale when things unfolded around my request for early tenure. With so many changes in the college (which I'll go into later), I believed I'd be more secure as a tenured associate professor. It would be worth the risk, I reasoned. Because I was an untenured chair, a chair outside the MAT program had to submit my review file. When I asked the interim graduate dean, Doug Morgan, who that might be, he said that Jim Wallace, the chair of undergraduate education, would be the one making the presentation. A red flag went up at that suggestion. Rumor had it that Wallace was upset about decisions made by the Mission Planning Committee (MPC), of which I had been a member, that impacted education programs. Despite all this, I concluded that I had no choice but to accept the dean's decision.

When I called to see if he would put my file forward, Wallace said, "I'm not sure I'll be able to do that."

I stood up from the chair in my office as heat rose through my body. "Why?"

"Well, I haven't been happy with your role in MPC."

"But Jim, I was only one member of a committee of ten. A committee with people far more powerful than I—the president, a trustee, three deans."

"True, but you were the only one in education. I think you have an agenda to get rid of the undergraduate education program."

"That's not true. If you won't put my file forward, Jim, it will immediately cast suspicion on the quality and value of all of my work, my whole record. Please give my request fair consideration."

I put down the phone; looked out my office window at Mt. Hood, its bottom half obscured by a cloud; and thought, *Now what?* I might not be able to get early tenure. They might make me wait another year! Eventually, Wallace agreed to put my file forward. In January 1985, I received a copy of his letter, which waffled but in the final analysis supported me for tenure. When I read the contents of the letter to Marc, he said, "If you're going to stab someone, you don't use a rubber knife." As I laughed, I saw a rubber knife plunged into my back, the rubber folding in on itself, not into me.

But it seemed someone was working behind the scenes. After my file had gone in, Morgan received a letter from the dean of the undergraduate college, saying I could not go up for tenure without the permission of the college's chair of the Committee on Promotion and Tenure. Earlier, I had met with the undergraduate dean for advice on my early application for tenure; he made no mention of this rule. I decided to check the tenure and promotion review policies to see where, and if, there was such a provision. I found none, perhaps because the policies had not been changed to consider the formation of the graduate school.

Next, Morgan called to say that the Committee on Promotion and Tenure had drafted a letter to be signed by the deans and the department chair, asserting that that committee had the sole right to review files. Morgan felt that this new hurdle left us with three options: go along with them and be reviewed solely by the college committee, be reviewed by the graduate committee only, or withdraw until next year. I found his options, especially the last one, unacceptable because I felt I was ready to be considered for tenure and promotion. "I can't give you an answer to these options, Doug, until I know their legality and I've heard from the Graduate Tenure and Review Committee."

I decided to put my energies into positive things: spending more time with Marc and Chantal, writing in my journal, and taking better care of myself by running and swimming. Years later, when Chantal recalled that time, she said, "Sometimes when I looked at the circles under your eyes, especially the bag under your right eye—you know, the one shaped in a *V*—I was afraid you would die."

My mention to Morgan of legal issues diffused the complexity of who should review my file; the Graduate Tenure and Review Committee did so. The letter came on March 8, 1985, saying that I was awarded tenure and promotion: they concluded I was a strong teacher and substantial scholar, with a record of unusually committed community service. The heat was off; I could be self-directed. I now felt like a true member of the faculty who could speak up, secure at the college until I retired in 2005. But dissatisfaction crept in with the position of graduate programs in the overall college structure. Those of us in graduate programs, no matter how scholarly or how valued as teachers and colleagues, would always be second-class citizens, because the undergraduate college was the heart of the institution. Did I want to be in such a marginalized position for the next two decades? Typical of the things that woke me up in the middle of the night were these thoughts recorded in my journal in November 1985:

> What motivates me? What am I afraid of? I do feel a commitment to the women's movement. I'm inspired by people who've worked to change the world, to make it a better place. I think one's life should make a difference. So there is a social reason for what I do.
>
> I find it intellectually fascinating—most of the time—to try to solve the intellectual problems I set for myself. I would get so bored if I only had the ordinary stuff of life before me. They remind me too much that things die, decay, and lose their luster. Beyond my personal relations with Marc and Chantal, which are richness unparalleled, I value most the products of my research—*Women in America*, the study of U.S. history textbooks, all of the feminist phase theory work. I'll keep doing what I am doing because if I didn't—what else would I do?
>
> Is it childhood deprivation that drives me to succeed? I don't think so. It's more the notion, gained from my parents, that if you do something, you should do it extremely well.

The Allure of Improving Quality and Learning as I Go

While I had only reluctantly decided to be a high school teacher, the University of Chicago's MAT program gave me two things that contributed to my success as a high school teacher and eventually as a professor of social studies education at Lewis and Clark—a deep love for intellectual inquiry and the ability to see, particularly in the university's Laboratory School, how innovative, creative teaching contributes to student learning. These values were out of step with Lewis and Clark's education courses, which were unimaginatively imitative of state certification requirements. While I didn't initially grasp this, my success as an administrator there was tied to the reforms I, along with others, made to the MAT program.

The path for such reform opened up when we hired a third faculty member in the fall of 1981 to cover language arts. With the addition of Carole Urzua, who specialized in language acquisition, Marge Clark and I were now part of a triad that could address weaknesses in our program. Setting aside several Fridays, regretting that it took precedence over my research day, we met around Carole's kitchen table, the room suffused with the smell of the simmering mole sauce her husband was preparing for lunch. Beginning with a blank poster board on an easel, we eventually agreed that we wanted a program that enabled students to integrate their intellectual and personal development with their professional development. With this mission in mind, we designed new courses—Teaching and Learning in the Secondary Schools, The Personal and Social Dimensions of Teaching, Self and Society, and New Perspectives in the Social Studies. We also added a cumulative seminar to help students integrate what they had learned in their courses by defining and answering a question related to their teaching or an aspect of their development. Searching around for a title, I asked Marc for ideas. Thinking a moment or two, he said, "Why not call it the QED Seminar?"

"QED?"

"Translated from the Latin, it means 'that which was to be demonstrated.'"

"Promising," I said. Marge and Carole agreed it was a creative name for our cumulative seminar.

The discomfort I had felt in most of the classes I taught my first year gave way to connected teaching and learning. For instance, in a unit on Western women's history in my New Perspectives in the Social Studies course, a young man connected women's struggles in the past with the ones his mother faced as a receptionist at the local Kaiser Permanente. This awakening led him to include readings on women in his American history courses. These kinds of experiences not only improved my teaching evaluations but increased my connection to my students as well.

⁓

As I was getting my stride as a teacher and a scholar, I had no idea how Lewis and Clark was about to change or how those changes would contribute to my development. Jack Howard, who had been the president for more than two decades, resigned shortly after I arrived in the fall of 1980. Following a national search, the college dean, John Brown, was passed over for an outsider. James Gardner had credentials highly prized in academia. He was a graduate of Harvard College and Yale Law School, a published author, and the Ford Foundation's Country Representative in the Caribbean and later in Brazil.[3] His work at the foundation involved scholarships and planning and financing of higher education and international studies in the United States and abroad. One of his first actions in the fall of 1982, something common to most new presidents, was to announce a two-year planning initiative.

Responsibility for that work resided with the newly formed Mission Planning Committee (MPC—mentioned earlier in this chapter around my tenure fight), which was chaired by the president, staffed by Paul Magnusson, and composed of a trustee, five faculty members (three from the undergraduate college, one from the law school, and one from the graduate programs), and the deans of the law school and the undergraduate college. Each tenure-track faculty member was eligible to vote for faculty representatives in the three units. Once the process was made public, Robert Wilson went to work, first to campaign for his election to the MPC and then to influence the choice of the other faculty representatives. Shortly after an announcement went out to the campus, he knocked on my office door. Flashing a smile, he asked, "Well, what do you think of this planning process?"

"Should be interesting," I said. "It sounds like a good balance among the three units. What do you think the issues will be?"

"Establishing some standards for faculty performance, rousting out some of the deadwood, getting a handle on the mission of this place, increasing the endowment, attracting better students, and of course, the place of graduate programs."

"Are you interested in being on the committee?" I asked. "If so, I'll lobby for you with some of my colleagues here in graduate programs."

"Good, good," he said. "The one thing I want to ensure is that some of the faculty who represent the old order here—the laid-back, little hippie college in the Northwest, the anything-goes culture of the faculty—aren't elected. What I'm interested in is what you think the place of graduate programs has in the scope of things. But my main question is this: Are you willing to serve on the committee?"

"Me on the committee? I'm not sure I could be elected as an untenured faculty member."

"There's nothing in the guidelines that stipulates members must be tenured. Let me worry about your election."

When Wilson left, I took a deep breath and thought, *What an opportunity!* I could work to get feminist ideas integrated into the mission and position graduate programs more favorably in the college. I stopped these thoughts, believing that one of the other graduate department chairs—all men except for me, more senior than I, and far more sophisticated about academic politics—was likely to be elected. To my surprise, when the election results were announced, I was the graduate programs' representative. Wilson facilitated that result, something he was unable to do for himself. None of my colleagues congratulated me on my election. I overheard one of them say, "Imagine electing an untenured faculty member to such an important committee."

My election to the committee fed my feelings of belonging in academia, of being able to make a difference. I was ill prepared to understand that dancing in the minefields of power in a college with barely more than one hundred tenure-related faculty members would have its costs. The popular girl of the 1950s, the sophomore class secretary photographed with the other officers (all male), believed I could play such a leadership role and not collect enemies as I occupied a place at the table of institutional power. When I imagined what I would learn from this service, I had no idea it was that I had become important enough to have enemies.

The first MPC meeting was held in the president's conference room in the manor house on campus. The sun shone through the English Tudor windows onto the long table as the committee members quietly took their seats. Gardner and Magnusson came in at the last minute, both carrying thin leather cases. The president called the meeting to order and said, "We have an unprecedented opportunity to set the direction of this college, to build on our strengths, and to craft a Pacific Northwest college that is distinguished."

Ah, I thought, *here is what I like doing best*—figuring out what to be, seeing what is possible, aiming for distinction. Our work was not only to attend the biweekly meetings but to consider the college from numerous perspectives: reviewing past mission statements, pouring over enrollment data and various budget scenarios, and even examining brochures promoting international education.

Being the graduate representative to the committee often left me feeling marginalized. When MPC members talked about the mission of the college, it was the mission of a traditional liberal arts college, something Lewis and Clark had never been. Yet not having a tradition of Western liberal arts curriculum became a springboard for other ideas: that our international programs were unique because they embodied both Eastern and Western perspectives, that placing gender at the center of the curriculum could be a distinctive mark, and that the history of the college had been one of liberal and professional education. With the emergence of these ideas, I gained confidence in presenting my thoughts to the committee, and from the feedback I received along the way, I was satisfied that they were being respected and accepted. I liked being at the center of institutional work. I enjoyed the camaraderie of the planning committee, championing ideas that mattered to me, and coming to understand how change initiatives succeeded—or didn't.

Toward the middle of our second year of deliberations, the MPC took up whether to continue graduate programs. President Gardner was an advocate for establishing a graduate school of professional studies. The most controversial question to emerge in our discussions was whether undergraduate and graduate teacher education programs should merge. We three faculty in the graduate program were proud of the ways we had improved its quality and saw the undergraduate program as too traditional, lacking innovation. The undergraduate professors were adamantly opposed to the idea of the programs merging, believing that if their program merged with us, they would be as marginalized as we were. I began to hear rumblings from the undergraduate faculty. "Tetreault is responsible for the idea of a graduate school. She's in favor of the merger. She's hard to get along with. She's only interested in her own power." These charges against me had physical costs. I started noticing broken veins on my upper inner arms. Asking a physician friend to have a look, he said, "It looks like phlebitis to me."

I bent over backward to be collegial in the face of this and viewed the attacks on me as a result of the undergraduate education faculty feeling threatened. An entry in my journal for March 18, 1983, noted that this experience taught me the following:

1. Everyone watches out for themselves when they fear institutional change.
2. One has to be strong and inner directed to survive in that environment.
3. I especially needed to try to get along better with weaker people.

In the spring of 1984, the MPC concluded. At the unveiling of the new mission statement, I felt that my two years of participation had resulted in things of importance to me: the college's mission included "high standards of academic excellence in liberal arts and professional education." The philosophy statement noted that the institution was particularly distinguished by its commitment to "balanced exploration of the perspectives, traditions, and contributions of women and men." And the Graduate School of Professional Studies was established.

There began to be signs that there was trouble in paradise once the MPC work was concluded, some of it directed at the president. At the graduation ceremony in June, I sat among the faculty, reading my students' exams. Some minutes into Gardner's remarks, a student shouted, "Bingo!" Each time he uttered some of his favorite words associated with planning—*distinction, liberal, professional, gender,* and *international studies*—a student would shout bingo.

Once the graduate school was formed, there was some jockeying for position among the faculty to see who would be dean. Paul Magnusson, the associate dean, was at the center of speculations, although he told me, "There's talk of promoting you, but I can't say what kind of promotion it might be." Oblivious to how unusual it would be to appoint an untenured person as dean, I was flattered that I was being considered for an administrative appointment.

One of the graduate school program chairs invited me to lunch soon after the public unveiling of the college's mission statement. *Hmm,* I thought, *He's never invited me to lunch before.* Once inside the restaurant, a shabby lunch place in Lake Oswego, seated in a booth that was on a raised platform, suggesting a stage for the high drama that was to follow, my colleague came to the point. "I'd like to be the dean of the graduate school and would like your support." I looked at him and said, "I'm not sure I can support you, because I may be interested in the position myself." He drew back as if I'd struck him. "Well," he said, "that makes things completely different." I thanked him for lunch as we parted, but he added with spite, "Have you calculated how much mission planning cost you? Probably a couple of books." I ignored his remark, believing that by managing my time, I could do both administrative and scholarly work.

When several weeks passed with no word of the appointment of an interim dean, I began to suspect I was not in the running. My hunch was confirmed when Doug Morgan, chair of public administration, was late in joining Marc and other

Lewis and Clark colleagues at our home to watch the Portland Trail Blazers in a playoff game in June. I noticed Doug's cheeks were flushed and that his body had a new posture. "Sorry I'm late. I had a meeting with the president." He had accepted Gardner's offer to serve as interim dean.

Doug in turn appointed me as assistant dean for graduate programs in November of 1984. Magnusson later told me that Morgan wanted to give me the title of acting assistant dean. "Too many prefixes," Magnusson said. "The position is weak enough as it is." When Doug called to offer me the job, he stated that I had responsibility for working with the faculty to develop a graduate core curriculum and writing a federal grant to support that work, as well as developing an innovative MAT program for preservice teachers. He also wanted me to somehow downplay my administrative role lest I be too threatening to the men in undergraduate education. I didn't know quite how I could possibly downplay my role and still do the job, but I accepted his offer anyway.

It became painfully clear that my administrative advancement opportunities at Lewis and Clark would go no further when the school held a national search for a permanent graduate school dean in the spring of 1985. With little to lose, I behaved unprofessionally by letting out my anger. I argued strongly against hiring the first candidate, a friend of Paul Magnusson's, a slick, beefy man. The candidate understood the politics that graduate programs labored under but considered feminist issues "just another passing fad." Compared to most men at Lewis and Clark, he was a throwback.

When the second candidate, Roger Paget, was interviewed, I made a point of sitting next to him at his dinner with the faculty because it was my chance to get to know him. A stocky man in his early fifties, with a young second wife and an infant, I was struck by his strange demeanor. His face took on a distant look, and he made no eye contact as he told stories of being a descendant of the pioneers who had settled Oregon, serving in the Central Intelligence Agency, and being a player in the mid-1960s in deposing Sukarno, the president of Indonesia. Fearful that he might be hired, I gave him a stern look as I felt anger rising up inside me.

Searching for some way to relate to me, he said, "Mary, Mary—you must be a Catholic. I recently converted to Catholicism." Before he could continue, I jumped in.

"Actually, I hate being called Mary. Too many girls were named Mary in my classes in Catholic school. I don't like any religion all that much, if you want to know the truth. Marc and I were raised in very religious families, but the University of Chicago changed all of that. For us, Catholicism is totally irrelevant."

He dropped his gaze, looked at his plate, and said nothing.

There was strong support for Paget; I didn't feel I could resist the hiring of yet another candidate, so I kept quiet and he was hired. One of his first acts was to appoint Carolyn Bullard, who had chaired his search committee, as associate dean. When he announced that administrative change to me in a private meeting, he explained that he felt comfortable with Carolyn because he'd gotten to know her during his interview.

He went on to sing Carolyn's praises, emphasizing how highly regarded she was in the community. Paget then told me that some faculty blamed me for the decline in enrollment in the MAT program and that one of the undergraduate education faculty members had resigned from a committee, accusing me of recruiting students away from the undergraduate program.

Shocked at how unfair many of these accusations felt, I defended myself. "People blame me?" I said, frowning, repressing my anger. "True, the number of students in the MAT program is slightly down. I may have alienated some students over the past several years because I believe that they deserve more than a program with few standards. I couldn't go along with what I found when I arrived in 1980, which was a tacit agreement between some of the faculty and the students that little would be required of them as they pursued a masters' degree with uninspired courses that duplicated topics mandated by the state."

He raised his eyes to look at me and said, "Why don't you fight back? It's all very sexist, you know. The institution has treated you quite shabbily." I felt my body relax. Did Paget really understand what I was up against? Was I naive in thinking I could take positions that to me were "right" and not have the undergraduate education faculty resist? After a while, I had begun to feel it might be my fault. If I ignored the abuse, it might go away. I had been allowing my colleagues to treat me in ways I would never allow in my personal life; I grew up in a family where the ideal was strong women who stood up to men. Yet I had been unable to apply this value to my professional life and believed I had gotten as far as I did because I worked to get along with colleagues.

Despite the new dean's consciousness of gender politics, his supportive nature could quickly turn to a wounding one. In mid-October, I made an appointment to talk with him about perhaps taking a sabbatical the following academic year to do some research. I was no longer the assistant dean and needed to focus on my advancement as a faculty member. Ignoring the purpose of the meeting, he launched into an evaluation of my administrative performance. "Your work is excellent, outstanding. Had I gotten to know you better before I appointed Carolyn as associate dean, I would have appointed you."

Surprised, I said, "Well, thank you, thank you. I am having fun working with the chairs on the graduate core. Although at some point, I do want to talk with you about my future options as an administrator."

Suddenly his tone changed. "Your problem is that you give people the impression you are condescending, a schoolmarm, an elementary schoolmarm. And you speak too rapidly, almost incoherently at times."

Rereading journal entries from this time, I see that Paget may have had a reason for speaking as he did. It later became clear that he had someone in mind

to hire as a director of development for graduate programs, a woman well connected to influential and wealthy people in Portland. Being able to combine that
with a faculty appointment would make his offer even more appealing. But his
strategies weren't all negative. He held out a "carrot," the promise of sabbatical in
fall of 1986 without the expectation that I would return for the following year, an
exception to college practice. His articulation of "my problem" did not jibe with
the way I saw myself. He struck me as a man who would use invective to get what
he wanted, and I can only conclude that he wanted me to move on.

But my existence at Lewis and Clark wasn't only one of marginalization. I was,
at the same time, in the center of planning activities mandated by the college's
new mission and my assignments from the acting dean. The graduate chairs
and I began our work on the graduate core curriculum with my proposal to
establish a series of faculty seminars that would discuss basic questions around
the development of the program: What kind of education do we want for our
students? What is the relationship between cognitive and adult development?
Where should the issues of gender and race be considered?

Once the chairs read my proposal, they began to resist. They had little or no
interest in these questions and thought my proposal was premature. Finally, Dan
Duke proposed that each chair talk about his or her own departmental curriculum to see where there were similarities in what we all did. "We might find a core
for graduate programs there," he said.

The other chairs agreed with Duke's suggestion, so I went along listening to
each program's presentation. Time spent in that way caused the chairs (all fellows but me) to relax and to begin to engage with ideas for a common core. They
started seeing ways in which concerns about preparing students for their professions in education, counseling, and public administration overlapped. I had
the utmost respect for them. Beginning with my first year as chair of the MAT
program, they taught me by example how to do quality administrative work: do
your homework and put forth clearly written, persuasive arguments supported
by data. But mostly they gave me confidence in my abilities, confidence that I was
a member of the team.

Another thing that brought the chairs beyond a fixation on, and defense of,
their programs was a series of seminars that the graduate faculty attended with
noted scholars in the 1985–1986 academic year. Supported by a grant from the
Fund for the Improvement of Postsecondary Education (FIPSE) that Doug Morgan and I had written, Lewis and Clark now had money to bring noted scholars
to campus, including Donald Schon, a professor of urban planning and education at MIT. Schon proposed that the paradigm of privilege in universities
should be turned on its head and that those disciplines working to solve society's most critical problems—poverty, unequal education, mental and physical
health—deserved the same status and resources as the sciences, for instance. His
epistemology of practice, "knowing in action," seemed particularly relevant to

our students. Schon contended that skillful professional practice often depended less on factual knowledge or rigid decision-making models than on the capacity to reflect before taking action in cases where established theories did not apply.

Barrie Thorne, a feminist sociologist then at Michigan State University, also led a seminar. She drew on the latest in feminist theory to demonstrate how gender was central to each of our graduate programs. A third scholar was Gunhild Hagestad, a Norwegian sociologist doing research on aging at the National Institutes of Health. A brilliant scholar, she drew on anthropology, history, demography, sociology, and psychology to destroy myths about aging and to argue that age was a social construction: "We don't have a life course (eighty years or more) perspective on aging, and we need one, because for the first time people are living beyond eighty." Sitting in a large seminar room listening to Hagestad lecture on the tasks of each developmental stage, I looked around at my colleagues, most of us in our thirties or forties, and saw faces fixed on her every word, colleagues at ease, having moved beyond concerns for our students to focus on ourselves. We were able to slow down and feel less urgency about things that were happening at the college. It felt like a community at peace with itself.

The richness of these seminars and discussions led to the design of two required courses, one on organizational behavior and another on life span development, to be taken by all of our masters' students. Critical issues seminars, held several times a year, brought in students from the law school as well. Our rationale for including a mix of students was that if you brought them together for part of their education, they would work together more readily once they were practicing in the field. The first critical issues seminar featured one of the authors of *Habits of the Heart*, William Sullivan, who lectured on the conflict between individuality and community. In another, Ros Feldberg, a sociologist whose specialty was demographic research on gender and work, came with a central question: Are women in female-dominated jobs earning less because the work they do is not as valuable, or is it less valuable because women do it? This was a particularly relevant question for programs in education and counseling, mostly considered "women's professions."

Despite the gift of time that my sabbatical in 1986–1987 gave me, Lewis and Clark increasingly came to feel like too rarefied an environment, one with most faculty turned inward. The pond I was swimming in seemed increasingly small. A chance to escape from my anomalous existence at Lewis and Clark came from an unexpected place: a dinner party in the spring of 1987.

Virginia Darney, an English professor and administrator at Evergreen State College's satellite campus in Vancouver, Washington, gave the dinner party in question. Marc and I were invited to meet Virginia's sister, Grace Grant, and Grace's husband, Dennis Tierney, both education professors. She was at

Occidental College in Los Angeles, and he was at California State University, Fullerton. Also invited were Pam Webb, the first director of Blackfish Gallery, an artists' cooperative that Marc directed from 1982 to 1985, and Pam's partner, an adjunct professor in the English department at Portland State University.

The dinner had been pleasant: well-prepared food, good wine, and talk about the art scene in Portland and how important Blackfish Gallery was to aspiring artists. "So you're at Lewis and Clark," the adjunct professor said after we had finished dessert. "What is your discipline?"

"Well, I teach in the MAT program; my specialty is social studies education, but my publications have all been in women's studies."

"Education? You're in education?"

"Yes, secondary education, secondary social studies."

He let out a laugh that was more of a bark: "Education isn't even a discipline. Some of the worst, most mediocre faculty at Portland State are in education. The university ought to get rid of all of its education programs." I looked up at a shelf on the wall across from my side of the table, a shelf decorated with beautiful Italian serving platters. *Stay calm*, I cautioned myself.

"Well, I don't know anything about the School of Education at PSU, but students choose our program at Lewis and Clark because they say it is of better quality. Many of them have undergraduate degrees from Oregon universities, so it could be they want a private school experience."

"Education, no matter where it is offered, isn't even a discipline. Teacher education doesn't belong in a university, and the thought that lightweights offer a doctorate in education at PSU makes me nauseous. It's a worthless use of tax payers' money."

Suddenly, I felt anger rise up in me. How many times had I heard education demeaned? Education courses were a waste of time, a form of vocational training at odds with the primary purpose of colleges and universities because knowing how to teach didn't involve more than knowing your academic discipline. Rarely spoken, but there nonetheless, was that teacher education was of little value because education was women's "true profession" or one suited for working-class men who lacked the intelligence, confidence, or resources to study "manly" disciplines such as the sciences or social sciences. What this adjunct professor was saying was not all that different from some of the more subtle put-downs I had experienced—less blatant than this one but nonetheless as demeaning. Even I had internalized these perceptions of inferiority. I had been attracted to my administrative role at Lewis and Clark because it took me out of the position of inferiority I felt I was in because I taught mostly education courses. I preferred team teaching MAT courses with colleagues in the social sciences and humanities rather than teaching more straightforward education courses for the same reason.

I let out all I had wanted to say to some of my colleagues in more traditional disciplines: "I can't speak for the education programs at PSU, but I know that important learning goes on in the MAT program at Lewis and Clark. Teachers getting their degree there take courses in both education and their discipline." *Slow down*, I said to myself, catching my breath. "Since I've been there, we've revised the program to be more innovative."

He shifted his eyes away from me.

"Have you ever been in a secondary classroom yourself?" I asked. "Have you ever tried to help teachers improve? Can you point to anything you've ever done to improve public education? I find your remarks offensive."

Everyone else at the table was silent. He turned to Pam and said, "It's about time we left."

Within the week, I had a note from Grace Grant: "Dennis Tierney thought you might be interested in this position." The position was dean of the School of Human Development and Community Service at California State University, Fullerton. The one-page description laid out basic information: the school encompassed departments in elementary and secondary education, marriage and family counseling, human services, reading, nursing, physical education, and the university's ROTC program. The faculty numbered 125, about the same as the undergraduate and graduate faculties at Lewis and Clark combined. The university, located in northern Orange County, enrolled more than twenty thousand students and included teacher education as central to its mission.

CHAPTER 8

A DEANERY OF MY OWN

In April 1987, I was speeding away from the John Wayne Airport, along the 55 Freeway, with Diane Ross, a physical education professor and a faculty leader at California State University (CSU) Fullerton, at the wheel of her Firebird. This was the first leg of my interview for the position of dean of the School of Human Development and Community Service (HDCS). The clusters of high-rise buildings bore signs with names such as Monsanto, Bank of America, and Wells Fargo. Agricultural fields spread out toward the horizon, eventually giving way to rows and rows of tract houses. I didn't feel I could ask Ross about the well-known conservatism of Orange County, a hothouse of right-wing movements such as the John Birch Society. It was reputed that evangelical churches flourished here, spreading their messages of abhorrence for communism, sex education, and abortion rights.

"Do you like it here?" I asked, my voice sounding uncharacteristically timid.

"I love it," she said, turning to look at me as she steered with one hand. "The weather's great, there's all that LA has to offer, and Orange County is becoming quite a cultural center. If you look over there to the left, you can see the performing arts center. Now, you're having dinner with the president tonight. She is a microbiologist and has to be in DC for some National Science Foundation panel on Monday, but she wanted to make sure to meet you. She's African American, you know. You'll be eating at her favorite restaurant, Marcel's, which has jazz on Saturday night."

I arrived at the restaurant at the appointed time and saw no one who could be President Cobb. Suddenly, there was a flurry at the door, and the maître d' said, "Ah, President Cobb, how wonderful to have you here tonight." Her laughter and his words were nearly drowned out by the jangle of her bracelets. "You must be Mary Kay," she said, taking my hands in hers. "Jewel Plummer Cobb. I'm sorry I'm late, but I couldn't find my keys. I was out gardening this afternoon and mistakenly left them in one of the flowerbeds. It took me some time to find them."

As we walked into the dining room, President Cobb stopped at several tables to greet people. Just as we were seated at a choice table ourselves, a man came by and, after giving her a hug, said, "Call me Monday about the urban renewal funds. I think I've found some way to deliver on a new football—er, sports—stadium, for the university."

With a smile, President Cobb turned to me and said, "I see football as a way to boost school spirit and forge ties with the community. Now tell me about you."

"I'm an associate professor and assistant dean at Lewis and Clark College, a small liberal arts college in Portland and. . . . . . ."

Before I could finish my sentence, a young man, the pianist in the jazz band, came over to our table. "President Cobb, how wonderful to see you here." They chatted for a few minutes, and when he left the table, she said, "He's one of the students in our jazz program. Very talented, very talented. And he understands that you get the best bang for the buck at Cal State Fullerton."

I got back to answering her question about me. "When I was a teacher in Chicago, on the South Side, I . . . ."

"You taught in Chicago? I'm from the South Side of Chicago. Where did you teach?"

"Parker High School at Sixty-Eighth and Stuart."

"Amazing. I graduated from Englewood, which is at Sixty-Second and Stuart."

For the remainder of the evening, talking with President Cobb was a cross between being in the presence of a local celebrity and one of your best girl-friends. When she drove me back to the motel, she put her warm hand on mine and said, "So nice to meet you. I want you to know that I want the next dean to help the faculty in Hudcus—we pronounce the school's name that way—to feel better about themselves, to understand that research is a reasonable expectation in a university."

Sitting in the sun by the motel pool the next day, preparing for my campus interviews on Monday, and reviewing materials about Cal State Fullerton, I reflected back on why I wanted to be a dean. As signaled by the photograph of junior class officers in the 1955 *Shamrock*, I liked being in the center of things, where the power was. My reasons were also tied to who I was as a person—constructed as "the responsible one" in my family and called on, for example, to accompany my mother one late night to pick up my father at a bar, his face bloodied from a fight, or to drive more than two hundred miles with my father to eastern Nebraska to pick up Aunt Pearl, a nurse, and bring her back to North Platte to help my mother, who was hemorrhaging after Patty's birth and threatening a nervous breakdown.

My time at Lewis and Clark had given me not only the experience of power and its costs but also a taste for what could be accomplished by working with others—namely, to paraphrase Adrienne Rich, to work toward a woman-centered university and imagine how it might be different if women were in positions of responsibility and authority.[1] There was another reason I wanted to be a dean that I shared only with Marc. I was no longer interested in doing what I had been hired to do: be an education professor. I was reminded of my ambivalence every time I was asked about my discipline and I answered, "Er, secondary education, social studies education, but all my publications are in women's studies." Becoming a dean and a feminist scholar gave me a way out of this dilemma. None of these were reasons I could give in an interview. Instead, I tried to think through an answer that drew on some of my successes at Lewis and Clark.

⋘⋙

The next morning, Diane drove me to campus, traveling at seventy miles an hour along the freeway, saying, "We're certainly going in the right direction this morning. Just look at those cars crawling along on the other side." The morning sun gleamed brightly off their windshields. A large freeway sign, reading, "California State University, Fullerton," announced our exit.

The university was founded in 1957; 452 students were admitted two years later. Nearly 40,000 were enrolled in 2016. Today, students can select from more than two hundred undergraduate majors and more than one hundred masters' level degrees. When I arrived on campus, Fullerton was one of twenty campuses in the CSU system. I later came to learn that the CSU system was created when the state legislature adopted their Master Plan for High Education in the 1960s. This plan established a three-tiered university system in the state. The University of California would accept the top 10 percent of high school graduates and offer doctoral programs, and CSU would accept the top third of high school graduates. The majority of students in the CSU system, however, transferred from community colleges. Originally limited to offering degrees at the undergraduate and masters' levels, many campuses began to offer the EdD, a doctorate in education, in 2000. Community colleges were the third tier.

My first impression of the campus was of a sea of parking lots, cars lined up to get the next open space, and buildings more than ten stories high, looking like cheap versions of those I had seen along the freeway near the airport. "The campus was carved out of an orange grove," Diane said. "The only remnant of that grove today is a small cluster of trees preserved in the middle of campus." Frowning to signal the importance of what she was about to say, she continued, "You have a map in your folder to show you where each of the buildings is. Don't miss the jacaranda trees near the student union that are starting to bloom. That's a sure sign that graduation is not far behind. Ah, here we are at the building where Hudcus is housed," she said, taking a ramp down to a small parking area of six spaces. "Your first interview is with the department chairs."

Once on the fifth floor, a secretary proudly showed me the dean's office, with floor to ceiling windows facing east and Mount Baldy visible that morning, dusted with snow. The interim dean, Eula Stovall, rose to greet me with a smile and a Texas twang as warm as her handshake. Her shiny navy-blue sweat suit reminded me that she was the chair of the Health, Physical Education, and

Recreation department when not serving as interim dean. "Let's go down to the dean's conference room. The department chairs and the associate dean are waiting for you. You will need to make your own judgment about Parker, the associate dean. I never knew what the hell he was doing, how he spent his time, mostly staring at a computer. He's good with budgets, but that's about all." As Stovall turned to go back to her office, I thought that it was common for a new dean to bring in her own person. Parker might have to go.

I entered a room with no windows, and there around the table were eight men and three women. The temperature in the room felt chilly. Or was I imagining that from the stiff postures and unsmiling faces of the people around the table? As they began their introductions, I thought of the movie *The Bad News Bears*, a comedy about a nearly hopeless youth league baseball team that wins in the end. The chairs of elementary and secondary education, respectively, began by giving only their name and titles—suspicious, aggressive, and waiting for me to prove myself. A youthful man introduced himself as the chair of counseling psychology. His professional attire was in sharp contrast to the student I had seen wearing the department's sweatshirt with an image of a California vanity license plate across the front that read ILISN2U. The chair of human services, impeccably dressed in a well-tailored sports jacket set off by a colorful shirt and tie, leaned into the desk, smiled broadly, and said, "I'm really more of a counseling psychologist than a social worker, seeing as how I have nearly half the market in textbooks for that field. In fact"—his eyes darting around the table—"I'm usually at home at this time writing."

Next was the chair of educational administration. His florid face and arms bulging against the sleeves of his polyester suit matched his description of himself as a former high school principal and football coach. The last two chairs to introduce themselves were those of special education and the reading program. The eighth male in the room, perched at the end of the table opposite me, introduced himself as Michael Parker, the associate dean, a longtime faculty member and former chair of counseling psychology. He looked like some kind of a throwback to the 1970s, his thick, nearly white hair forming a cap around his face, reminiscent of the rock group the Monkees. (Thankfully, he had put his bell-bottom trousers away and, shortly after I arrived, was transformed by a trendy haircut and business suits to match.)

The chair of nursing sat on the edge of her seat, wearing a welcoming expression. The other female chair, Judith Ramirez, had earlier been associate dean and was now chair of child development. Her correct posture, no-nonsense professional attire, shoes that could have been worn by a Catholic nun, and clear speech suggested that she was a woman I could depend on to build a winning team. My instincts were the opposite for the dean's executive assistant, who had a choice office in the dean's suite, better than the associate dean's. When I met her briefly before the meeting, she handed me a written catalog of activities that the previous dean had delegated to her: the dean's convocation, graduation, supervision of office staff, "and so on." Because of all her responsibilities, she quickly told me, the dean had approved of her leaving the office at three thirty so that she could be on time for her second job as a security guard at Disneyland in nearby Anaheim.

Finished with introductions, the chairs wondered mostly how I would be their advocate for getting resources that came from student enrollment—resources, they declared, that were their due but unfairly allocated to the sciences. "Why is that?" I asked.

"It is an issue of unequal teaching loads. A new faculty member in biology teaches only one class his first year. Meanwhile, ours have heavy teaching loads, often three courses per semester in addition to supervising student teachers."

"Where is your provost on all of this?" I asked.

"Jack, Jack Coleman. We're not sure what he values, but you have to remember, President Cobb is a scientist."

"Well, my next appointment is with Coleman, so I'll ask him his thoughts about funding the various schools." As I walked across campus to the provost's office, the chairs' claims about the unequal allocation of resources weighed heavily on me. When I told Coleman about the chair's worries, he brushed them aside by saying, "Every department believes they're not getting their due."

Several days after I returned to Portland, I picked up the phone and heard a voice say, "Jewel Cobb here. I'm delighted to offer you the dean's position in Hudcus. The salary is seventy thousand dollars. You'll have the rank of full professor—you'll need to present your file to our tenure and promotion committee, but that will be a mere formality with your strong publishing record. Oh, and the benefits in the Cal State system are excellent—health care, dental care, and a fabulous retirement plan."

This offer improved my fortunes in several ways. My salary at Lewis and Clark was in the low forties; here was a raise of more than 60 percent and promotion to full professor. It would be at least five years before I achieved that rank at Lewis and Clark. But more importantly, I was being given the chance to try to put Don Schon's promise of a different university into practice, hopefully gaining more status and resources for HDCS.

What I hadn't anticipated was resistance at home.

My sabbatical was near an end when I accepted the dean's position at Fullerton. There had been time for the V under my left eye to fade, time to relish Chantal at seventeen. The conscientious student she had been in middle school returned her senior year, as she received all As except for second-year calculus, missing that grade by only one point. She took a French class at Reed College—she had completed all that her high school had to offer—writing her college application's personal essay in verse, patterned after The Canterbury Tales: "The Tale of My Journey to Reed: The Story of a Modern-Day Pilgrimage to Higher Education."

Figure 13. School of Human Development and Community Service graduation, 1988

Marc and I congratulated one another on our good judgment in not even thinking about leaving Portland until Chantal graduated from high school. One morning in June, I was urging her to clean up her room. It was not possible to take a step without sliding over layers of clothes, books, papers, and dirty dishes. "Isn't it about time you did something with this mess?"

"This is my room. I'll be messy if I want."

"Yes, but—"

She interrupted me, her brown eyes glaring. "I'm furious that we are moving to California in August, and Southern California at that—La La Land!"

"But it won't matter," I said. "You're off to Vassar in September, off to the East Coast, off to New York. Portland will wane in importance."

"But I don't want us to move."

"Look, Chantal," I said, growing impatient. "You have to do things in life you don't want to do. My family made five moves between the time I was eleven and when I graduated from high school. It's just something you have to do."

"I don't care what happened to you. I care about me," she said, tears beginning to stream down her cheeks. "You've taken away my friends, you've taken away my school, you're taking away my house, and you're taking away my town." Silenced by her outburst, I quietly walked over the uneven mass underfoot and left the room. Until that moment, I did not understand that her boyfriend and her female friends would never be more important than the summer after graduation.

I had yet to learn how Marc and I would feel after Chantal departed for college in the fall. Marc captured our mood in a self-portrait he did at the time. It is one of a forlorn man looking off to the right, with a sober mouth, a Tour de France baseball cap pressing down on his graying hair, and Lucien Freud–like painterly strokes emphasizing shadows of worry. Our beloved daughter was gone. From everything we could garner, she was having a good time—so good, in fact, that a dean met with her to inquire about her failing grade in Introduction to Chemistry, since she had done so well in math and science in high school. Chantal had entered Vassar thinking she would major in biochemistry. In a telephone call toward the end of her first semester, she explained that the way her chemistry course was taught had "nothing to do with who I am as a person." Later, she explained that she might have pursued science if she had first taken a course that demonstrated the relevance of science rather than the one she had taken. Fortunately, Chantal took Introduction to Anthropology, taught by the feminist professor Coleen Cohen, which set her on a path to majoring in that discipline.

As Marc and I adjusted to our new life together, I wondered if I had taken anything away from him too by asking that he move again. "Noooooooo," he said when I asked him again nearly thirty years later. I was able to "give" something to Marc because of my unbelievable salary. He would be able to paint full time and join a gallery, LA Artcore.

"Now that I'm painting full time, I'd be happy to do all the cooking," he said.

In my head was an image of my father returning from work, expecting that dinner be ready promptly at five thirty, and my mother, lipstick newly applied, having set the table so he'd think dinner was imminent. "I think not," I said. "I don't want to do to men what they have done to women. There is too great a possibility of anger when you're the only cook. Let's continue to trade off each week."

Figure 14. Seminar on Feminist Pedagogy, Huntington Library, January 1990. Back Row: Barrie Thorne, Frinde Maher, Jill Tarule; Front Row: me and Marilyn Boxer.

At a going-away party hosted by the Magnussons, Major James Powell, a friend and an army veteran, on hearing that the university's ROTC commander reported to me, presented me with the trappings of authority in the military: a khaki-colored beret with an insignia—an eagle whose head was turned sideways, its wings pointing upward—and a wooden swagger stick with a bullet protruding on the end. Raising his hand in a sharp salute, he said, "You'll need these." I appreciated the humor in his gift but couldn't help connecting it to *Games Mother Never Taught You* (1977), advertised as "the definitive, hard-nosed manual on corporate politics for the career woman." A central thesis of the book was that the landscape of business had been drafted out of a military/sports model and that it was imperative that one understood where one fit in the hierarchy.

My earliest lesson about the chain of command came from President Cobb, the first female and one of four black presidents I would serve under in the next seventeen years. In my first weeks on campus, I decided I had to deal with my nagging worry about finding the time to continue working on my feminist pedagogy book. Frinde Maher and I had agreed to study at least six institutions in order to have a mix of small liberal arts colleges, a research university, and two comprehensive ones. By then, we had a plan of attack. One of us would be the lead researcher, spending three weeks on campus, while the other came for one overlapping week. Frinde could take the lead on the next three—Towson State University in Maryland, Spelman College in Atlanta, and her own campus, Wheaton College, in Massachusetts. I would need one week off campus for each of those visits and time to observe classes and interview faculty and students at my third campus, San Francisco State. My sabbatical the previous year had enabled me to spend three weeks each at the University of Arizona and Lewis and Clark College.

I broke into a sweat when I realized, in addition to the time spent off campus, that I would need time for transcribing tapes, writing a case study for each of the eighteen professors whose classes we would observe, writing the book proposal, and—egad!—writing the book itself, all while also being a dean. The one thing that calmed me was that both Frinde and I knew by then that if either one of us flagged in the project, the other one would take up the slack. Remembering how connected President Cobb and I had been the evening we met and her assertion that research was a reasonable expectation for faculty, I anticipated no problems when I sought her approval to carve out time to work on the book.

I called the president, emphasizing that the faculty needed an example of how to get "work" done. Just as I moved on to specifying when I would work on the book and also attend to my administrative responsibilities, she interrupted me and said, "You shouldn't be talking to me about this. You don't report to me; you report to Coleman. He's the person you should be talking with." She slammed down the phone, making me wonder why I hadn't learned that lesson about the chain of command from reading *Games Mother Never Taught You*. My misjudgment on this speaks volumes about how much I had yet to learn.

Talk to Jack Coleman, I thought. How could I approach a man who was an accountant, a former vice president for finance and administration at San Jose State, a retired air force pilot, whose specialty had been flying airplanes into the eyes of hurricanes to gather data? I had been told that I was not his favored candidate, that he had wanted an associate dean already within the Cal State University system but that President Cobb had made the final decision to hire me. Everything about my first encounters with Coleman suggested he thought the president had made a mistake. But not to call him meant dropping the study and severing a part of my heart, my mind. Research had been essential to who I was as a person ever since I began working on *Women of America: Half of History* in the early 1970s.

When I reached Coleman on the phone, I imagined him sitting behind his large desk, looking through his aviator glasses at the couch on the opposite wall. "President Coleman, I mean, Provost Coleman, I'd like to talk with you about an idea I have for continuing my research on university teaching." My tongue was unable to utter the phrase "feminist pedagogy" as I made my case.

"And what is that?"

"Well, what I need most is time. I thought I'd propose to my department chairs that I work at home two mornings a week, for a total of eight hours, and then make up those hours by working from five, when the office closes, until seven Monday through Thursday—you know, exchanging eight hours for eight." I heard my voice catch. "I will also give the department chairs my home phone number so they can contact me if anything comes up. I live only eight minutes from campus." I didn't tell him I usually worked in my pajamas at home.

"How do you imagine doing that when you have a school to run? Not come to campus until noon two days a week? I don't want you doing that."

Panic. If I didn't persist, I would never be able to finish the book. "One of the biggest issues in Hudcus is that there is no culture of faculty scholarship. By signaling to them that it is important to me, I hope to begin changing that culture, leading by example."

There was a long pause. "I still don't like the idea. Your first priority should be your work as dean. That is, after all, what we pay you for. Know that I'm opposed to your staying home to write a book. But if you can run that school, which the past dean found almost ungovernable, I won't object." I hung up the phone and put my hand on my beating heart.

At the next department chairs' meeting, I presented my plan, careful to speak from an outline I had composed beforehand. When I finished there was silence. Then the chair of elementary education, whose perfect penmanship reflected the cursive method he once taught, said, "You have my support. I think it is a good idea; a good example for the faculty." And it worked out. Never in the six years I was dean did I hear rumblings of dissatisfaction with my plan; a chair called me at home only once.

Always aware of Coleman's begrudging approval, I stayed home two mornings a week, climbing up to my study by eight to transcribe tapes, writing case studies of each informant. Though Frinde and I wouldn't finish *The Feminist Classroom* until 1994, rumors about my work habits began to circulate. The one that amused me most, likely spread by Parker, the associate dean, was that I rose each morning at four thirty to write. Had he spread such an idea to put fear in the hearts of the department chairs?

My study was a small loft high above our second bedroom. The only way up to it was to step on the first rung of a vertical ladder, my hands tightly gripping its side railing as I ascended. After negotiating the ladder, I crawled to the right onto an open landing about four feet wide, suppressing my vertigo, until I was able to stand alongside the railing that enclosed the rest of the space. It made me think twice about going to the refrigerator. It was nothing short of a miracle that Marc had gotten my bulky oak desk over the railing of the loft. I'd watched as he had tied one end of a rope around the desk and another around the railing along the front of the loft. He had managed single-handedly to hoist it up to the open

A DEANERY OF MY OWN

space near the ladder, being careful not to crash into the glass sliding doors that covered the closet below. Once the desk was upside down in the open space, Marc had slid it into my study. Looking up in wonder from below, I thought, *The things this man knows how to do.*

My room with a view had a high window, and by standing up, I could look out on the garden, where a brilliant coral tree bloomed each March. Off to the other side was a deck with a seating area, throne-like as one ascended four steps. A redwood hot tub, large enough to hold six people comfortably, sat in its center. At night, the jasmine vines that grew above the latticework permeated the cool night air, a contrast to the warmth of the tub. "There goes the 10:10 to Paris," Marc would say as we saw planes from LAX high overhead. There was another structure at the end of the garden, originally a tack house built in the 1920s, measuring 385 square feet. Converted later into a residence, it was the perfect place for Marc's studio. Our address, 812 Lois Lane, inspired Marc to name his studio "Clark Kent Studio." Occasionally, we would receive a call inquiring about the sale of his artwork: "Is Clark there?"

"Lois here," I'd say. "I'll get him right away."

I learned yet another lesson on the chain of command from President Cobb as my first year as dean ended. The occasion was the HDCS graduation in May 1988. The ceremony was my executive assistant's domain, and she resented any questions, let alone ideas, I had about the event. When I first learned that the faculty was seated in rows behind the thousand or so graduating students, I objected.

"That's how we've always done it," she replied. I decided not to back down. "We're changing it. They will sit in the front rows. It is their day too."

Another bone of contention with my executive assistant, who embodied all the patriotism of Orange County, was her practice of showcasing the ROTC cadets at graduation. I became increasingly alarmed at our rehearsal as I watched the cadets march in, the two in front ushering in the colors—the United States and California flags. Marching two abreast at close intervals, the morning light illuminating their young faces, the other twenty or so cadets carrying rifles and sabers paused from time to time to cross and twirl them, as their "faculty" advisor shouted, "Halt! About Face!" When I expressed my alarm to Mike Parker, he said, "Let's wait until next year to curb the ROTC show. Getting the faculty up front was enough for this year."

The day of graduation, after the platform party, which included President Cobb, the department chairs, and me, was seated, the cadets, looking even more militaristic in their uniforms than they had at the rehearsal, marched in. The low tent covering the graduates and their guests made their swords and sabers more menacing. I cringed. As soon as President Cobb saw this display, she leaned toward me and whispered, "What is going on here? We're not a military academy."

"I know, but I decided to tackle one issue this year. I had to insist that the faculty be seated in front. Next year, I'll minimize the role of the ROTC."

Figure 15. Celebrating Chantal's graduation from Vassar, Gourde, France, 1991

"Why would you bow to her? You're the goddamn dean." And why *had* I bowed to her? I'd wanted to avoid conflict, not sure how powerful she was. And more importantly, Parker had cautioned against curbing the show. This and the earlier "lesson" from President Cobb in the chain of command taught me that she might feel like my best girlfriend at times, but we were definitely differently positioned in the administrative hierarchy.

The initial fear I harbored about whether I could possibly succeed as a dean quickly transformed as I started learning what I needed to do as the dean of HDCS. The sports/military model was not a uniform I easily wore. I was much more comfortable enlisting the chairs and their faculty into new ways of collaborating, imagining new possibilities, and seeing the importance of our work to society. I decided the time to do that was at my first dean's convocation.

I made my way through the student union to the room where the convocation was being held, still surprised by the sale items that met my eye when I entered the bookstore: sweatshirts with the CSUF logo, baseball caps touting the year our team had won the college world series, and coffee mugs, eventually giving way to the shelves of textbooks for sale, organized alphabetically by course title. There was a small section of general interest books near the rear shelved under categories such as "Literature," "*New York Times* Bestsellers," and "Religious Themes." How different this bookstore was from the one at Lewis and Clark, where classic literature and current general interest books predominated. When I reached our meeting place after walking up the stairs to the second floor, Mike Parker at my side, I saw that the room was packed. "Quite a turnout," I said.

"Enjoy it. You'll never again see so many of them together at one time. A new dean always brings them out."

I moved toward the podium at the front of the room and began. "One of the best things about academia is that each year offers the possibility of fresh beginnings: faculty who are rested and new students with high hopes for what their education will bring to them. And in your case, a new dean." A ripple of self-conscious laughter spread across the room. "With our fresh beginnings in mind, I want to tell you what is important to me and for us to decide together if these ideas can inform what we do. In turn, over the next few months, I want to learn what is important to you."

Borrowing what I had learned from Donald Schon while at Lewis and Clark, I made the case that HDCS had the perfect configuration of programs to work to solve society's most critical problems by educating our students to function differently as professionals. The chairs of nursing and child development were nodding their heads in agreement. Their counterparts in elementary and secondary education crossed their arms in front of their chests.

When I finished, faculty members came forward to introduce themselves; in some cases, they offered how an idea had resonated with their teaching. Corey, the chair of human services, said, "I want you to come to our next department meeting to see how we are implementing many of the ideas you mentioned." Beginning to poke his fingers into my briefcase, he asked, "Is your calendar there in your purse?"

"I'd love to come. Call Dolores; she keeps my calendar." I noticed some of the education faculty in small clusters near the back of the room. I was reminded of advice that Schon had given me at Lewis and Clark: "Don't expect everyone to buy into an idea; establish small centers of excellence that faculty can resonate to." It was unrealistic to expect everyone to get on board. I felt a satisfying high as I approached the wine table. *Silences*, I thought. I had stopped short of telling them why gender was important to me. My interest in gender was no secret on my résumé, circulated widely on campus when I was interviewed, listing articles with titles such as "The Treatment of Women in U.S. History High School Textbooks: A Decade's Progress" and "Feminist Phase Theory: An Experience Derived Evaluation Model." Yet my experiences since the 1970s had taught me that I needed to know my constituency before suggesting where gender might be relevant. I found this to be true for predominately male groups and ones such as the HDCS faculty, with a higher percentage of female students and faculty members than any other group in the university.

In no time, I came to see that I needed a "wingman" in my associate dean, not only someone who would help with enrollment predictions but someone whom I could trust to tell me the "truth"—someone who was loyal and politically astute and had the confidence of the faculty. I came to see that the associate dean I had inherited, Michael Parker, was all that and more. He had a more than twenty-year history as a faculty member and department chair and knew who took which side in pitched battles and where all the bodies were buried. I could send him out in two directions—first, to meet with other administrators, especially other male ones, in the larger university, usually about resources, and second, to troubled departments within HDCS. Parker and I became partners. It had been the right thing to do to wait and make my own judgments about the fit between this inherited associate and me.

All the promising ideas in the world mattered little if HDCS lost the competition for resources. It took less than a few weeks on campus for me to notice that when I asked someone for an idea, they gave me a relevant financial number as well. Parker taught me why this was so. The CSU system, which had been strongly supported by Governor Pat Brown, was undermined by other interests and had suffered neglect when Ronald Reagan succeeded him as governor in 1966. As a result, and out of necessity, funding became an obsession within the system from the smallest programs to system-wide ones. There was an elaborate formula applied based on "mode" (large lecture classes or small seminars, for instance) and "level" (lower and upper division undergraduate and graduate classes). This created an atmosphere in which everyone tried to game an unrealistic system that had never been funded as planned anyway. Also, mode and level formulas did not prevent disciplinary hierarchies from influencing funding on individual campuses. Californians generally considered programs such as those in HDCS important, but they were resented by most of the campuses in the CSU system as expensive and of little prestige. Conservatives deprecated such programs, and the gender bias associated with the "women's work" of teaching and service also fed into the marginalization of these areas.

Following the legislature's allocations to the CSU system, the chancellor's office passed funds on to campuses based primarily on enrollment targets every semester but was also influenced by a campus's history of funding. Once resources were allocated to the campuses according to all of these factors, university presidents and vice presidents had the discretion to allocate the money as they saw fit, ensuring that certain disciplines with low enrollment were still offered and taking into account that some disciplines, such as the sciences and engineering, were more valued than others. Negotiation then ensued between the provost and the deans about how much enrollment we "could make." One thing was certain: not meeting enrollment targets could lead to a reduction in resources the next time around. Every dean quaked, imagining what it would be like to announce such cuts to their faculty. All of the time Parker spent staring at a computer screen involved determining the student credit-hour target HDCS could achieve and, subsequently, what each of the ten departments could deliver. He prepared me to go to deans' meetings armed with data to support our proposed targets and with historical data that showed that HDCS was not getting its share according to the system-wide formulas.

But Parker wasn't only good at that. I also began to see that it was important to know what I should be doing and what others could do better. Judy Ramirez came into my office at one point in 1988 and said, "I just got back from a conference where I heard the most wonderful presentation by one of the authors of that new book, *Women's Ways of Knowing*. It is totally relevant for our students and faculty. I think we should bring one of the authors here."

I knew about the book because Frinde Maher was a friend of one of the authors, Jill Tarule. Tarule and the other three authors had set out to understand why so many women doubt their intellectual competence. Interviewing more than a hundred women, rich and poor, young and old, well-educated and unschooled, they found a common chord: they described a struggle to be heard in schools and families that valued neither a woman's voice nor her ideas. They argued that women are "voiceless" because they are at odds with the traditional male model of knowing, which establishes "truth" by objective, dispassionate methods. As the stories showed, women "find their voice" when they enhance objective knowing by using intuition, personal meanings, and self-understanding, not proof alone.

"Hmmm," I said. "How do you think the other chairs will take to the idea?"

"I can tell you right now who will object—the chairs of education programs."

"How can we test the water? Find out what will fly?"

"Send Mike out," Judy said.

"Perfect."

I approached Mike with Judy's idea and asked about his willingness to feel out the department chairs for their receptivity to having one of the authors of *Women's Ways of Knowing* come to campus. A couple of days later, Mike came back to tell me what he had learned by wandering the halls and department offices. "I was right," he said. "The department chairs mostly don't care. A few were even enthusiastic—the chair of nursing, for example. But the people you should worry about are conservative, male-defined women faculty."

"You mean such as that blonde in elementary education, the one with the beehive hairdo?"

"She's the one. And she said to me, 'Let her know that if she brings in one of the authors of that book, she'll be seen as a one-issue person.'"

"OK, I guess that is that."

"No, not at all. Have Ramirez be the lead on this one. There is no love lost between her and that other woman, so it won't matter." Tarule came to give a talk and was so positively received that I supported her return as a visiting scholar in HDCS the following semester. Younger faculty in education and those in child development gained new perspectives on collaborative learning from her seminars.

Early on, I turned my attention to the ten department chairs and urged them to set aside the old resentments they had harbored since 1975, when their programs were forced to merge into HDCS. The resentments were many—especially infighting over resources, with those outside education believing those programs were selfishly taking more than their share. For example, faculty in physical education were certain that athletics was being supported with funds intended for their own courses.

As an exercise, I asked the chairs to imagine HDCS in the year 2000, when the school would celebrate its twenty-fifth anniversary. We did this imagining at department chairs' meetings and retreats. At first, they were skeptical: "Here is another dean with lots of ideas, this one talking about integrated services and arguing that the school's particular configuration of departments was one of its strengths." Remarkably though, the department chairs' resistance was short lived.

At the first chairs' retreat, held at the UCLA conference center at Lake Arrowhead, we did brainstorming activities that imagined the best for ourselves: an alive faculty, a shared sense of purpose, control of our own destiny relative to the curriculum and the school's organization, and peer support for research and course development. We also imagined new ways of educating our diverse student body. "Remember that student," I said, "at one of those celebrations Jewel made us hold, who, after receiving her reward, surprised us by saying, 'We've made it in an institution that wasn't made for us.' What would we have to change in order to offer an education that *was* made for her?"

Fueled by mountain air, comfortable accommodations, good food, and high-quality Scotch, we came to know one another and to plan for a better HDCS. We bit off digestible challenges and wrote down where we would like HDCS to be in five years: "We will further a more integrated approach to the education and care of children and adults by offering a course that brings students together from all of our programs so that they will work collaboratively once they are in the field."

Planning also included the faculty. At a school-wide retreat in the fall of 1990, we made progress in articulating a philosophy for HDCS, excited by the idea of collaborative learning and the social construction of knowledge—namely, that knowledge is constructed in individual classrooms out of the interaction of different perspectives rather than found as "truth." Mike Parker's pessimistic observation at my first dean's convocation that I'd "never see so many of them together at one time" was proven wrong as faculty showed up at the retreat and engaged with new ideas.

In an email to me after reading a draft of this chapter, Diane Ross, the faculty member who had shepherded me to and around Fullerton my very first time there wrote the following:

> In the beginning, there was resistance from the faculty and much criticism of "your focus." But your direction, goals, perspectives, and activities also changed our attitudes. An openness to change began to develop and even words such as *collaboration* were added to our everyday vocabularies during faculty interactions. You introduced new ideas to many who had not heard a new one in years. Not only did faculty from different disciplines talk to one another, but also those of us who are white came to see others who do not look like us in new ways.

Parker recalls thinking at the time that because of our collective effort, the school moved from the 1950s to the present.

But change didn't happen just because we had imagined it and wrote it down. Help came from one of Provost Coleman's associate vice presidents, Michael Clapp, who called one day in 1990 and said, "There's someone I'd like you to meet, a guy named Sid, who is new to the LA Basin and is heading up the West Coast office of the Annie E. Casey Foundation. When I listen to you talk and I listen to Sid, it sounds like you're talking about the same things. He's looking for a place to locate his office." Clapp went on to tell me that he and Sid Gardner had been roommates at Occidental College. Gardner had been a city councilman in Hartford, Connecticut, and an advisor to the Clintons on health care and services to children while Bill was governor of Arkansas.

Gardner showed up for our initial meeting looking reserved in a three-piece pinstriped suit. His slicked-back black hair added to his corporate look. The only hint that he might be more than a corporate type was the cowboy boots that peeked out from under his suit pants. I wasn't exactly sure what he was looking for or what he was proposing, but I gave him an office and introduced him to faculty who were interested in new ways of thinking about their programs. In no time, Sid was talking about a different paradigm for serving children, arguing that he knew of a child from a dysfunctional family who was treated by seven different agencies in isolation from one another. "You have to ask," he said, "how did our professions come to divide a child up into seven separate parts?" His message for those of us in HDCS was that we had the rare opportunity to educate our students to imagine a more effective approach to serving this child. "There is a new movement called integrated services for children that seeks to do things differently. We are positioned to be in the forefront of this movement."

Together, we came up with the idea of CSUF's Center for Collaboration for Children (CCC), which opened in 1991. Faculty seminars, symposia, and extensive planning led to the development of a course in integrated services for students across all the academic programs, with the exception of those in teacher education. That branch of the faculty was more focused on classroom management, claiming that educating an increasingly poor and diverse student population was all it could do. There was no time to teach prospective teachers about collaborating with other child-serving professionals. The CCC continued under Gardner's direction until his retirement in 2001, when it was renamed the Center for Community Collaboration. According to its web page, it continues to be a major change catalyst, both locally and statewide, for universities and communities to embrace interprofessional education, community collaboration, and results based on accountability.

Our collective work helped us stand out from the crowd when the Western Association of School and Colleges visited campus in 1990 as part of the accreditation renewal process. When the visiting team, composed of university administrators and faculty from around the country, gave its oral report to Provost Coleman and his administrative team, they were critical of the campus: there was a business-as-usual approach; the faculty had no idea of what was to be done about the impending and frequent fiscal crises. The one exception was HDCS, where there was a clear focus on mission and vision. When I heard this, I was startled but pleased to hear this recognition. I dared not look at Coleman.

When the campus received the accreditation team's written report and comments were solicited from the campus, Coleman objected to the statement about planning in HDCS: "Hudcus is not the only place in the university where planning takes place." Despite Coleman's objections, the accreditation team stuck to its evaluation, noting that no other school in the university was doing the kind of planning we were.

The progress we had made in HDCS toward becoming a vital, collaborative community is captured in one of Marc's watercolors. Parker and I decided that we needed a brochure to signal the idea of HDCS, a document, along with related materials, that we could use to recruit faculty, students, and donors. I had seen a painting by Jacob Lawrence, titled *The University*, on a conference brochure that pictured a grand spacious hall, with human figures at sharp angles, distant from one another. I showed the image to Marc and asked him to duplicate it, wondering if I could be sued for plagiarism. I need not have worried, as he worked off a photograph of the faculty assembled at one of our retreats. From that, he painted an abstract watercolor with larger images of faculty in the foreground ascending into blurred images at the top. It perfectly depicted my idea of the school:

a multilayered, complex mix of people who, by coming together, had created a sense of community, one in which they could take justifiable pride. It illustrated how the "Bad News Bears" of CSUF were becoming a winning team.

⋘⋙

My responsibilities weren't only to HDCS but to the larger university as well. Resources may have been the coin of the realm, but personal relationships mattered, especially those across campus with the associate provosts and the deans. "Get to know Dennis Berg and Mike Clapp," was one of the first things Jack Coleman said to me. Together, they were responsible for things that particularly mattered to the faculty: curriculum, faculty and staff appointments, and grievances. They were representative of a group of straightforward fellows, good citizens active in the faculty senate, and reminiscent of the positive attitude I saw among bright high school leaders. They were men known on campus, generally free of sexist attitudes, part of the egalitarian faculty culture that predominated in the CSU, and committed to enabling a diverse student body to succeed. Other male campus leaders also reached out to me. Keith Boyum, a faculty senate leader and coordinator of the Educational Policies Fellowship Program (EPFP), quickly recruited me to be one of two campus participants. EPFP was a yearlong professional development program focused on policy, leadership, and networking that combined activities specific to each state as well as nationally focused ones. The other participant, Tom Klammer, an associate dean in the School of Humanities and Social Sciences and also a campus leader, would become one of my most trusted colleagues.

The table that the deans sat around at our biweekly meetings next to the provost's office seated twenty, even though there were only six schools at CSUF in 1987. Most meetings were restricted to the provost, the deans, and the director of institutional research, Dolores Vura, who came with spreadsheets that calculated various scenarios of enrollment targets and related budgets. When appropriate, Parker prepared scenarios for me to present. At one meeting that I recall, I waited until the right moment to begin and spoke in a firm voice. "I said at our last budget discussion that graduate programs in Hudcus have supported programs in the sciences and humanities for the past decade. Some of you asked if I had data to support my assertion. You will see from these spreadsheets I'm passing around that the teacher education program has been funded at less than 80 percent of system formulas over the past ten years. So rather than taking cuts at this time, we should receive additional resources."

The dean of the arts, Jerry Samuelson, slammed his fist on the table. He was the most senior dean, a thin man who was always impeccably dressed with two-toned saddle oxfords, a full mustache, and perfectly clipped white hair, looking like the prototypic dean of the 1950s. He was the person who ensured that public events at the university had class, such as deciding how the stage would be arranged for each school's graduation, the color of the slips that covered each chair at university fundraising dinners, and that sort of thing. The other deans looked up but were quiet. Hunching his body forward, Samuelson said, anger in his voice, "I don't want you to say that ever again."

Before I had a chance to respond, thinking that Samuelson's outburst was an objection to my proposal for a fairer distribution of resources to HDCS, the dean of humanities and social sciences, Don Schweitzer, a psychologist, said to him, "You can't say that to one another. It is only dysfunctional groups or families that forbid one another from saying things." The deans were not a dysfunctional group. Provost Coleman ran too tight a ship for that to happen. A master of the chain of command, something he most likely brought from the military, he kept us all in line. It would take having other managers for me to see how clearly fair he was.

⸻⸺⸻

President Cobb brought a perspective to Cal State Fullerton that expanded my understanding of the workings of class and race and gender. Even though I had taught in all-black high schools in Chicago in the 1960s, Cobb introduced the faculty and staff at the university to the multilayered realities of race in America. Her family had been a part of the black bourgeoisie for several generations: her father was a physician, and her grandfather a pharmacist. Cobb's prominence as a scientist was depicted in a large poster that was part of a national campaign by the National Science Foundation to promote women in science. She laughingly told the story of how her son Jonathon, a radiologist, awoke one morning in the bedroom of a date and, glancing at the door, saw a poster depicting prominent women scientists: "Oh, my god, there's my mother!"

Parties at Cobb's home subtly suggested that her social class and background were several notches above most of us at the university. Her guests, however, affirmed her strong identification as a black woman. Bobby McFerrin's mother, Sara, who was an opera singer and music professor once married to Robert McFerrin, the first black vocalist to sing a major role at the Metropolitan Opera, came to one of her Christmas parties. Marc and I attended a private luncheon honoring Rosa Parks, who was in Los Angeles to receive an award and traveling to Orange County to visit her friend, Jewel. President Cobb brought prominent academics to campus as well, including Johnetta Cole, the anthropologist and president of Spelman College, and Ronald Takaka, a historian at Berkeley, who had written a multicultural story of the United States.

Cal State Fullerton was a school with a very diverse student body. African American students made up about 3 percent, the same as their overall percentage in Orange County. Students of color came primarily from the Chicano and the Asian American communities—Little Saigon was near the campus. Ever conscious of the diversity of the students, Cobb was a strong advocate for diversifying the faculty by race and gender as well. An event honoring faculty years of service in the late 1980s was a visual representation of their shifting demographics. The event was held in the university's arboretum, acreage at the north end of the campus that was a peaceful set of gardens, including a desert collection, a Mediterranean one, and the woodlands plantings. The president, the other deans, and I sat on a covered stage erected for the event to protect us from the hot, late afternoon California sun, high above the faculty, who also were under a tent. Because of the height of our platform, we looked out on a natural, uncultivated area: brown earth, sun-scorched plants and weeds, and drought-tolerant trees, mostly California oaks.

After her introductory remarks praising the faculty, President Cobb rose and began to call forward those with the most years of service, thirty years or more. Seven white men rose and walked toward the stage, looking as though they had long abandoned their dream of the university becoming the "Harvard of the West." When the twenty-year cohort rose, a lone white woman moved forward, followed by several men. Sandra Sutphen, a political scientist hired in 1967, told me that she and another woman were hired in her department that same year. "We joined two other women, and the next year we hired two more, which brought us to six women out of a faculty of sixteen. That made us the department with the highest percentage of women at Fullerton and the highest absolute number of women in any poli-sci department in the country. Governor Pat Brown expanded the state college system so rapidly that departments were desperate for hires, so even women could get jobs."

As the next cohort hired in the 1970s came forward, the first man of color appeared, an African American, followed by a Japanese American. As President Cobb and I stood at the end of the ceremony, she leaned toward me and said, "Twenty years from now, I want to see the faculty of color be of the same percentage as our students. What are you doing to make that happen?"

Chairs in HDCS departments with no diversity had a common explanation for their homogeneity: "We can't find any people of color who are qualified." Yet where there was diversity, there was an energy and sense of richness that had been absent at Lewis and Clark, where the faculty had been mostly white. The stories of some of these faculty members of color at Fullerton schooled me in both the courage of these first hires and the prejudices they faced.

The department of human services had two African American faculty members who were indeed qualified—Jerry Wright, the first black man to earn a PhD from the Department of Anthropology at Harvard, and Soraya Coley, whose PhD in social work was from Bryn Mawr. Her early days as the first black female professor in the department hadn't been easy: "When I began teaching, students would challenge me. They couldn't believe that a black female professor knew enough to be an authority." The elementary education department had one Latina, Ana Garza. There was a lone African American woman on the reading faculty, Ruth May, whose father, Lorenz Graham, was related by marriage to W. E. B. DuBois and was at one time his personal secretary.

If I could talk with President Cobb today—she died on January 1, 2017—I would tell her what I had done to "make it happen," to diversify the faculty. Most importantly, I did it in tandem with department chairs who understood the importance of diversity. Judy Ramirez, the chair of child development, led the way. The first diversity hire in that department occurred in 1990, taking on Ellen Junn, a Korean American psychologist with a Princeton PhD. It took years for me to learn the cost to her of being "the other." After reading the chapter, "Voice," in *The Feminist Classroom*, she told me how she identified completely with Noreen Nakagawa, a Japanese American student at Lewis and Clark who we interviewed for the book. Nakagawa quoted Emily Dickinson's poem "I'm Nobody! Who Are You?" to illustrate how she felt watching Haley Mills sing "Femininity" in the 1963 Walt Disney movie *Summer Magic*. As Junn said,

> I grew up near Holland, Michigan, where my father, who was born in South Korea, was a political scientist at Grand Valley State University. There were no Asian families in our small farming town. No one in town looked like me. As Noreen said, [in your book] "Everyone was tall and blond and then there was me." I wept when I read how the dominant culture's construction of race and gender had warped her. That was me. I also wept because of the Western name my father took—Bob. Bob. And the name my mother took was Sue, seemingly straight out of popular TV comedies and consistent with the assimilation "melting pot" paradigm of that time in American history.

Junn's hiring was followed by that of Sylvia Alva, also a psychologist, with a PhD from UCLA. My relationship with Sylvia started off on the wrong foot. Perhaps I was distracted in our initial interview, because she told Ramirez, "I don't think the dean even knows who I am." Later, she was forthcoming about who she was, the child of Mexican immigrants who sent her "home" to Mexico to avoid the dangers of Los Angeles. "Home," she said, "where we had far more freedom than we ever would have had in LA."

Other departments made progress as well. Secondary education hired a Mexican American, Maria R. Montano-Harmon, who was doing pathbreaking research on Latino adolescents' command of English. The daughter of Mexican immigrants, she grew up on the Arizona border. Once she told me, "When I was young, I vowed that I would never do two things—marry an Anglo-American man and live in LA. I became best friends with such a young man in a class at Arizona State University. And now he's my husband." She laughed. "And you know where I live." Even the males in educational administration broke the gender barrier by hiring a woman, Louise Adler, who had extensive experience as a school district curriculum specialist. They dug in their heels at first because she was not just like them, someone who had been a school principal or an athletic director, but she proved to be as tough as they and eventually worked her way into their hearts.

How I wish I were able to ask President Cobb to go to each department's website to see how the faculty and chairs made it happen. The website of the educational leadership department shows that someone did so: nine women and five men are tenure-related faculty, four of whom are Asian and one black. Among the part-time faculty, four are black and one is Asian. Secondary education also moved toward greater diversity in its faculty, with two Latinos, one black, and one Asian added to its ranks. But I would want to tell Cobb one more thing: Soraya Coley is now the president of Cal Poly Pomona, where Sylvia Alva is her provost, and Ellen Junn is president of Cal State Stanislaus. It is slow, Jewel, but it is happening.[2]

CHAPTER 9

SECOND CHANCE
TO BE A PROVOST

ADMINISTRATIVE CHANGES

The trumpets of the mariachi band blared, celebrating the achievements of Chicano students at CSUF. We deans were attending this yearly event to honor those who had beaten the odds by graduating from high school, enrolling in college, and making the honor roll. Every time I glanced outside the restaurant, named Tlaquepaque, and saw low stucco buildings, each with an overhang, I felt I was in a midsize Mexican town. It was spring 1991, and I was at a table with the recently appointed president of the university, Milton Gordon, and the affirmative action officer, Rosa Maria Gomez-Amaro, herself the daughter of immigrants, as were most of the students. I strained to hear what the president was saying as the trumpets reached a high note, but I caught this much: "And then I'll make Mary Kay the provost." He looked at me.

"But you'd certainly want to have a search first," I said. Could it be, I wondered, that he was considering me as acting provost?

President Cobb had been forced to retire when she turned sixty-five. Rumor had it that she was furious with Ann Reynolds, CSU's chancellor. True, there was a mandatory retirement age, but some of the male presidents had been allowed to continue past it. Cobb had just acquired a president's house for the university, the former mansion of one of the founding Fullerton families, the Chapmans. She'd imagined living there and hosting community and university groups in style. But Reynolds did not change her mind. Cobb left campus, bought a Jaguar and an apartment in LA overlooking the space where the Disney Performing Arts Center would later be built, and went into therapy.

The search for President Cobb's replacement had been contentious. Despite Gordon's strong credentials—he had a PhD in mathematics and had advanced up the ranks, first as a faculty member, later as a dean at Chicago State University, and most recently, as provost at Sonoma State University—he had not been the favored candidate among the faculty. They were taken with a candidate who was an established scholar, an articulate visionary, and an associate vice president at California Institute of Technology yet a much less experienced administrator. At a meeting of the academic deans to discuss the three finalists, the dean of continuing studies summed up her impression of Milton Gordon. "He's nothing but a pretty face." He was indeed a pretty face, an African American man with slightly wavy gray hair and a Grecian nose. Only his irregular teeth detracted.

It was difficult to warm up to Gordon—he was reserved, seldom spoke in meetings, and if he had a vision or an agenda for the campus, he was playing his cards close to his chest. He did surprise his naysayers when he discontinued football, a money-losing enterprise despite the massive stadium that had been built during Cobb's presidency. President Gordon's first year on campus was controversial, including his inauguration. The 1990s were a time of repeated budget cuts in California's public universities, and on the day of the inauguration, some of the support staff staged a demonstration to protest what they saw as a waste of money. As the platform party progressed toward the stage, there among clerical workers and maintenance staff stood the president's younger son, a sophomore at Berkeley, holding a sign, "No cuts to secretarial staff." The older son, an engineer with an MBA, did not attend the event.

I spent my time at the reception following the inauguration talking to the president's two sisters, both teachers living in Hyde Park, which I fondly remembered from my days there in the 1960s. From them, I learned that their father had been a Pullman sleeping car porter, most likely the source of the family's middle-class status, and that in adulthood, their brother had lived near John Marshall Harlan High, an affluent neighborhood on Chicago's far south side.

When Provost Coleman announced his retirement less than a year after Gordon's appointment, he said of the president at a deans' council meeting, "I think he is a nothing." A few days later, I received a call from the president: "I'd like you to consider an appointment as acting provost for the next academic year while we conduct a national search." Thoughts rushed in, but the strongest was that I didn't want to work for a president who was prejudged so negatively by some on campus. I declined his offer, saying I wanted to concentrate on writing *The Feminist Classroom* and continue as dean. When Gordon appointed Don Schweitzer, the dean of humanities and social sciences, I had a twinge of regret because I believed that I would have been a more visionary leader.

My journal entry from March 3, 1993, records my ambivalence about many things: I was deeply invested in various initiatives in HDCS yet uncertain about my own future.

I'm in an excruciatingly boring deans' meeting and really feeling some pain. Why? I'm scared to death that I'm not going to be able to get a job as a provost and wondering how I want to spend the last years of my professional career. Where can I make a contribution? What will feed me in the short time I have left?

President, provost, dean, women's studies professor?

The book *Strangers in Paradise* has really depressed me. It has depressed me because the authors hold that working-class academics embody the class anomalies in this culture—both the notion that you can advance and how few actually do. There are those who (like me) often suffer under the illusion that we've made more progress than we have. I have to give up the illusion of upward institutional mobility and acknowledge the constraints and ceiling placed on me.

I need something new but ironically may be on the cusp of the best ten years of my career if *The Feminist Classroom* is successful. How could I have gotten myself into a position where I feel so bad about myself? I've sort of bumbled through my life having no sense that I would achieve as much as I have and yet continue to have increasing expectations for myself.

June 1993: Another academic year was over. A feeling of escape permeated the car as Don Schweitzer, Marc, and I drove to the Ontario International Airport, which was east of Fullerton. It was the first leg of a journey to Washington, DC, to attend one of those conferences on daunting and largely irresolvable topics that take place at that time of year: improving the public schools, engaging the university with the community, achieving institutional transformation in higher education. I suppressed feelings on the futility of such topics and decided to enjoy the pleasure of going against the morning traffic. I anticipated the perks of the conference—a four-star hotel, wine receptions, good food, and chances to connect with national friends and colleagues. Once the conference was over, Marc and I would have time to visit the National Gallery.

Don was at the wheel of his red Toyota Supra. A large man, his corpulent body had settled into the plush leather driver's seat. Only his belt restricted the expansiveness of his stomach, separating the soft flesh into lower and upper territories. His face was flushed, and when he smiled, which was frequently, the space in the middle of his two front teeth always caught me by surprise. In his early fifties, Don had spent his entire academic career at Cal State Fullerton, first as an assistant professor of psychology and later as an administrator working his way up the hierarchy—department chair, associate dean, dean, and now provost. We had worked together for five years, first as fellow deans. Mostly we circled one another, he wary of my feminism and I of his conservatism. I had reservations too about his discipline, psychology, known for its empiricism. But mostly I disliked his cautious way of being the chief academic officer.

Don and I were guarded with one another on our drive to the airport as we talked about what we had in common, mulling over the worst-case scenarios circulating about budget cuts and replacing retiring faculty. Silence permeated the car once he and I had exhausted these topics. "How's your daughter?" Marc leaned forward to be heard from the back seat.

Don's face brightened. "She's great. She graduated a few weeks ago from Northern Arizona State with a degree in business, and she already has a job working for a cable company. She and her boyfriend are even talking about buying a house."

"Wow," I said, marveling at how quickly some young college graduates achieved the marks of adulthood. Chantal was on a different track, having just begun a PhD program in anthropology after spending a year in France on a fellowship that Vassar had awarded.

"She sounds like a great daughter," Marc said.

Turning into the airport parking lot, Don said, "She's the perfect daughter."

Don, Marc, and I shared a taxi from the airport into DC and agreed to meet for dinner at seven. Our luxury hotel did not disappoint. We entered through an expansive arcade into a lobby with marble walls. Graceful white orchids were placed throughout, creating a sense of peace and being away from the street noise of DC. Our nonsmoking room was bright in the late afternoon sun; gauzy white curtains and a large antique writing table contributed to my feeling of luxury. I wondered where I would sneak my one cigarette a day before going to sleep. When we gathered in the lobby for dinner, Helen Taylor, the director of secondary education on campus, and Carmen Zuniga, one of the promising bilingual, bicultural faculty members we were beginning to hire, met us.

We walked to dinner at the City Grill, a popular restaurant with Washington's power brokers. As we entered a narrow hallway, the walls were lined with the photographs of celebrities—senators and representatives and people I didn't recognize, most likely lobbyists. We settled into a leather banquette that surrounded us like a safe cocoon, each ordering our favorite drinks—manhattans, martinis, and whiskey sours, a true deviation from the white Chardonnay we sipped at gatherings in Southern California. Our conversation ranged from stories about our families and rumors on campus to what the next few days might hold, always respectful of the power hierarchy—provost, dean, spouse, department chair, and junior faculty member. Don was more relaxed and connected to people than I had ever seen but clearly remained the dominant person. He paid the bill, and we left.

Even though we had all agreed to meet for breakfast, Don did not appear. Helen was the first to speak. "Where do you think Don might be?"

"I have no idea," I said, relishing the taste of an almond croissant. "I have no idea what his habits are. He may be out for a walk, he may be sleeping in, or he may just be enjoying a moment to himself."

At noon, the conference participants gathered in the same banquet room for lunch. The room was nearly full by the time I arrived. I didn't see any of my

Fullerton colleagues and had decided, after skimming the list of participants during a lackluster plenary session, that I would seek out some of the prominent feminists, who would be critical to getting the word out about the soon-to-be-published *The Feminist Classroom*. I was deep in conversation with Beverly Guy Sheftal from Spelman College when I saw Helen approaching out of the corner of my eye. Her look was more serious than usual. "The director of the conference wants to see you immediately."

Helen and I were ushered into a small dark office, elegantly furnished with oriental rugs, wingback chairs, and dark tables. The president of the American Council on Education (ACE), the organization that sponsored the conference, shook my hand during our introductions and said, "I have some bad news for you. Don Schweitzer was found dead in the shower about eleven this morning. He died of a heart attack around seven thirty. His wife tried to reach him on the phone for several hours. Fearing something was wrong when she got no answer, she insisted that security break into his room. It was not easy. The door was double bolted."

"Has President Gordon been informed?" I asked.

"Yes, he knows."

"Is there anything I can do?"

"We may need someone to identify the body at the morgue before it is flown back to California. There were a few things in his room that someone needs to take back to California—keys, a notebook, and his wallet. There was a bottle of sake in the room; the hotel will dispose of it." There was little for us to do. When I returned to campus, faculty and administrators were in shock over Schweitzer's death. "What happened? Did you have any idea this was coming? He was overweight but still."

Several weeks passed, and there was speculation about who the president would appoint as interim provost. Mike Parker walked into my office in late June and said, "There are rumors that you're being considered for provost."

"Rumors? Rumors from where—the Academic Senate, some of the deans?"

"The usual suspects," he said. I felt a rush of excitement. Here was my opportunity to be the "responsible one," to set aside my reservations about working for Milton Gordon, to get administrative experience as a provost that would put me in a good position for elsewhere or—who knew?—for being appointed "permanently" to Fullerton's position. But would my male colleagues accept me?

Two days later, I met with the president. He said, "I've consulted with some of the deans and the chair of the senate and would like you to step in as provost. The appointment would be for this academic year."

I thanked him and then asked, "Will I be able to apply for the position when you have a national search?"

"Yes," he said. "And by the way, you need to get the deans in line to agree on budget cuts. I'd like to have a proposal by next week."

As I walked from his office on the ninth floor of Langsdorf Hall to the elevator, a feeling of fear started in my head and seeped through my body at the thought of getting the deans in line. *They're mostly a collegial group; none of them is a bully*, I thought. It would be more than a year before I began to understand who the university bully really was.

LEARNING ON THE JOB

My first morning as acting provost, I sat at my desk in McCarthy Hall, which had been the president's office when the building opened in the early 1960s. It still had some grandeur. My desk backed up against a wall with a door that opened to a large conference room, holding a table that could seat more than two dozen. Windows on the north wall, rumored to be bulletproof, a response to student protests and police and National Guard activity during the late 1960s, had a view of a central square, swirling with the diversity of Orange County: white students intermingled with Latino and Asian students. A bookcase covered the wall opposite the windows. I took delight in replacing Jack Coleman's accounting books and Don Schweitzer's psychology manuals with my library of feminist theory, American history, and higher education books. A nondescript door, next to another that led to the outer office where four secretaries sat, housed a private bathroom. You wouldn't want the faculty to know that administrators at the highest level had normal bodily functions!

I pulled the job description I had saved from an earlier search from my file marked "Possibilities" and read the following:

> Reporting to the president, the provost serves as a member of the president's executive staff. He or she is the chief academic officer and serves as the chief executive officer of the university in the absence of the president.
>
> The provost is responsible for the implementation of the university's academic plan, the advancement of the academic mission, and the continuous improvement of the quality of the academic experience at California State University, Fullerton. He or she also is responsible for overseeing academic budgets, enrollment management, and student success, as well as enhancing academic research, scholarship, and creative activity and the diversity of the institution.
>
> The offices reporting directly to the provost include the academic deans of the seven colleges; the university librarian; the Office of Research and Graduate Studies; undergraduate studies; international studies, diversity, and extended studies. The provost works with the academic senate on policies of interest to the university community.

This description of duties was left over from the 1992 search for provost. I recalled a question a faculty member had asked during one candidate's interview:

Figure 16. CSU Fullerton provost, 1993–1998

"If you're appointed provost, what kind of a relationship do you imagine having with the deans and the faculty?"

His response: "Everyone worries about those relationships, but the most important one a provost has is with the president."

I had looked up back then, surprised, and known he was correct.

Glancing again at the announcement now, I thought, *How am I ever going to manage all of this?*

The job announcement I had just perused was an aerial view of my responsibilities. I needed a strategy for ensuring that things ran smoothly on the ground. Here was a new beginning, and I intended to take up some of the best practices of the men who had worked as associate provosts in the office. One of them, Michael Clapp, who had responsibility for personnel matters, kept an 8½-by-11-inch spiral notebook. When I watched him talking with me in his office or at a meeting with the deans, I never could see what he was jotting down. But I could imagine its salacious content, rife with tales from the underbelly of the university: affairs gone sour, grievances that a Shia faculty filed against a Sunni colleague, the complaints my executive assistant had about me when I was dean of HDCS.

Deciding that adopting Clapp's practice was a way to keep track of all my meetings and promises or denials, I got up, opened the door, and asked my secretary to get a stenographer's pad from the supply closet. Looking skeptical, she headed for it. As a girl of the 1950s, I had taken shorthand instead of chemistry in high school and had worked three years as a secretary, but I had only rarely used that skill. This seemed a humorous postmodern reversal, the lady boss with her steno pad, pen ready at any speed.

I flipped back the cover, and on the right side of the first page, I wrote the date and the name of the group I was soon to meet with: "June 22, 1993—President's Advisory Board (PAB)." I set this information off with a rectangle for quick identification, and below noted what I needed to do to follow up. On the left, I recorded things I wanted to remember from the meeting or relevant thoughts that popped into my head. In my entry from the first PAB meeting, I wrote the following:

- Note who is sitting at what places at the table.
- Sherri (the chief budget officer) gave overall budget estimates, wants to avoid layoffs; university will assist in any way possible.
- Come up with timetable for faculty grievances arising from tenure and promotion decisions.
- Discussed President's Convocation.
- Infrastructure planning—discussed how to ensure heating system works. I'm struck by the diversity of things that need attending at the university.

On the right were reminders:

- Consult with academic affairs budget man.
- President's Convocation wants theme of beginnings and will need names of deceased faculty in the past year.
- President returns on July 20.

Once I completed a task, I put a slash through the entry. Knowing that my notebooks could be subpoenaed in a lawsuit, should I ever be a party to one, I continued to keep a private journal at home.

The morning of my first meeting with the deans as provost, I walked into the conference room on Wednesday at eight thirty sharp, the early morning sun timidly reflected through the dirty windows. The room seemed larger and yet shabbier as I sat at the head of the long conference table. I felt my perspective shift—it was now up to me to deliver on the president's charge, to get the deans to agree on budget cuts. I sat down, smiled at them, and said, "No one is leaving this room until we have achieved fair and equitable budget cuts. Some of you," I said, looking straight at the dean of natural sciences and mathematics, "have figured out how to work the system, which is to put forward only staff cuts—in some cases, secretaries, and in others, lab assistants—when the president has been clear that there will be no staff cuts. So let's begin by looking at each school's proposed cuts to determine if they can actually be used to reach our target in academic affairs."

I looked at Mike Parker, even though he was no longer my wingman but the acting dean of HDCS, to see if I was doing OK. He gave no visible response, but I felt more confident. The other deans were equally poker faced. "Now, I'm going to go around the table and ask each of you to tell me and your colleagues how you are going to meet the percentage of the cuts that are your responsibility. Let's go in alphabetical order. School of the Arts is first." When it was natural sciences' turn, the dean said, "It's going to cut into faculty's research productivity, but I can meet my cuts by reducing our equipment allocations."

Much to my surprise, the deans didn't fulfill my worst fantasies by telling me that they wouldn't change their proposal, hinting that I wasn't up to the task of being provost, wondering why I had been appointed rather than one of them, threatening to go to the president, or signaling that I should resign. One by one, they proposed how they would meet their percentage of cuts to reach our target of two million dollars. I left the meeting feeling confident. But more importantly, I felt a sense of acceptance; I could risk being a collegial "boss" with those who had been my peers. The deans had chafed under Jack Coleman's authoritarian administration and drifted under Schweitzer's. When Coleman was provost, numbers, not ideas, predominated: spreadsheets on enrollment targets, graduation rates, budget allocations, and equipment needs. When President Gordon first met with the deans' council in 1990, he asked what was on our minds, and there was an utter and embarrassing silence. No one spoke. *We have no voice as a deans' council*, I thought. Here was my chance to help them fashion their voices.

Coleman's posture as our commanding officer had been felt most keenly every Thursday afternoon at three when we "reported" to his office, on time, for a "deans' informal." This was a practice Coleman brought from his days in the military. The deans would crowd into Jack's office, some of us sitting on the overstuffed couch covered in a shiny velvet floral pattern; others made do in folding chairs arranged in a semicircle. Wine and soft drinks were set out on a low coffee table. I watched to see which deans chose the wine—all of them, thankfully—and how much they drank. Every eye in the room was on Jack and how much he drank, which was exactly one glass of white wine at each gathering.

In contrast, the first informal I hosted had the feel of adolescents at a party when the parents were away. Our laughter caught fire when Jerry Samuelson leaned over to me and, in a loud whisper, said, "Couches were once banned on campus because bad things could happen on them." The deans and I filled our wine glasses frequently without a backward glance; no one was counting how many glasses the others had. One dean began to complain about how unreasonable his oldest faculty member was—he was nearly eighty, with only a few students enrolled in his classes, and his student evaluations were the lowest in the school. "And he's now suing the associate dean—and, oh, yes, *me*—for age discrimination. He overheard my associate say, 'We have to get that old fart to retire.'" He laughed and reached for the bottle of white wine.

"I have an idea," another dean said. "Let's have a faculty exchange in which we offer up our most problematic faculty member for reassignment to another school." Loud laughter erupted as each of us imagined the scenario.

Two months later, on August 21, 1993, I wrote the following:

So what have I learned these past weeks?

1. Allocating resources is extremely difficult because you inherit patterns, and even though you try to be fair, there is never enough, and recipients are often unhappy.
2. You have to be exceedingly organized in the job and make the best use of those on your team. A constant question I ask is, What should I be doing and what should I delegate?
3. Personal will and persuasion matter. You have to charm the snakes, the bullies, and the gnats alike.

PLANNING AS A VEHICLE FOR INNOVATION

In January 1994, without consulting with the academic senate, the president appointed a University Planning Committee (UPC) with twenty or so members from among the faculty, administrators, and community members, as well as two students. Since my days as a member of the Mission Planning Committee at Lewis and Clark, I had been a strong advocate for the positive value of planning and was pleased, as acting provost, to be a part of Fullerton's initiative.

A short while later, the president brought a consultant, Ray Hass, to campus to meet with the UPC. My steno pad at the ready, I began to take notes during his introductory lecture, quickly realizing that here was a man who had a much clearer conception of planning than anyone at Lewis and Clark. He presented his philosophy of planning to guide us: "Planning is an iterative process. It is the conversation that matters. It has to be inspirational and aspirational, and it has to be practical." Hass understood the mission of the CSU: "You are a pathway into the American mainstream for those who wouldn't otherwise get there." Once a mission statement was crafted, he said, "You have to keep asking, is it useful? Does it help you make decisions, especially budgetary ones? The role of a planning committee is to set priorities that guide resource allocation. The committee needs to construct a plan that includes statements that guide decisions, becoming a 'gate' for proposals for funding to go through. There is a need for a process that will validate the plan."

Someone raised this question: "How do we deal with objections, especially those among the faculty who believe planning resides with the academic senate?"

"You need to think about ways to involve them. There are collegial rules operating in each institution. What needs to be asked and made explicit within your ground rules is, Do you buy in or not? It is important to remember that you can bring no more order to an institution than it can tolerate."

With Hass's departure from campus, it was now clear that the first thing the UPC needed to do was craft a mission statement that would guide decision-making. The president, nominally the chair of UPC, asked me to chair the meeting that took up this challenge. I saw this assignment as an indication of the president's confidence in me, although I recall no conversation with him nor do I have notes in my steno pad of his expectations. His decision effectively gave me the power of a "permanent" provost along with the vulnerability of an "acting" one.

I saw a way to advance my idea of what our mission statement might contain and honor Don Schweitzer's memory. Several months before his death, Schweitzer brought to the deans' council the draft of a mission statement that had been developed by the PAB. The first sentence—"Learning is preeminent at California State University, Fullerton"—surprised me because I had never heard Don express such an idea. He was championing a paradigmatic shift from faculty members' fixation on teaching to proposing that what really mattered was students' learning. I searched through a pile of papers in my "In Basket" and found a Xeroxed copy of the draft that he had circulated. I calculated that an idea that originated with Schweitzer might win the support of scientists and social scientists, who were likely to be skeptical of the same idea had it originated with a female administrator whose discipline was originally education.

At the UPC meeting, I handed out copies and said, "Here is Don Schweitzer's draft of a mission statement, prepared by him and circulated before his death. I propose that, in his honor, we consider his idea that student learning be central to our mission." Steve Murray, chair of the biology department, a UPC member who was facilitating that portion of the meeting, stood at a podium. The large white screen behind him reflected what was on his computer screen. Both were blank.

"How about this," I said, "for the first sentence of our mission statement? 'Learning is preeminent at California State University, Fullerton.' The idea is broad enough to encompass student learning but also includes faculty learning through teaching and research. It might even apply to our work in the community."

There was silence as Murray typed the sentence in, and it appeared on the large screen. "Learning is preeminent at California State University, Fullerton." No one proposed a change.

"How about the next sentence?" It took some time to craft one, every faculty member a wordsmith: "We aspire to combine the best qualities of teaching and research universities, where actively engaged students, faculty, and staff work in close collaboration to expand knowledge."

President Gordon was mostly silent throughout the meeting, never weighing in with what he felt was important or worthwhile. At times, this felt uncomfortable to me but grew less so as I remembered how much time the posturing of Lewis and Clark's president had taken up. When a draft of the mission statement was sent to the president for his approval, I felt great satisfaction that we had not only a statement that I valued but also one that UPC committee members had crafted collaboratively. Following the president's approval, the UPC took up the task of writing goals and strategies that supported our mission, eventually articulating eight goals and forty-nine strategies. President Gordon had the idea of printing our mission statement and goals on a wallet-sized card that could be carried by the several thousand members of the CSUF community. While I always carried the printed letter-sized statement of mission, goals, and strategies in my briefcase for quick reference, I never could bring myself to carry the wallet-sized document. It smacked too much of Mao's *Little Red Book* or an Orwellian *1984* world. Ironically, one of the faculty members would later attribute the pocket copies to me.

There was now a flurry of activity that expanded beyond the UPC and addressed the difficult work of getting each school and department on board. At one of the first meetings of the deans' council after the president approved the mission statement, the dean of humanities and social sciences said, "I liked the idea someone had to ask each dean and his chairs to come up with a list of the 'marks'

of a graduate, first for each school and then for the university. Wasn't that what
we were to bring to this meeting?"

"It was," said the dean of business, tapping his fingers on a stack of tattered
sheets. "Let me tell you what my chairs and I came up with."

Damn, I thought, *now we're in for a presentation of quantifiable business jargon.*
Instead, he read the following:

> CSUF graduates of the School of Business and Economics possess the habit
> of intellectual inquiry, succeed in challenging professions that contribute
> to the economic well-being of Orange County and beyond, build strong
> relationships to their communities, and contribute productively to society.

"That's so comprehensive," the dean of the School of Communications said,
"that it could be the marks of any of our graduates. The only thing I see missing
is an international perspective." The deans, each in their own way, worked to
bring their department chairs along. The chairs were key to facilitating buy-in
and implementation of the new mission statement by the faculty as well as the
goals and strategies the UPC had crafted and determining how all this applied
to faculty work and the distinguishing characteristics of graduates in individual
departments. Many did not share the enthusiasm for planning that predominated the UPC. An idea for how to get the chairs on board came from an unexpected pair: Tom Klammer, the associate provost for academic programs, and
Soraya Coley, who was serving as the first faculty fellow in my office.[1]

Both Klammer and Coley had attended a department chairs' workshop sponsored by ACE that had featured Walt Gemelch, a professor of higher education
known for his ability to articulate the challenges faced by department chairs and
the chairs' centrality to the university's work. Gemelch's presentations were characterized by participants as group therapy peppered with raucous humor. Soon
after returning to campus, Soraya and Tom met with me and got right to the
point. Klammer said, "We have an idea for you." Coley's nervous laugh made
me suspicious. I was very fond of both; I admired how tirelessly they worked
to ensure that all students and faculty succeeded. Tom continued, "We propose
holding an academic affairs retreat for the seven deans, several associate provosts,
and the department chairs to work on priorities for our newly crafted mission."

I couldn't imagine how that might work. There were more than forty-five
department chairs. After going back and forth, I finally said, "OK, give me a proposal arguing why this is central to our planning, what will happen during the
two-and-half days, and how much it will cost." I wasn't sure that I would see
them again.

In less than a week, they were back with a carefully thought out proposal
detailing what would happen each day. The first day and a half would be devoted
to a reproduction of Gemelch's chairs' retreat; the remainder of the time would

be set aside for chairs to work together on school or departmental priorities. They went on to propose that it be held at a luxury retreat center in Rancho Santa Fe, California. The cost of the retreat, twenty-five thousand dollars, took my breath away. I almost picked up the phone to ask them, "Are you out of your minds?" But I concluded that their idea was worth the money. I agreed with Klammer's observation that it might mediate the chairs' real feelings of being overworked, unappreciated, and disaffected. But first I had to get the president's sign-off. I sent the proposal to him and waited.

A couple of days later, my secretary buzzed me: "The president is on line one." Before I had a chance to say anything, he said, "What the hell are you doing, proposing to spend twenty-five thousand dollars on a retreat?"

"Well," I said, buying some time while I thought, "you will see from the proposal that the three days are designed to help department chairs think more broadly about their roles, to see the frustrations they face in common, and to see all that with humor. The final outcome will be a proposal from each chair about how his or her department is going to implement the university's plan. All seven of the deans will be there to listen and think about what all this means for their school."

"Twenty-five thousand dollars is a lot of money."

"I know," I admitted, "but it will yield far more than that amount in returns." I reiterated my rationale, adding, "And we'd like you to join us for dinner the last night."

"I'm going to approve this," he said, "but reluctantly. I don't like your spending this much money, but I like your style."

When we arrived at Rancho Santa Fe for our retreat on a beautiful September day in 1996, the adobe architecture, lush lawns graced by white lawn chairs clustered in groups of four, and pathways brilliant with flowers led me to hope that providing the best for the department chairs would pay off. Once they settled into their five-star accommodations, the chairs warmed to Gemelch's sessions on the role of department chairs; good food and generously flowing wine worked away at their resistance. When they were first told it was time to develop departmental priorities, the resistance on some faces reminded me of my brothers' faces when I proposed they do some housework. I chalked this up to the challenge of tying their disciplinary allegiance to university-wide priorities or being burned out by earlier projects that took precious time and energy only later to fall by the wayside and yield little. Yet when the time came for chairs to present ideas for implementing the mission, I was surprised to see that they competed for who could be the most imaginative, who could focus most on learning, and how their departments were central to the process.

The last evening of the retreat, our group gathered for a cookout on the beach. As I looked out over the fifty or so people gathered in clusters, illuminated by the setting California sun, drinking wine and talking animatedly, I felt we were

Figure 17. Book publication party for *The Feminist Classroom*: Michael Parker, President Milton Gordon, and me

indeed a community of teachers and scholars committed to the value of learning. It was a moment of great satisfaction that deepened as I watched Coley and Klammer continue working with the department chairs.

FURTHERING A CLIMATE OF INNOVATION

The deans and I took the consultant Ray Hass's dictum that a mission statement should guide budgetary decisions seriously, providing a "gate" for funding proposals to go through. Less than six months after the retreat, we wrote a statement,

"Principles of Resource Allocation and Reallocation." Our nine principles, stopping short of Ten Commandments, focused on academic affairs and called for incentives that encouraged "creativity, collaboration, entrepreneurship, and new ways of working." They also tied resource allocation to program reviews and accreditation, program quality, meeting enrollment targets, and student demand for a program.

The president's response to the call for allocations that furthered our mission was to initially provide a million dollars for new initiatives, innovative annual projects that could emerge from the ground level and encompass multiple ideas and tracts. In subsequent years, the amount was six hundred thousand dollars. Despite the energy and imagination behind these projects, I know of no reallocations of dollars throughout the university as proposed in the 1996 Principles of Resource Allocations and Reallocation, raising the question as to how deeply the process affected the institution.

Planning did create a climate of innovation, however, which yielded new ways of thinking about teaching and learning. For instance, there was talk that one of the chemistry professors was transforming teaching and learning in his general chemistry course: "We need to look at what Pat Wagner is doing. Let's bring him to one of our meetings!"

"Why don't we go to his lab to see what he is actually doing with students? Isn't it up and running?"

For the next deans' meeting, we gathered in Wagner's lab, tucked into the bottom floor of the library, a large room with forty stations equipped with the latest computer technology. There was a student at each monitor. As we looked on, Wagner told us, "This classroom is designed to facilitate different instructional strategies. I never lecture anymore. I, along with some colleagues at UCLA, have prepared a presentation of content, all online, that takes up six topical threads throughout the course. This is diametrically the opposite of the traditional chapter-by-chapter presentation."

As Wagner talked, students began to organize themselves in pairs and groups of four. He said, "These group activities let students discover the concepts and principles of chemistry by exploring carefully constructed sets of data and models guided by appropriate directions and queries. They're learning chemistry by exploration and discovery."

"Are you having better success than the old lecture method, where more than half of the students usually fail—a mark of rigor for some faculty?"

"We are. All but three of the students passed the course last semester; overall they scored a full grade-point higher than a control group."

Inspired by Wagner's work, Kolf Jayaweera, the dean of natural sciences and mathematics, said, "Now we've seen what a smart classroom looks like. Indeed, this is the smartest classroom I've ever seen. I'm offering to chair a committee to take a look at our classrooms. Let's all meet next week in one of the typical science ones."

We gathered in a large lecture hall with fifty ascending seats; a lectern stood silently at the front of the room, where a large, tattered white screen was pulled down over a barely erased blackboard. "Now that we're gathered here in a typical classroom, do I need to say more about the need for a plan for smart classrooms?" Jayaweera said, laughing. "We could call our effort the 'Smart, Smarter, and Smartest Classrooms Project.' Who is in on the committee?"

It took surprisingly little time for a subcommittee of the deans to bring forth a proposal, complete with a budget, for outfitting classrooms. Some people say that collaboration is sexy. Here was sexy work at its best as each dean talked about the implications for various disciplines—the visual arts, teaching how to write, analyzing business theories, and using models in geography. We were ready to take our proposal to the PAB, which fell to me.

The following Monday morning, I passed out the work of the deans' committee to the president and other members of his cabinet. "Here's a proposal for state-of-the-art classrooms developed by the deans' council after observing Pat Wagner's General Chemistry course. That meeting spurred them on to assess the condition of the technology in all of our classrooms. To say the deans who worked on this are proud of their 'baby' would be an understatement." It took only a few minutes for me to see that the president wasn't pleased. When I completed my presentation, he gave me a steely look and said, "And how do you propose to pay for this?"

"You'll see on the last page that we've included a budget. A student technology fee and dollars from the deans' equipment budgets could cover some of the costs. We had hoped you might chip in as well. The deans and I see this proposal as a central way to advance our goal of making learning preeminent at Cal State Fullerton." The other administrators around the table were silent.

The president's response was simply, "Let's move on to the next agenda item." In my enthusiasm for our collective work in academic affairs, I had not anticipated his negative response. Only later would I learn that computers and technology *were* on his agenda, albeit for faculty and staff. The deans and I moved forward on the project, paring down its scope to fund classrooms that met our priority of serving the most students. In retrospect, I should have presented the proposal to him in a private meeting. Perhaps then we could have figured out a way to work together.

The one area where the deans' collegiality was challenged every year was in difficult budget negotiations. There was a pattern to most budget cycles, beginning with initially dire predictions of cuts that sent everyone reeling. It was common for the deans to wear themselves out speculating about how much would be available, how that would drive course offerings, and how much one could wrangle out of the provost, all while keeping an eye on fellow deans to make sure they weren't getting more than their share. Then there would be a small ray of hope, news from the chancellor's office that it wouldn't be as bad as predicted, and eventually a final budget would be developed that provided funding to carry out the central activities of teaching and research. I came to see this ritual as a terrible waste of human energy.

I decided that there must be a better way to do business. Despite voluminous spreadsheets, it was never clear to me what resources each dean had. I decided to take this question to the chief budget and planning officer, Sherri Newcomb, in the fall of 1996. Sherri, one of President Jewel Cobb's brilliant hires, was a woman barely in her thirties from South Dakota.

"Can you give me an idea of the resources each dean has?"

"That's easy. The bulk of the money is in faculty positions. If you want, we can begin the process of determining the value of each position and then make each dean responsible for all of his or her spending, not just the money around the edges—you know, equipment and supplies."

"Wouldn't that be hard to do?"

"Sure, but not impossible."

"Would it give the deans some flexibility, make them more fiscally responsible? They spend much more responsibly since we now let them carry over money in their supplies and equipment accounts from one fiscal year to another."

"Sure."

"But I need to make sure I have some resources to support my priorities."

"Easy. Once the deans and I calculate each school's totals, you will also have the amount for all of academic affairs. You can then decide how much to take off the top for your priorities."

I looked at the calendar on my desk. "Are you free to come to the next deans' meeting? I meet with the president later today. I want to make sure he approves of this."

Just before Sherri and I walked into the conference room the next Wednesday morning at eight thirty from the private door of my office rather than the public one in the hallway, I said, "This should get their attention." I sat down at the head of the table with Sherri on my left and looked at the deans. I imagined them thinking, *Now what? What budget shortfall has Sherri come to impart? At least it's not the president.*

"Sherri is here to discuss how we might determine the value of each faculty position, including vacant lines, with an eye to giving each of you the responsibility for managing those dollars."

The first dean to speak asked, "Do you mean we'd have control over those dollars? No tricks here, no hidden agendas?"

"You'll have control over the dollars. Sherri will make appointments with each of you to determine the value of each position. I will determine how much I will take off the top to support university-wide initiatives, those that we've agreed to as we're implementing our planning priorities. And of course, I'll share that with you before it is finalized to get your input."

The deans relished this newfound responsibility for their school's resources and yet couldn't resist, once all the dollars were securely in their accounts, humorously referring to the dollars I took off the top as a "tax." I mostly ignored them or humored them by calling them "tea party revolutionists," reminding them that we were a university, not just a loose affiliation of schools, and that we had common purposes.

Our sense of common purposes in creating a better university, better for faculty and students, sustained me. The dean of business and the science dean, who had been deans elsewhere, said they had never seen a deans' group work better. The dean of the arts, who had been at Fullerton for more than two decades, said, "It has never been better for deans than since you became provost."

⋘⋙

I soon discovered that what was most appealing to me as the university's chief academic officer was the broad canvas of academic programs and units. Here were worlds I had only seen from afar like the world of engineers, who took pride in showing me huge, sculpture-like constructions designed to measure the magnitude of earthquakes. I attended a concert and reception for the opera singer, Deborah Voigt, who had attended CSUF. There were mathematicians committed to figuring out why freshmen who had done well in high school math could not pass a proficiency exam that would keep them out of remedial courses. Scientists enthusiastically gave me tours of their labs, emphasizing how their research and grants were instrumental in preparing a new generation of scientists, a diverse group including women and students of color. The humanists and social scientists showed me their publications. For example, the psychology department held the nation's best record for journal articles published by faculty in a masters' degree institution. A political scientist was nationally recognized for his study of black/white relations in Los Angeles.

There were things I believed needed to be done to ensure that academic affairs felt like a "real" university. While he was provost, Schweitzer had hired an interior decorator, a member of his fundamentalist church, to redo the large lobby that housed the four secretaries in academic affairs. Somewhat to my amusement and horror, she had installed small bookshelves high up on the wall, so high that, at five feet, four inches, I had to stand on my tiptoes to barely read the titles. They were books that had no relationship to the university, the faded golden gilt on their spines suggesting an antique store or garage sale. She had also bought a dozen or more artificial ficus plants and placed them throughout the lobby. One of my first acts was to remove those books and the shelves and to send a call out to the faculty for anyone who had published a book in the past year to provide one for prominent display on a bookshelf in the lobby of academic affairs labeled "Faculty Publications."

I valued getting to know the faculty better and learning what was on their minds. I hit on the idea of holding a series of faculty soirees in my office. Mostly,

I invited faculty across departments in all the schools at the university. Occasionally, I put together targeted groups: female faculty, campus leaders, those who had been at Fullerton for most or all of their careers, or junior faculty of color.

At the first one, I heard a psychologist say to the woman next to him, "Wow, this is the first time I've ever been in this office when something pleasant might happen. Feels like the principal's office."

"Yeah, in junior high," she said.

Perhaps because they were paid to think and write and talk, or perhaps because of the wine and no agenda, they told me what was on their minds: understanding the nature of teaching and learning, forging a new culture of learning on campus, and determining how information technology could be used to further student learning.

They also brought up topics that affected them: the culture of tenure and promotion review on campus and the economic stresses faculty faced in Southern California with their long commutes and high-priced housing. Mostly absent were the chronic complaints about the uncertain budget climate in California universities or the tensions between faculty and administration.

Midway through my tenure as provost, a finance professor wrote me a three-page, single-spaced memo that criticized me for burying my best idea on page four of a six-page memo that assessed academic affairs' progress in implementing the university's mission and goals. He concluded by writing, "You've got the whole place thinking in new ways." While this reaffirmed what I was advocating, not every faculty member agreed with him. The summer following the president's approval of the mission statement, I arranged a luncheon with women department chairs. Sitting outside, in the garden of a local restaurant, talk turned to institutional planning. The chair of political science, Sandy Sutphen, in a voice gravelly from smoking, blurted out her objections to the talk about student learning: "Whenever you start talking about student learning, you make me anxious."

"Why is that?"

"I felt in control when I believed teaching was preeminent. But now with all this talk about students' learning, this 'shift,' as you call it, I don't feel in control. How can I know what students are learning except when they take my tests?"

Ellen Junn chimed in, "That's what the assessment of student learning is about."

"Don't get me started on that," Sandy said. "It's an attempt to erode my subject matter expertise."

Sutphen's resistance seemed benign compared to that of some others. In "The Sound of One Voice Dialoguing," an article published in fall 1996 in the *Senate Forum*, the official publication of the academic senate at CSUF, Stanley Woll, a professor of psychology and someone I had not met until I invited him to one of the faculty soirees, suggested that Cal State Fullerton, "a once respectable

174   LIVINGWHENEVERYTHINGCHANGED

universityinthebestsenseoftheterm,isbeingturnedintoamediocreone...."
continued:

> For example, the main accomplishment of this administration is the Mission and Goals Statement, and that is a dubious accomplishment at best. First, it starts with that brave assertion, which has now been repeated with mind-numbing regularity, that "Learning is preeminent at CSU, Fullerton," an assertion which, to the extent it conveys any meaning at all, is, shall we say, a misstatement. FTES (student credit hours) are preeminent with this administration. Despite repeated attempts at the exegesis of the word "learning" ... the fact remains that the assertion is devoid of any substantive meaning, an empty mantra which seems to comfort with its constant repetition. . . .
>
> . . . the Mission and Goals Statement has more of the feel of religious doctrine or a cult incantation than it does of a set of reasoned principles worthy of an academic institution. In fact, since we have all been provided with pocket copies, I propose that we combine it with a nightly prayer: "God is good, God is great. Learning is preeminent at Cal State."[2]

Woll was seen by many faculty colleagues as one of the most extreme and negative of the old guard, yet his characterization of my work suggests a number of anxieties at work. Most likely he saw the emphasis on learning as further eroding his status as a professor—a professor at a comprehensive university with a lower status than a Research I university. Faculty members in the social sciences and hard sciences charged that I had an agenda—that I was trying to make the university mediocre, make it more like HDCS, when I allocated twelve new faculty positions to the school based on enrollment growth, even though faculty lines went to other schools where there had also been growth. At five in the morning on December 7, 1996, I wrote these thoughts in my journal:

> Woke up thinking about the worrisome things I heard today about what the faculty are saying about me. Maybe I shouldn't have given HDCS their fair share of faculty positions; maybe this community won't allow me to do that. . . . It is not as though I took positions away from some departments. This is an interesting lesson in how you bring about change in an institution. You can't get out too far ahead of the faculty; you've got to understand their agendas and their fears. I need to say to the faculty, "What are the issues? How do we address them without tearing one another apart?"
>
> The cautions of Ray Hass, CSUF's consultant on planning, come to mind: "Remember that you can bring no more order to an institution than it can tolerate."

It gives me some comfort that at this writing twenty years later, the mission we crafted still guides the university's work.

CHAPTER 10

OPPORTUNITIES
AND AMBITION
OVERSHADOWED
BY AMBIVALENCE

I had wanted to attend Harvard University's Institute for Educational Management (IEM), a three-week, total immersion program for presidents, provosts, and vice presidents since the mid-1980s, but the year it was my "turn" at Lewis and Clark, there was a budget shortfall and the money allocated to send someone was one of the first things to be cut. When President Gordon proposed I attend at CSUF, I asked him if he could cover the three-thousand-dollar tuition.

"I'm not about to do that," he said. "You'll have to figure out some way to pay for it."

I called *Jamie Jenkins, the vice president for student affairs, to see if the president had supported her attendance a year earlier.

"Well, sort of," she said, laughing. "I applied for a scholarship, and Harvard awarded me one thousand dollars. Milt coughed up one thousand dollars, almost choking to death when he told me, and I paid one thousand dollars." We began calling ourselves the scholarship girls when I got the same package.

President Cobb had hired Jamie in 1989. Back then, Cobb couldn't contain her enthusiasm about her: "She's brilliant and capable of shaping a student affairs division that works for our diverse student body, something her predecessor never got." Jamie's persona always reminded me of Toni Morrison: statuesque and dressed in loose, flowing clothes offset by bold designer jewelry. There was an aura of loneliness about her. She once told me, "I don't mind living alone. I'm a news junkie and always have CNN on. That's my company." Jamie and I would laugh about how we came to feel, borrowing Morrison's phrase from *Sula*, "the ease of old friends" as we forged a closer relationship between our two divisions once I became provost. We saw the world, and particularly the workings of privilege and diversity, similarly.

I looked forward to the Harvard seminar in the summer of 1995, eager to be in Cambridge for three weeks and see how I compared with others who aspired to be university presidents. My enthusiasm dampened when a packet weighing more than five pounds appeared on my desk. When I ripped it open, brochures touting the virtues of attending the IEM, my dorm assignment, and the week's schedule slid out, revealing a huge, three-ring plastic notebook of case studies to be read before the seminar. The central place of case study analysis was also there in the schedule: breakfast at seven, followed by a meeting of my discussion group at seven thirty to "master" the case studies for that day, then on to a full day of presentations, concluding with yet another discussion after dinner.

Marc and I decided that he too should come to Cambridge. Many of our lifelong friends were in New England, and one of them, Nan Hass Feldman, an artist, offered us her house and studio in Framingham. Marc would be able to work, and we imagined an occasional wild night together in a Harvard dormitory. Once in Boston, we made our way from Logan Airport to my "house," farther from Harvard Square than I had imagined. The reality of college dormitory life hit me once we opened the door to my room to see gray cinder-block walls, a narrow single bed, a desk pushed up against the window, a few shelves for books, and a battered dresser. Even though all the IEM participants were middle-aged adults, we had a dorm monitor, a stern-looking undergraduate who caught my eye as Marc carried my bags up the stairs. Her disapproving gaze intensified on the few nights Marc followed me up to my room.

The program's brochure promised that participants would assess their leadership skills and develop strategies for long-term institutional success. I had been a big fan of reflecting on my own administrative work since a conversation back in the mid-1980s with a friend, Richard Schmuck, who had written extensively about educational administration. Marc and I had been hiking along the Columbia River with Dick and his wife, Pat. As we rambled along, I'd asked, "What can I read to be a better administrator?"

Dick was silent for a minute and then said, "Nothing."

"Nothing." I laughed. "But you've published lots on the topic."

"That is so. But I wouldn't read any of that. Keep a journal, and when things don't go as you wanted them to, write about how you could have done things differently."

The organizers at IEM didn't seem to think that the ninety or so administrators in attendance could be authorities to one another. Instead, the authorities were Harvard stars that they paraded before us. One of the most memorable was David Riesman, the noted sociologist and author of *The Lonely Crowd*, published in 1950.

Sitting at a table lower than the first tier of seats, Riesman looked diminutive and elderly as I peered down from my seat in the top row. Perhaps to signal my alienation from the institute's approach, I sat near the back of the large seminar room, yearning to hear the real-life stories of how my fellow students, all holding senior executive positions, had dealt with issues on their campuses. Were there any among us who also had a difficult relationship with their president? Riesman's presentation ranged from broad assertions about universities—"the faculty and the trustees don't understand their institution"—to practical tips about how to succeed in snagging a college presidency: tailor your application letter to "the institution as an institution" and "do a blitzkrieg ethnography while on a campus interview." He continued, "Once you obtain a presidency, have other interests and cultivate friends in another line of work."

Mentally, I checked off the points with some skepticism. Was it true that all faculty members didn't understand their institutions? All trustees? Who did Riesman think *did* understand? Presidents, provosts? I was relieved to note that I had interests other than administrative work, mainly my reading and writing in feminist studies. Given all Riesman was saying, I raised my hand and asked, "Why would someone want to be a college president when being a provost puts you in touch with all that is appealing about the academy—students, faculty, teaching, and research?" My voice trailed off. He looked up at me from the depths of the area below and said, "Oh, that's easy. The people on the outside are so much more interesting. The world out there is more interesting than the world inside."

I sat there, baffled. My old ambivalence about being a college president washed over me. I had a hard time envisioning myself in that role. My politics led me to imagine that I'd have to suppress my true positions among conservative business types, currying their favor as I tried to raise money for the university. I thought of Ed Royce, the congressman from Orange County, and executives such as the CEO of Marie Callender restaurants, who were graduates of Cal State Fullerton.

Another concrete opportunity came my way in November 1996, when I was selected to attend the American Council on Education National Identification Project (ACE NIP), which had been established to increase the number of women college presidents. The two-day seminar was held at ACE headquarters at One DuPont Circle in Washington, DC, which was seen by many as the epicenter of higher education in the country. Entering a conference room for our first meeting, I wondered who the thirty or so racially diverse women of various ages seated around a large table were. Just then, I spotted Blenda Wilson, the president of CSU Northridge, who fluttered her fingers at me as we made eye contact.

A series of speakers were featured who provided an overview of trends in American society that impacted higher education: the "cost/price spiral"; reasons the work force was stressed; the new social contract that offered no guarantees for lifetime work; and the need for structures in universities that build community through cross unit collaboration. The director of ACE NIP, Donna Shavlik, who was part cheerleader, part strategist, and part earth mother, talked about the devaluing of women in society. The forums ACE NIP sponsored had male mentors and supporters as well as female. Shavlik was rumored to be behind a practice at ACE that provided shelter for a few female presidents and other administrators who had been fired, giving them a small office and the title "Fellow" until they recovered enough to move on to something else.

When these presentations ended, I was ready for the headhunters, employees of search firms hired by universities to manage presidential searches. The two whose remarks impressed me most on an earlier panel were from Academic Search. They had larger questions for each candidate such as, Why do you want to be a president? What are you looking for? They also had practical advice for once a campus contacted you—talk about them as well as yourself, get to know headhunters, and don't take the first thing that comes along. They prompted me to write my answer in a journal:

> Why do I want a presidency? Because I want to do what Johnetta Cole did at Spelman and Judith Ramaley at Portland State University—take an institution that is average and make it stand out above the crowd because of imaginative ways of educating students, supporting faculty, and engaging with the community. Wasn't Ramaley the one who coined PSU's motto, "Let Knowledge Serve the City"?

When I got my headhunter assignment, I saw it was Barbara Taylor from Academic Search. I was pleased at my good fortune. Taylor and I sat down, and she looked at my résumé and began her critique. "Good experience in a liberal arts college and a comprehensive university." She looked at me over her reading glasses, "You've worked your way up from department chair to dean to provost and have some impressive publications. What about your experiences in being more external? You know, working with the business community, serving on boards, raising funds?"

"Not as much as I'd like," I said. "Any suggestions you have for how I might do that are welcomed."

"Get your president to nominate you for boards and strategize ways to interact with leaders beyond your campus. You've probably done more than shows here on your résumé."

"My president doesn't seem to get the concept of mentoring." I refrained from telling the convoluted tale of my relationship with President Gordon.

She looked up again with the expression of someone who'd just had a good idea. "There's a presidency opening up in the SUNY (State University of New York) system, a university system much like the California State system," she said. "That might be a good fit for you. It's also a highly centralized system; the chancellor is the one who is out front with the legislature, not the presidents. It's at SUNY Brockport, a promising campus west of Rochester. The chair of the search committee, who is also chair of the President's Advisory Committee, an attorney, is a great guy. He would like to see some new directions—increased enrollment, increased fund-raising. I suggest you apply. Salaries are low, so you may not make much more than you are now making." Pausing, she said mostly to herself, "But there may not be enough there for you."

Her last sentence planted the seeds of doubt, but I decided to apply anyway. Before I had my application in the mail, Peggy Atwell, the associate provost for faculty affairs at CSUF, walked into my office. "You're being talked about for the presidency of San Bernardino. Milt got word of this and called me in a lather, wondering if you were going to apply."

"Tell him there is not a chance. I don't want to go to San Bernardino."

Don Schweitzer had hired Atwell just before he died in 1993. I'd first met her over lunch at one of my favorite restaurants in Orange County, Café Piemonte, thinking as I entered, *She's mine now, whether I like her or not.* I'd spotted a perfectly coiffed blonde in professional attire who projected her reputation as a highly regarded education professor at the San Bernardino campus. "I guess you know you've inherited me," she said.

Before lunch was over, I was beginning to feel I had inherited a jewel, a solid addition to my team—someone bright and tough enough to handle the gnarly issues and badass infractions that crossed her desk. Beneath her professional, "teacherly" demeanor was an earthy woman with a foul mouth that never ceased to amaze me.

A few days later, Molly Broad called and said, "You may know that the presidency at San Bernardino is open, and the chancellor wants to know if you're interested."

I imagined myself there, in the Inland Empire, pushed up against the mountains in one of the most polluted cities in California, stuck on Interstate 10, traveling more than seventy miles to the chancellor's office in Long Beach for meetings. I wondered how a president would ever raise money in such a place. Better to level with Molly now. "I'm interested in entertaining a presidency in the CSU but not in San Bernardino, I'm afraid."

A tone of incredulity entered Molly's voice as it rose like that of a valley girl: "Not interested?" Secretly, I thought to myself, *I think I can do better.* I also didn't want to further exacerbate my relationship with President Gordon. Perhaps he worried that I could end up as one of his colleagues capable of undermining him.

What I didn't know then that I now know is that I should have feigned interest. Rarely was someone hired their first time out in a presidential search in the CSU, but it would have gotten me into the pool of contenders in the chancellor's and Molly's minds.

The search for the presidency of SUNY Brockport followed a customary pattern. About a month after I submitted my application, Barbara Taylor called to say I had made the first cut, moving from one of the two hundred or so applicants to the top dozen candidates, those invited to an "airport interview," usually an hour-long talk with the search committee in a nondescript conference room at a hotel near an airport. There is a culture of secrecy surrounding this stage of job searches because most candidates are either sitting presidents or provosts who do not want their home campus to know they are applying. The one person a candidate will tell is her boss. When I told President Gordon, his only reaction was to say, "I see."

The concept of speed dating didn't exist in the 1990s, but in retrospect, these interviews were like a speed date with a group of disembodied people reading from a list of preordained questions, with few smiles and no deviations. The chair of the search committee, the attorney that Taylor had described as "a great guy," looked more like Mr. Chips than a corporate lawyer in his tweed jacket and bow tie. With a soft voice, he delivered a message similar to that of the head-hunter: the university had promise and needed to better serve the community not only in Brockport but also in nearby Rochester.

When I left the room and wandered through the LAX parking lot to find my car, it was hard to know if I had done well or not. It wasn't until March 1997 that I received a call from Taylor: "I'm calling about the Brockport search. The committee wants you to come to campus for an interview. You came in as a very strong candidate. They want your husband to come along as well."

In the mid-1990s, one could not do a Google search. While I waited for a box full of printed materials, I called one of the faculty at CSUF in physical education who had attended Brockport as an undergraduate, turning down Welles-ley, much to her ambitious mother's disappointment. "I wonder if you can keep my question confidential. I've made the cut for the president of Brockport and wanted to ask you a few questions about the campus."

"I know. I just got off the phone with one of my professors there. She wanted to know what I thought of you." My Fullerton colleague spoke in vague generali-ties about her impressions of Brockport, leaving me with no more than I had before we talked.

When I got the box of materials, I saw some promise: the school seemed to have an emphasis on quality, technology, globalization, and outreach, and it maintained a balance between the liberal arts and professional education. I pre-pared for the interview by listing in my journal all the ways I was a good candi-date for the job:

I have a record of achievement and advancement in two institutions. I'm a person of vision and collaboration, who cares passionately about higher edu-cation and its value to individuals and to communities. At fifty-eight years old, almost fifty-eight and a half, I feel my life is finite and precious. So why do I want to go to a new place and work my heart out, give my energy and life to a place? Because I want to make a difference and have my life mean something.

The first morning when I walked about the campus from interview to interview, the historic buildings, somewhat run down, stood out. The campus had been founded as the Brockport Collegiate Institute in 1841 and designated a state normal school in 1866.[1] The sky seemed heavy overhead; snow flurries enveloped me. The sun and diversity of California seemed far away.

The retiring president had worked to expand Brockport's influence by establishing the MetroCenter, a classroom complex in downtown Rochester. When Marc and I visited, the director was enthusiastic, but I had a difficult time understanding what was there—a culinary program for disadvantaged students seemed the most concrete thing. There were other worrisome signs: Kodak, the major corporation in town, was on the downslide.

Before leaving the campus for the state capitol, Albany, to meet the chancellor of the whole SUNY system, I was shown the president's office on the top floor of the administration building. The room attempted to look executive, with paneled walls and a long narrow conference table. A large desk sat at the end up against the windows. I sat down at the president's desk and swiveled his chair around to look out the windows, surprised to see an expanse of green trees that went on to the horizon. A profound sense of loneliness washed over me. I couldn't imagine sitting in this presidential chair.

Yet I liked the faculty. When it seemed I was a viable candidate, those on the search committee began to coach me before my meeting with *Ralph Evans, the provost and vice chancellor for academic affairs for the SUNY system, whose office was in Albany. They worried that my feminist publications would alarm him or signal that we were on opposite sides of the curriculum wars. They gave me a copy of his latest book, *Assimilation American Style*. My last meeting was with the chair of the search committee, who said, "The committee was hoping for someone to dazzle them, and you have done so."

Marc and I flew to Albany late in the day, and once out of the earshot of anyone on campus, I turned to him: "What do you think?"

"The campus is pretty depressing; even the sculptures are mediocre."

When I met Evans the following morning, he was pleasant enough, spending most of my interview talking about his plans to reign in faculty who shared my values about educating the new majority of diverse students on SUNY campuses. He favored a common core curriculum, system-wide exams to measure student knowledge, and a second language requirement, yet he was opposed to bilingual education for non-English-speaking students. The Brockport faculty members' fears were unfounded. He didn't question my publications, peppered as they were with research on feminism and multiculturalism. But I left thinking I didn't want to work in a system that seemed headed for such centralized control. Yet as president, I would report to the chancellor, not Evans.

I had barely sat down at my desk the next morning, happy to be home, when Barbara Taylor called to tell me that the chair of the committee would be calling to offer me the presidency. "I know the salary is low, $110,000, but the chair is able to enhance it with $10,000 from the foundation account. There are other perks related to compensation, including the president's house and a soft money account for travel and entertaining."

"I'm afraid I'm going to have to withdraw; the campus just doesn't feel like a good fit for me."

"The chair is going to be very unhappy about this."

Minutes after I hung up the phone, it rang again. It was the chair of the search committee; Taylor had already spoken to him. "I can't believe you've turned us down. I have only one other viable candidate. What am I going to do?"

"I appreciate your offer, but I don't feel like the job is a good fit." I couldn't say that I couldn't take a job I didn't want, in a place that depressed me, just because he had only one other viable candidate.

The most important professional relationship I had at CSUF was with the president, Milton Gordon. During the year I was interim provost, 1993–1994, we enjoyed a harmonious working relationship. We agreed on the direction of the university that our planning initiative was informing as well as on tenure and promotion decisions and also budgetary ones. Our harmony was captured in a picture taken at a party during that year to celebrate the publication of *The Feminist Classroom*. Looking relaxed in his Helmut Lang sweater, the president is standing close to me and smiling. At the end of the gathering, Gordon said to me, "You're going to become famous, and they're going to take you away from me."

I laughed and said, "I wouldn't worry about that."

"No," he said, "Laurel Wilkening at UC Irvine is likely to do that."

But worrying that someone would take me away didn't push him to make a quick decision following the national search for provost that year. Weeks passed before he contacted me, inviting me to lunch. I wasn't sure what to expect. "Would a president invite you to lunch at an expensive restaurant in order to tell you that he has offered the position to someone else?" I posed this question to one of my feminist friends at the University of Washington, Betty Schmitz, who had been an executive assistant to another president and was quite astute about these matters. "No." She was correct. He did offer me the position, but at a salary far lower than I had anticipated. I countered with a request for several thousand more; he refused to compromise, so I accepted his offer of $115,000, deciding to set aside the fact that many of my colleague provosts had higher salaries than mine even though Fullerton had one of the largest student enrollments in the system. Perhaps because we had worked harmoniously together the year I was interim provost, neither of us initiated a conversation about what he expected of me. Later, I would come to see that our different expectations mattered a great deal.

Figure 18. Sharing a humorous moment with Associate Vice President Tom Klammer at the academic affairs retreat

Nevertheless, I was on top of the world in the fall of 1994. I was the newly appointed provost, no longer with the prefix of "acting," and *The Feminist Classroom* was getting national attention. For instance, I gave a keynote address on feminist pedagogy at the University of Vermont's conference on gender issues in higher education. Taking a vacation, I stayed in New England for a few extra days to attend Frinde Maher's wedding to John McDermott.

Flying home from Boston, I jotted down ideas in my journal of things I wanted to accomplish as provost. I was eager to get my feet on the ground. As I looked out the window, I wondered why the president had selected me. I thought perhaps it was because I had been able to do some innovative things as dean of HDCS, initiatives recognized by the visiting university accreditation team. Or perhaps he thought I was the most qualified of the candidates, a known quantity, and saw that I had effectively chaired the University Planning Committee. Or was it that he wanted to hire a woman?

When I walked into my office the next Monday morning, my secretary said, "You have a meeting with the president at one o'clock."

"Did he tell you why?"

"No, nothing from his appointment secretary."

The president's secretary ushered me into his office and, just as I was about to sit down, he said, "You've been off campus too much. You didn't do that last year. Why are you doing it now?"

Settling into the couch, I began to explain why I had been away. He cut me off. "There were some important meetings last week. I needed you here."

"I understand," I said. "I'll be very careful about the times I'm away from campus."

Thus began a dual existence. When the president and I met about issues in academic affairs, I would have notes jotted in my steno pad, either items that I felt he needed to know about or those needing his support—the merits of a particular action or policy, how to handle a difficult personnel decision. Almost without exception, we were in agreement about what should be done. When finished with my agenda, I would ask, "Is there anything you need?" Most often, Gordon would say, "No, no. That's fine. Nothing."

But I felt that he was increasingly distant and suspicious of me, revealing less and less over time. Outside those meetings in his office, there was another reality: phone calls to one of my subordinates instead of talking first with me, public reprimands—for example, claiming that I hadn't kept him informed about our plan to meet enrollment targets—and assertions about me that he wouldn't discuss once he hurled them at me, such as, "People are afraid of you."

I decided to meet with the president once classes were over in December 1994, in that moment when the entire campus seemed to relax, to air my grievances with the way he was treating me and to deal with my feelings of anger and powerlessness. I also hoped he would tell me how I might improve my "performance." I was nervous when I sank down into the large couch in his office, hoping the evergreen wreath on his window had put him in good spirits. "I want to talk to you about some things that have been bothering me."

When I finished with my list of concerns, he said, "I think you're being too sensitive. I intended none of this as a rebuke of you. I see the way I'm treating you as routine."

Conceding that I might be too sensitive, I left our meeting thinking I had put him on notice that I wouldn't take his abuse. Now I too could begin to relax.

⋘

The twenty or so provosts in the CSU system met several times a year at the chancellor's office to listen to the system's chief academic officer drone on about funding battles with the state legislature, enrollment growth across the campuses, and campus accreditation. Breaks during the formal session and meals were times when the provosts let out our frustrations with the meeting and talked shop. For some, it was a time to complain about their president. "I think Blenda is about to fire me. I come into her office with an agenda and she resents it. 'What about mine?' she asks. We've finally decided to hire Barbara, an executive coach, to help us find out what the issues are." I thought, *Perhaps that is my problem with my president—my agenda.*

Another person said, "Boy, am I on a steep learning curve. One of my biggest problems is my associate provost. She thinks she should be the boss, not me. I feel like she undermines me whenever she can."

"Where is your president on all of this?"

"Oh, he's terrific. He gives me strategies for dealing with her."

In all of these conversations, tongues loosened by wine, I never once mentioned my president. I believed that he would fire me if word ever got back to him that I had uttered a negative word. I came to learn later that I would have understood the president better if I had talked to one of my colleagues, Don Farrish, who had been a dean who reported to Gordon when he was provost at Sonoma State University. When I finally talked with Farrish about Gordon, he said, "Oh, he's paranoid. He always thought the deans were hiding money."

A few days before Christmas 1995, my third year of working for the president, his secretary told me to come to his residence at ten the next morning. When I walked into the reception room on the first floor, he said, "Sit there on the couch." I was beginning to see that when he told me to sit, I was in trouble. "You have been disloyal to me. I demand complete loyalty from everyone who reports to me."

"I've always been loyal to you," I said. "What are you talking about?"

"When the faculty objected to designating an elephant as the symbol of the university, you weren't supportive enough."

The previous spring, the university had engaged in a marketing campaign to better capture the essence of Cal State Fullerton. When the outside consultant presented his proposal, he showed mock-ups of university stationary with an elephant in the top left corner, ears fully extended. The origin for this idea stemmed from elephant races held on campus shortly after the school was founded in the 1950s. Passing around grainy newspaper clippings of students atop elephants, the president joked, "Look at those crew cuts! Who around the table besides me remembers those coed bobby socks and saddle shoes? Talk about capturing the era." This struck me as a desperate attempt to engender campus spirit on a newly formed university that was still being carved out of orange groves. To use this student stunt as the symbol of a university in the 1990s that was trying to be taken seriously and to be seen as a legitimate teaching and research campus seemed ludicrous to me.

"When the idea was first proposed, the only thing I said to you was that I didn't like the objectification of animals." I hadn't revealed that the idea came from Ursula LeGuin's short story "Unnaming the Animals." "Once you decided it was the university symbol, I told the deans to fall in line and not criticize your decision. And they didn't."

"That's not enough—that's not complete loyalty."

"But I wouldn't give complete loyalty to anyone, including Marc and Chantal."

"You've heard what I expect." The image of Charlie Chaplin spinning a globe in the film *The Great Dictator* flitted through my mind.

⋙⋘

The president's support for me continued to slide. In May 1996, he announced at a President's Advisory Board (PAB) meeting that he had appointed a member of the board to a new position, university executive vice president. When he announced this, I asked, "What does this mean?"

"I don't know," he replied. I wonder now if it was a strategy to prompt me to resign.

At the end of the meeting, I walked out with Willie Hagan, the vice president for administration and finance, a man with exceptional academic values, and asked, "Do you know what this means? Are we going to have to report to him?"

"If we do," he said, "we'll all resign."

The president's designation had no bearing on our reporting relationships. The only difference I could see was that his new appointee appeared at more academic affairs gatherings than previously. The only person who ever spoke to me about this appointment was Ephraim Smith, the business dean, who said, "Once he made the announcement, nothing changed. Weird!"

Shocked that the president hadn't told me about his decision before the public announcement, I decided to meet with him to clear the air. Uppermost in my mind, I wondered how he thought a president and a provost should relate and whether there was something wrong with my own performance.

When I met with him, he was quick to point out that he was unhappy with certain aspects of my performance, such as the way I handled giving him requests for implementing the new planning initiatives or the way I submitted merit pay recommendations to him. I defended myself by pointing out that I was a mere hour late in getting more than eight hundred recommendations to him for merit pay across all of academic affairs. I felt that his grievances centered on minor things, again wondering if he wanted me to resign. I left, thinking, *I'll bet he's not worrying about the chancellor of UC Irvine stealing me away from him now!* Temporary rescue came in an unexpected way in the spring of 1996. Tom Klammer, by then my associate provost and "main man," walked into my office one morning with news about the vice president for student affairs: "You've been given some extra time. Milt just fired Jamie."

Early in my days as provost, President Gordon had said, "I don't know what to do about Jamie. What do you think of her?"

"Hmm," I'd said, feeling conflict between my friend and my boss, basking in the glow of being the favored daughter, "she's been very open to working with me and others in academic affairs to improve services to students."

"She seems to take forever to get things done."

"I don't know about that, but if there is anything I can do to be helpful, just let me know." That was the last conversation the president and I had about Jamie. And now she had been fired. Jamie Jenkins left campus at the end of the academic year, never telling me why the president had fired her. When last I saw her, she was sitting alone in the main quadrangle of the university, watching students line up to march across campus to the sports stadium where graduation was being held. They bore large flags she had purchased from all the countries in the world as a departing gift to the campus.

⋘

Help in dealing with the president came from a consultant I hired in the fall of 1996 to serve as a resource to one of the deans. His faculty members were in near revolt, wanting to meet with me to criticize every aspect of his administration: writing a mission statement that was solely his creation, favoring some departments and faculty over others, and mismanaging the budget. A naturalized citizen who wrote clearer prose in English than the native-born deans, the dean approached me for help in dealing with the problem once it became overwhelming.

The consultant, Sue Schaeffer, had been a vice president for human relations at United Airlines and came highly recommended. At our first meeting, she had good suggestions: "Establish a clear picture of what you want from the dean this year; clarify measurable outcomes of what you want to achieve. Don't give him any mixed messages. Also decide what the president and you should do to solve the problems." On the right-hand column of my steno pad, I wrote my initials by these two suggestions, with a note to fax an update to her. She also had ideas for the faculty's responsibilities. "Deliver a challenge to the school that they develop a specific picture of what they want to be like in the year 2000."

I soon saw that Sue could help me think through my relationship with the president as well. After listening to my issues, she said, "It sounds as though you have tried to accommodate him around each of these incidents. You've been too accommodating. I think he is a bully, and if you stood up to him, he'd back down. What would happen if, in private, and right after an incident, you told him you didn't want him to treat you that way or to speak to you like that in public? When he passes over you to a subordinate, say to him, 'I want to be told about this, consulted as provost.'"

Following my meeting with Sue, I wrote in my journal:

> I feel liberated! I don't have to waste my energies being a victim! I hate that role; I have been spending too much time telling Marc and even my associate provosts of my complaints. I've never had therapy, but this feels like the best of it. I can get out what is bothering me and hear another person's

observations about how I might change my behavior. I'd never be a victim in my relationship with Marc. Why here?

Shortly after meeting with Sue, I received a couple of demeaning emails from Gordon and became aware that the president was again going around me to consult and to solve problems in academic affairs. The next time we met, I told him how I felt about these incidents, asked for his respect, and requested that he talk with me first about anything involving academic affairs. He initially objected but listened and said he would do so. "It felt good," I wrote in my journal. "I can let people know what I want. Perhaps I have to give up being the manipulative girl of the 1950s, who expects others to figure out what I need."

Because administrators' salaries are public in the CSU, I saw that Willie Hagan had been hired at a salary higher than mine. I wrote a long letter to the president outlining my various accomplishments and arguing for a salary increase. When we next talked, he said I had unrealistic expectations for a salary increase because, he said, "I see you struggling as provost."

"Is this about gender? When I was hired, you didn't want to give me a salary higher than Sal, the then vice president for administration and finance, but when you hired Willie, you brought him in at a salary higher than mine?"

His only response was to dismiss my assertion with a wave of his hand.

I went back to his claim that I was struggling. "What did you mean by saying I am struggling?" He brought up some recent contentions over the use of space, and when I explained how I had handled the issues, he said, "I don't think you supervise your people enough." I left thinking, "I can't win." He seemed to have a secret negative ledger of my performance that he shared with me only when I confronted him. When I told Marc about this conversation, he said, "You should demand a performance review."

"Ha," I said. "Do you think he'd do it? He has never reviewed me and never will."

I continued my conversation with the consultant, who urged me to focus on the future and to think about what I wanted. Sue also suggested I let the sleeping dog of Gordon's failure to evaluate me lie. "Let him know that you are disappointed in his rejection of your salary increase, believe you deserved better, and his actions don't jibe with all you've been doing."

But doubts about my performance crept in. When Sue gave me an article by the organizational theorist Chris Argyus, I felt like a failure. Perhaps I was one of the managers he wrote about who gave signals that were confusing to workers, glossed over problems because of not wanting to explore their own weaknesses, and didn't reflect enough in "knowing in action." But I concluded that if these things were true of me, I wouldn't have such a good working relationship with the deans.

University policy called for a campus-wide review of senior administrators every three years; mine was scheduled for fall 1997. This meant that a questionnaire was sent out to all administrators, faculty, and staff in academic affairs, as well as all PAB members. The questionnaire didn't worry me because I could point to numerous positive accomplishments in my self-assessment; I believed that I was a team player and recognized as such by my colleagues. What did worry me, in private, was that I was afraid of being unmasked for the increasing anger I felt toward the president, despite Sue Schaeffer's advice to let it go. I began to feel that he and I were playing a cat-and-mouse game in which he was setting up traps and ready to pounce at any infraction in my behavior. In May 1997, for instance, at exactly the time when I was to give a keynote address at the American Association of University Women, which was holding its national meeting at nearby Disneyland, he scheduled a PAB meeting. When I learned of this, I contacted the program chair and said I would be unable to speak. I would be damned if I'd get fired over missing a meeting.

The day before my fifty-ninth birthday, October 26, the president called me to his office and said, "Your performance as provost isn't going very well, and I want you out of the position by January 30, 1998. I've looked at your campus-wide review, and you're not going to be happy with the results."

I took out my steno pad with trembling hands and began taking notes. "I need to see those reviews so I can determine that for myself. I'd like to see them now."

"They are in personnel, and you can't see them for two weeks."

"Two weeks? That's ridiculous. They're my reviews. Where does it say in our personnel policies that someone can't see their reviews for two weeks?"

I felt I was fighting for my professional life. I needed to convince him not to make me step down midyear. "Look, Milt, you know I'm looking for a presidency. Give me time to do that this year, and if I don't have one by spring, I'll resign."

He was silent for a moment. I thought I had convinced him.

"Why didn't you take that presidency at SUNY Brockport? I did a lot to help you become the top candidate."

"It wasn't a good fit, and I've certainly learned about the hazard of poor fits working for you."

He looked at me and said once again, "January 30."

"No one is fired in the middle of the academic year unless they have done something egregious. People will think I've absconded with funds or that I'm a closet alcoholic. Something other than that you just want me out of the job."

Then I thought of what I had wanted to say to him for years; it came out awkwardly as I stumbled over the words, "You're a bully, Milt. You're a goddamn bully."

I left President Gordon's office in shock and denial, fearing that I wouldn't be able to get another job of comparable responsibility. I found myself hoping for something that could rescue me, such as Gordon's sudden death or, barring that, his reconsideration of his decision. That fall, I read Mary Gordon's memoir, *The Shadow Man: A Daughter's Search for Her Father*, which recounted her journey

of discovering who her father really was. What interested me most were her pas-
sages about the "salvation" promised to Catholic children. Perhaps I was so angry
with President Gordon because I kept trying to do all I could to gain "salvation"
and he kept identifying yet another sin. I thought he wanted me to do the job of
provost when what he wanted most was unquestioned loyalty.

When I unlocked the outer door to the provost's suite—it was nearly six on
Friday—the only light was from Tom Klammer's office. Tom rose to meet me.
"He fired me," I said. "The son of a bitch fired me."

He just shook his head and said, "Maybe you should talk to Keith Boyum."
Boyum was the most powerful faculty member on campus, with an astute
understanding of campus politics. Shaking my head in the negative, I thought
to myself, *I don't want to pull the "children" into this divorce.* I was determined to
come out of this with my self-respect and vowed to perform as a professional
until I turned out the lights for the last time in my office.

Before going home, I called Marc. "Milt just fired me."

"Oooh, tough, but you'll be better off not working for him."

"Maybe. I should have trusted my instincts and not signed on to work for
Gordon." It was only later that I learned that his paranoia wasn't directed only at
me. When Gordon heard that former president Cobb had been in contact with
someone on the Foundation Board, he told her to stay off campus and to have
no contact with faculty or community members. There seemed to be a pattern
in his treatment of her, Jodi Jenkins, and me. Would I ever be able to untangle
the workings of race and gender in these relationships? How could this have
happened to me?

My only thread of hope was intervention from the CSU chancellor, Barry
Munitz, or the associate vice chancellor, Molly Broad, whom I had called on Friday.
Broad reached me early Monday morning while I was attending a seven o'clock
meeting in South Orange County for some organization or board whose affiliation I hoped would make me a stronger candidate for a university presidency. I
took the call in a private room away from the meeting and said to Molly, "Milt
fired me, and worse, wants me out of the position by the end of this semester."

"That's exactly what happened to Marilyn Boxer!"[2]

My reviews arrived from personnel midday that same day. With trembling fingers, I skimmed through them. They were mostly positive. A few people criticized
me: the director of research and sponsored programs for being averse to numbers,
a physics professor for paying too much attention to student learning. Assuaged
by the general tenor of my reviews, I met with the president on November 5, 1997,
and gave him my written proposal for termination in June rather than in January
of 1998. He rejected my proposal outright. I spoke with Molly Broad again to ask
her and the chancellor to intercede. "I need your help, Molly, to convince Milt that
I should stay until the end of the academic year. That will give me time to look
for another job and quell rumors that I've done something outrageous." Molly

assured me that she would do what she could. Next, I called Sue Schaeffer, who recommended a lawyer in San Francisco who dealt with such personnel cases. The president's case against me was weak because he had never given me a formal review and had approved a salary increase for me the year before.

When I went into the president's office on November 8, I knew he had talked with Munitz and Broad. He sat behind his desk; no lights had been turned on. There was a chair placed at the farthest edge of the desk. "Sit there. Sit right there," he said, pointing to the chair. I sat down, uncertain where to put my legs. "I will allow you to resign your position as provost on June 1. I will announce this to the larger community on Monday." I silently let out a deep breath, knowing I had prevailed because of the chancellor's intervention.

The chair of the faculty senate, Vince Buck, was the first person to call once the president began to inform the campus of his decision. "I hear the president fired you. When he told me this, I couldn't believe it." It gave me some comfort that my firing had surprised this political scientist, who characterized his way of expressing his views of some administrators as "emphasizing the negative without sugar-coating. My disdain was for those who were unwilling to respect the role of the faculty in shared governance."

It was time to inform the deans. Once they were assembled in the conference room, I decided to be direct, "I have some news. I'll be stepping down as provost on June 1. I leave knowing that we've accomplished many of the goals we set out to achieve. So that there will be a timely transition, a search for my replacement will begin now. I remember fondly my first meeting with you as provost in June of 1993 and how we rose above divisive budget cuts, how some of you had proposed cuts of staff that the president wouldn't allow." A weak laughter rippled down the table. "There is a time for everything, and it is time for me to resign for the good of the institution, the president, and myself."

The senior dean, the dean of the arts, appeared shocked and unbelieving. "The president never consulted us."

"If I made a list of one hundred things I expected you to say at this meeting, it would not be that you were forced to step down," the dean of communications added, guessing correctly.

But some felt otherwise. The one dean who said nothing, Don Castro, the dean of humanities and social sciences, was rumored to have said, once news of my firing spread across campus, "The faculty are dancing in the streets." He was also most likely the one who told the president that people were afraid of me. I should have attributed more meaning to his habit of scrunching his ample body into the farthest corner of the couch each time we met in my office.

Later that week, I attended a meeting of CSU system presidents and provosts. As I huddled among others, getting a cup of coffee, one of my colleague provosts whispered, "Milt is telling everyone that you're going to sue him, sue the university."

"What a fantasy life that man has. Sue him, and never work in this town again?"

As I went about doing my work in spring semester 1998, I couldn't help but brood about why this had happened to me. Was it some failure on my part, the cost of being a change agent, sexism, or the reality that if a boss doesn't want someone, there was no way to win?

My perspective during that last semester was bifocal. One eye was focused on meeting my responsibilities as provost. The other scanned the horizon for presidential openings—talking with headhunters, putting application materials together, meeting deadlines, and showing up for airport interviews. The floors of B gates in the Denver International Airport, where I often changed planes, came to have a soothing familiarity as I walked over areas of colored terrazzo depicting indigenous fossils and Native American symbols found in Colorado. The scope of time the fossils represented reminded me that my current drama was but a drop in the river of time.

I interviewed for presidencies that semester, crisscrossing the country for initial ones at Rowan University and Montclair State University in New Jersey, Parkside in Wisconsin, and Eastern Washington State University. Before going to meet a search committee, I got into the habit of taking one last look in the mirror and singing, "Another opening, another show." I would straighten my shoulders and coach myself as I walked toward the interview: *Imagine you're a president. Everything about you should reflect that—posture, voice, smile, and particularly your message.* Always hovering in the background was that this was my last semester as provost, that my future was uncertain. None of these opportunities advanced to the next stage, the campus interview.

The interview that stands out among this set of airport interviews is the one for Montclair State. A faculty member on the search committee, a white male who had once been provost there, announced early on that he had spent all the previous night reading *The Feminist Classroom*. With agitated speech and gestures, he almost shouted, "How can we have a president who has written such things, a president whom the legislature will surely go after. We're a state university. We depend on them for our funding."

"Yes," I said, "but I can't imagine being a president who would take her feminism to the state legislature. It wouldn't be an appropriate way to represent the university. And yet I do believe in the concept of academic freedom."

In the midst of these searches, I wrote in my journal:

How can I keep going under these circumstances? I have no choice. The emotional wear and tear is great. What is most troubling is how self-absorbed you become. As I concluded when I was working out last night, I'm the same person whether I get a presidency or not. The choice of going back to secondary education where I have tenure is unacceptable, a waste of my talents and experiences. I must keep going.

CHAPTER 11

SHIFTING MY
GAZE FORWARD

CONTINUING TO PURSUE PRESIDENTIAL ASPIRATIONS

I had on-campus interviews that covered the landscape of state universities: Fort Lewis, an undergraduate college high on a plateau in Durango, Colorado; *Great Lakes University; and Edwardsville in Southern Illinois, a campus carved out of the farmlands—green and beautifully landscaped but lackluster nonetheless. My first on-campus interview in early 1998 was at a private school, Adelphi University on Long Island.

I first learned that I was being considered for that presidency when Louanne Kennedy, the provost at CSU Northridge, called me and said, "I got a call from a headhunter about the presidential search at Adelphi, and before he could say anything, I said, 'She's terrific, she has vision, she knows the ropes, and you'd be lucky to get her.' But much to my surprise, the headhunter said, 'I wasn't calling about her; I was calling about Matt Goldstein.'"

"Who is Matt Goldstein?" I asked.

"He's currently the president of Baruch, one of the campuses in the CUNY (City University of New York) system. I knew him when I was a faculty member there." Adelphi, a private university on Long Island, had recently been in the news because it had the highest paid president in the country at the time, a campus with such financial troubles that the state's governor fired the board and appointed a new one that included the former Smith college president and author of *The Road from Coorain*, Jill Kerr Conway.

At the initial interview, held in some corporate tower in Manhattan, Kerr Conway asked the first question: "Tell us about your educational experiences, how they influenced the way you think about higher education."

I wove the story of the first assembly at my Catholic women's college and how the dean said that our education held out the promise of becoming a whole man, the promise of a liberal arts education. "A chill went through my body. A nerve had been touched. I was being offered something bigger than myself, something beyond the material world, a reason for being. Here was the first spark, my first yearnings for an intellectual life. That was my defining moment as a college student and continues to shape the way I think about the promise of a college education, appreciating now the irony of a woman becoming a whole man." Members of the search committee looked around the table and laughed.

The interview felt intimate after that question. Looking up the long interview table, I saw not only Conway but an African American woman, a highly placed administrator in the National Science Foundation, and a group of CEOs, including an outspoken man from the Edison Project, one of the earliest for-profit schools in New York. Still too close to my firing at Fullerton and feeling I had to explain, I spent far too much time chronicling the details of my troubles with the president, weaving a tale of his mistreatment as I moved the campus toward thinking in new ways. Now how I wished I then had known the consultant who later told me: don't focus on such things; it is like going on about the failure of your first marriage.

Despite that misjudgment, I was one of two candidates invited to campus for an interview. Once off the plane, as Marc and I were ushered into a stretch limousine for the drive to Long Island, I said, "It's not hard to understand why they are in such financial trouble." The same limousine later took us from the campus into Manhattan for dinner with a trustee. Lunches at expensive restaurants were the norm. Marc had one with the vice president for finance and administration, who after three Scotches of the rarest quality admitted how troubled he was by the institution's fiscal problems. At my last address to the campus, on a terrace resplendent in the spring sun, I spoke of the promise of the university. I felt a high as I sensed the crowd's response—wanting to be appreciated, wanting to be their choice. Several of the faculty accompanied us in the limousine to the airport and talked in code about the other candidate and how they preferred me. Yet Matt Goldstein was hired.

Fort Lewis College was a tightly knit community on the western slope of the Rockies. Getting there involved a heart-stopping flight in a small plane from Denver, bouncing up and down at the whims of the air drafts. The retiring president had crashed once: "But only in a field close enough to walk to the terminal." It was hard for me to get my head around the college; a conversation at dinner with the board seemed particularly strained. Members of the search committee, especially the faculty, signaled their support. It was difficult to know how I had done once Marc and I boarded a flight back to Denver.

"We'd like you to come back for a second interview," the chair of the Fort Lewis search committee said, "Just you this time, without Marc." Once back in Durango, I was met by whirring cameras from the local television station. The area was packed with people whom I later learned were ranchers, professional and business people, members of the college foundation board, and leaders from local Native American tribes. It made me wonder if this was an outpouring of a "tight" community or if something about me (too many publications with the *F* word?) was troublesome to these active supporters of the college.

I spent time walking the campus; a combination of the altitude—6,872 feet— and the locally quarried sandstone buildings gave the space a chilling lunar feel. Soon afterward, Michael Stratton, a member of the Colorado State University system governing board and the college's search committee, came down to sea level, traveling to the Fullerton campus with another man to interview a list of people I recommended. My sense was that it all went well; Stratton continued to be my supporter. When we shook hands as the committee departed, he pressed his card into my hand. On the back was written, "You have to deliver Putnam."

The next morning, sitting on the floor of our bedroom, the sun warm on my back, I called Anne Putnam, another member of the search committee, and said, "I'd very much like hearing from you what you find troubling about my candidacy."

"I didn't expect you to begin with that," she said. Her main concern was my "fit" with the local community. The fact that I had grown up in western Nebraska didn't seem to matter. "We want to find another Joel," she said. She went on to say that the current president had done a wonderful job in the last ten years—well, maybe except for the last two. He was their savior. His wife was also great. "There is so much about your candidacy that excites me, but the community is concerned about your fund-raising and development experience. There are a number of contributors who have very strong opinions of how things ought to be." I was unable to deliver Putnam. I couldn't figure out if it was something about my personality or my particular experiences or whether she was negatively influenced when the first thing Marc asked her was, "What do you do to escape?"

My experience at Great Lakes University had a different character. At my first on-campus interview, the chair of the board and the search committee said after shaking my hand, "Your friends in women's studies are demanding an interview with you."

"I don't know anyone on your campus in women's studies. What are their names?" When he said their names, I replied, "No, I've never heard of any of them."

As I walked around campus, I understood what the headhunter meant when she characterized the university as an oasis in a city known for its grit. The campus in the heart of downtown clustered along the river, its buildings well maintained. But the view from the president's office, the smallest I had yet sat in, looked out on a street showing signs of urban decay. The challenges seemed near impossible to me, even though there was a ray of hope here and there. A local foundation had a long history of supporting the university. The faculty members on the search committee were committed to educating their students and pursuing research.

In numerous ways, this search seemed interminable. Campus rumors reached me during the months after my first interview in fall 1998. The chair of the board had offered the position to a provost at an East Coast university, who had turned him down. I returned to campus for a second interview in mid-December. I was told that twice the search committee had recommended my hiring. Seizing the initiative, I sent the chair a fax detailing what I would do if he hired me; he responded that it didn't overcome his negativity toward me. He thought I lacked the energy and passion to do the job and worried that I wouldn't have the support of the community, even though I had that of the faculty. In retrospect, I could never have reported to a board chair who saw me that way anyway.

In late January, the chair sent a letter to the university community saying he was going to invite several other candidates to campus but was pleased that I continued to stay in the search. When a call finally came from the headhunter in late spring of 1999, I learned that the board had hired a man of color who had been the vice provost for student affairs at a similar university. I appreciated what may have been community pressure to diversify the administration. But when I told a colleague of this hire, she said, "Hired as a president? He's a great guy to go out drinking with, but a president?"

Reflecting back on this period, I now perceive that there were changes in both academia and the external world as I moved from the loss of my job at CSUF through my quest for the right fit in a presidency. One thing that changed was what I could aspire to. Twenty-five years earlier, I told a colleague at Wayland High School that I couldn't be department chair "because I am a woman." When I entered the academy in 1980, the percentage of presidents who were women was under 9 percent; when I searched for a presidency in the late 1990s, it was 19.3 percent. Today, it is 30 percent. I sometimes wondered if I was the "woman" candidate, there to make the search seem more diverse but never really having a shot at the job. Yet the fact that I got as far as I did in some of the searches is attributable in part to the women's movement's influence on the male-dominated medieval university.

But had *everything* changed? Far more difficult to measure than the number of women in higher education presidencies was the subtext of "fit." SUNY Brockport had concluded that I was a good fit, even though I disagreed, and a year after Matt Goldstein resigned, Adelphi offered me a one-year contract. But other remarks I heard along the way suggested that my gender and age might have been at play: Fort Lewis wanted to find "another Joel." Was the board chair's remark that I "lacked the energy and passion to do the job" tied to my age, which was sixty?

As to internal changes, I carried around an undercurrent of grief at the loss of my job at Fullerton that housed a range of emotions: shock, fear, anger that I had been treated unfairly, and shame. My victory narrative of success was blown asunder as I faced setbacks, and I had to face the recognition that destructive things happen. I thought often of my colleague Tom Klammer's remark: "You stay in the ring too long." I became more humble, more understanding of others who, qualified as they were, didn't always succeed. I often reminded myself that this wasn't my whole life. There also was Marc and Chantal, our friends, my research, and things that I loved to do—hike, swim, read, and attend art exhibits, concerts, plays, and movies.

One thing that did not change was my ambivalence toward the presidencies where I was a finalist. My journal observations speak volumes: the president's office was the smallest I'd seen; the campus was on the wrong side of Rochester; the campus had a chilling lunar feel, and so forth. Every time, I thought I could do better. I never really changed the point of view I expressed in my question to David Riesman at Harvard about the value of being a president rather than a provost. When I asked Jean Dowdall, a headhunter who was instrumental in advancing my candidacy in a number of searches, if she could tell me how I projected myself in presidential interviews, she said I was "too internal, too academic, more like a provost." Despite my ambitions to be a president, I cared most about the concerns of a provost: student learning, faculty work, and getting resources to support good ideas in academic affairs. A woman I'd met who had encouraged me to go to the ACE NIP meeting in the first place, herself a president who lasted only three years, characterized me thus: "You're not a deft enough politician to be a president. You're too honest and too creative." Throughout my search for my next act, I kept wondering who I was: a scholar, a feminist, and an administrator or someone who didn't easily fit into any of those categories.

I have volumes of journals from October 1996, when I first learned of the opening at SUNY Brockport, until I realized I was not going to get a presidency sometime early in 1999. They are riddled with notes imagining the thrill of leading an institution, figuring out how to do something better, and being in the thick of addressing the issues in higher education broadly and in a particular institutional context. They are filled with questions I asked headhunters about how I could have done better and what was missing. I prepared opening statements that let search committees know the impact I believed I'd had in my previous positions. I engaged a consultant who, one long day at her house in Oakland, urged me to prepare more pungent answers to questions and critiqued my ideas, my voice, and my posture.

At times, the things I thought to do differently were cynical and not true to who I was—think only of your career; never try to make any change in an institution because people will turn on you.

So why did I harbor this ambition to become a university president? I had little experience with the key emphases of a presidency, such as courting external communities, fund-raising, and development. Yet a part of me believed I could grow into that role and make a positive difference in a unique way as the president of a higher education institution. But if I'm being honest, I was also taken with the privilege—the higher salary, the status, and the influential people I would get to know. Both of these things can be true at the same time. And if I were a man, I probably wouldn't have been plumbing my motivations anyway. I would have just assumed the problem was with them, not me, and left it at that.

The first Monday in June 1998, my future was uncertain at best. Marc and I decided to make the drive from Fullerton to Santa Monica to visit the recently opened Getty Museum. Robert Irwin, who had designed the garden, described his task as making a contemporary "sculpture in the form of a garden aspiring to be art." It was more meandering than I had expected, with patches of brilliance—the cascading waterfall descending among huge copper-tinted stones and bougainvillea shooting out of twenty-foot-high steel rods, narrow at the bottom and opening wide, like huge bouquets offered up to the sun. At the bottom was a labyrinth of sculpted azaleas resting in water, no longer in bloom. Every path had a profusion of roses and perennials and silvery grasses. At lunchtime, we sat on the terrace overlooking the garden with the sun in our faces. Just as I finished my egg salad sandwich, my cell phone rang. It was Louanne Kennedy, the provost at Cal State Northridge, a social friend since the time she and her husband, a civil rights lawyer, had come to dinner at our home.

"I'm worried about what is going to happen to you. Do you have any idea what you'll do next?"

"Unless some miracle happens, I'll be teaching at CSUF in the fall. That bastard Gordon won't even give me a sabbatical for a semester to prepare to teach after more than a dozen years as an administrator. I have enough vacation to carry me through the summer even though he is contesting one day."

"I think I have something for you. The dean of education here at Northridge retired and we haven't been able to fill the position. I'd like you to come up here as interim dean for the 1998–1999 academic year. I know you're looking for a presidency and will need to be off campus for interviews. I'll need to clear this with Blenda, the president, but can't imagine that she wouldn't support you."

Looking out at the parade of garden lovers making their way along the paths, I said, "This sounds promising."

By August 1, I was the interim dean of education at CSU Northridge. Northridge was in the San Fernando Valley approximately fifty miles from Fullerton. If cars could travel at sixty-five miles per hour, the freeways' speed limit, the drive would be about an hour. But the average speed during rush hour on most LA freeways was less than twenty miles per hour. Clearly, Marc and I needed to find a room in between. We got out a map and decided that something in the Pasadena area would work. Remembering that notices for rental rooms were often posted at the Huntington Library, I inquired and learned of a small apartment in Pasadena.

"The apartment is up here," the owner of a home in a comfortable middle-class neighborhood said, talking as we walked up the stairs. "You can see all we've done to renovate the space." At one end of the attic was a sitting area, nicely furnished—a bit too ruffled and chintzy for us, but clean. There was no kitchen. Instead, there was a counter with a microwave, a toaster, and an electric skillet. No stove, no sink, no refrigerator. Any dishes would have to be washed in the tiny sink in the bathroom. At the other end, behind a drawn curtain, were a bed and a dresser.

When we got outside, having agreed to get back to the owner, I said, "We're never going to be able to cook in this place."

"True, but since I'm going to be working in my studio in Fullerton, I'll drive up with dinner Monday through Thursday, and you can drive back to Fullerton on Friday evenings." We would meet first at 24 Hour Fitness in Glendale, work out, take our twenty minutes (family shorthand for having a drink), eat dinner, put our dishes in the bathroom sink, and walk the few steps to bed. The next morning, Marc would load the dirty dishes and any leftovers into a cardboard box and drive back to Fullerton. I would zoom off to Northridge, driving against the traffic. Evenings in our pied-à-terre were glamorous for a while, but Marc began to feel like he was on a treadmill, driving to Pasadena, which often took well over an hour each way, washing the last night's dishes, and cooking the evening meal.

"This is taking too much time. We really should live in the Brewery."

"But there is a waiting list there of more than a year and, God willing, I'll have a presidency by then."

"Let me go by the rental office and see what I can find. Remember, I'm the guy who always drives to the front door and gets a parking place." Marc called after his visit to the office: "Can you meet me at the Brewery at four thirty today? A large studio apartment, recently renovated by two architects, just opened up this morning. The manager looked at me and said, 'It's yours if you want it.' She'll hold it until five tonight."

The Brewery Arts Complex, formerly the Pabst Blue Ribbon Brewery, was the largest artist-in-residence community in the country, just off the Main Street exit on the Golden State Freeway (I-5), minutes from LA's Union Station. Instead of the small bungalows with white picket fences that Main Street suggested, this section of East LA was a jumble of low industrial buildings, vacant lots, chain-link fences, and gas stations. Once inside the Brewery, however, another life emerged. Signs pointed to a restaurant and a coffee shop. Well-kept roadways wound through the complex; lush plants poked up above some of the terraces. Artists would walk about, a few standing at the bar just inside the restaurant.

When the manager opened the door to the studio apartment, we stepped into a hallway, approximately twenty-five feet long and eight feet wide. "You could have an art exhibition here," I said. The architects had renovated the space that opened up from the hallway into a studio; glass windows filled the entire south wall, letting in the glowing late afternoon light. The San Bernardino Mountains were visible, as was a tiny stream of cars barely moving along "the Five." Behind sliding-glass doors was the living space, a wide-open room, again with a wall full of windows on the south and a tiny alcove. A no-frills kitchen and bathroom were at the other end, as well as a room with a door, which the architects had used as a storeroom.

"I can see our living room furniture looking out at the windows, and this tiny alcove would be perfect for our books. Don't you think our dining room table would work in the space between the living room and the kitchen?"

"Let's take it," Marc said. Once settled in the apartment, he was able to spend the day in his studio, no longer the freeway-flyer chef stuck in traffic, thinking about the painting he had left behind. My commute to the Northridge campus was against the traffic on I-5; rarely did I go less than seventy miles per hour. We rented our house in Fullerton, unsure of our future.

We settled into life in Fermenter 43, the number written on the wall of what became our bedroom, comfortable except for the dust mites and the pigeons that roosted and cooed outside and occasionally found their way inside, frantically flapping around until Marc was able to open an outside door—a door with no stairs that dropped precipitously, several stories, to the cement below.

A bright spot during this time was a trip to Paris that Marc and I took in mid-February of 1999 to celebrate Chantal's thirtieth birthday. She was there doing research for her dissertation and what would later become her book *Transcultural Teens: Performing Youth Identities in French Cites*. Our time with her was a reminder of life beyond presidential searches as we wandered together through the streets and markets of the city. Just before we were to go to bed one night during our visit, Marc said to Chantal, "If we had tried together to imagine you, to figure out what our daughter should be, we could not have come up with someone as wonderful as you."

REALISTIC NEXT STEPS

As it became clear that I was unlikely to get a presidency by the fall of 1999, when I was scheduled to return to Fullerton, I was able to shift my gaze forward and think about realistic next steps. I applied for and was interviewed for a host of provost's positions, almost too many to recall: Hunter College, the College of New Jersey, Portland State University, the University of Maine in Orono, City College of New York, Miami University in Ohio, Pitzer College in Claremont, and Kent State University. At each on-campus interview, I would try to imagine the life Marc and I might have—for instance, enjoying all that Manhattan had to offer, especially the art museums and world-class music and theater; being nearer to our friends on the East Coast; and going on vacations to Cape Cod with Chantal. But given the salary, could we afford to live in Manhattan?

This period in my life was not as dire as one of my friends put it: "You're like a zombie, flying across the country from interview to interview." I didn't feel like a zombie as I reviewed the material sent from each campus. I felt very much alive on a flight from Newark to Los Angeles when one of the engines went out on the plane and the captain turned around and made an emergency landing at Dulles, fire engines lined up to wait. A woman across the aisle from me had a bouquet of lilacs. Perhaps this would be the last time I saw that sign of spring, the promise of new life.

Despite my multiple trips off campus, I became engaged with the faculty in the College of Education at Northridge, rolling up my sleeves and working with them to improve the ways their work was done. The challenges of preparing educators—teachers, school administrators, school psychologists and counselors—to work primarily in the multiethnic schools in the Los Angeles Unified School District added an extra dimension of importance. From a dean's perspective, this meant primarily paying attention to faculty vitality by getting to know them as individuals and members of a particular department.

It wasn't the job announcement for provost at Portland State University (PSU) that caught my eye but what I had learned from my earlier interview for the presidency. The previous president, Judith Ramaley, had put the university on the map because of an innovative general education program and a partnership between the university and the city that was talked about at national conferences. I decided to apply.

One morning in early spring, I got a call from the chair of the search committee at PSU, saying that I had made the cut for an airport interview. My enthusiasm for the job increased as I talked with colleagues around the country. Tom Erlich, once the provost at Stanford and later the president of Indiana University, said, "It's one of the most interesting provost's positions in the country." When a box of promotional materials arrived from the campus, I looked first at a slick brochure that featured the many partnerships between the university and the city. Photographs documented slogans an ad man could love. "Let Knowledge Serve the City" was emblazoned on a skywalk that crossed Broadway, a major street running through the campus, a slogan reminiscent of the Progressive Era but still inspirational for the late twentieth century.

At the bottom of the box were excerpts from an about-to-be-published manuscript, a history of the university, *The College That Would Not Die, 1946–1996*. Its author told the story of how the college began as an extension center of the University of Oregon and Oregon State College, housed in Vanport, the World War II shipyards north of Portland, to educate returning veterans. The State Board of Higher Education believed that once the returning veterans were educated, the college would fade away as students enrolled at one of the two flagship universities downstate. Students, whose work and families were in Portland, felt differently and made it clear that they needed a city university that accommodated them.

I landed at the Portland airport and was met by an ample brunette wearing a name tag with *"Sally" in bold script. She had majored in women's studies while a student at PSU and was the protégée of the most powerful staff member on campus, Donna Bergh, executive assistant to the provost. Donna's reputation was based on the quality of her work and her practice of measured reflection. I was told that there was a network of staff, mostly women, who were beholden to her for their jobs. At her instigation, the campus assigned a staff member to each candidate in high-level searches. When interviews were completed, the staff would meet informally and share their assessments of the candidates. It was then up to Donna to lobby for their favorites with the powerful people on campus, particularly those on the search committee.

Once we were inside Sally's aging red Toyota Corolla, she handed me the interview schedule, which listed a series of meetings in a dizzying number of airport hotels—Holiday Inn, Sheraton, Embassy Suites, and the Radisson. "I'm surprised to see the interviews are in so many different hotels."

"Oh, I can explain that. We decided to interview the twelve semifinalists at the same time, taking the utmost care to ensure confidentiality, so that none of you know who the other candidates are and so that no one on your campus knows. You can imagine what would happen if word got out that you were interviewing."

I saw that my first interview was with Michael Reardon, the retiring provost. Working to conceal surprise, I said to Sally, "Isn't it somewhat unusual for the provost to interview the candidates who might replace him?"

"Oh, no. Michael wanted to be available in case the candidates had any questions. Everyone loves Michael. Here we are at the hotel for your first interview. I'll just drop you off in the entryway. Remember, if the door is closed to the interview suite, just knock and wait for an answer."

I took the Holiday Inn's elevator to the fourth floor. Room 403 was indeed shut. I knocked lightly, and a male voice said, "Just a minute. We're just finishing up."

A few minutes later, the door opened and a tall brunette, a molecular biologist I recognized, stepped into the dimly lighted hallway. As we hugged, she said, "I haven't seen you since the National Women's Studies Association meeting. So much for confidentiality!"

"What's it like in there?" I whispered into the biologist's ear.

"You're on your own, sister."

Reardon, a man with a graying fringe of hair above his ears, sat at a table. His sharp, intelligent eyes peered out through glasses. I later learned that Reardon was an intellectual historian hired in the mid-1960s into a department that stood out because of its members' publications. Known for his Jesuitical approach to knowledge and his rhetorical brilliance, one colleague would later describe his lectures as "original works of scholarship."

We shook hands. "Has anyone ever told you that you look just like Helen Mirren?"

"It happens from time to time," I said, "especially after she's played a less-than-glamorous character. Same genetic pool." Hoping to get Reardon's perspective on the current status of University Studies, I asked how the four-year general education program was faring. He was vague, circumspect.

When my time with Reardon was over, Sally whisked me off to the next interview, held in a large function room at the Sheraton. Thirty chairs were lined up lecture style, their metal frames a shiny contrast to the regulation beige walls. I quickly checked my schedule and saw that the group was the Council of Academic Deans, labeled CADS by some wag, and the president's Executive Committee (EXCOM). Of the fifteen interviewers, all were white men, with three exceptions—James Ward, the dean of social work, an African American man with erect posture in an impeccably tailored suit, and two white women. They stood in clusters of three or four. Raucous laughter burst forth from one of the groups where a rosy-cheeked, dark-haired man held forth. His high laugh was broken by audible snorts when he paused in his storytelling. Robert Sylvester had performed as a world-class cellist, always ready for a story of his time in New York with Lennie (Leonard Bernstein), until a shoulder injury prevented concertizing.

The chair of the search committee, described in the university's history as "the father of the College of Urban and Public Affairs," introduced himself in a formal patrician manner. A member of an upper-class Egyptian family, Nohad Toulan had come to the United States as a young man to do graduate work in city planning. In heavily accented English, he called the group together, asked for introductions, and then assumed the posture of a professor about to give a fifty-minute lecture: "I'm pleased to welcome our fourth candidate, Mary Kathryn Tetreault. She comes to us from California, which should make her no stranger to the budgetary ups and downs of a state university. But what she probably doesn't know is the history of insecure budget cycles in this state. Right now the state budget is good, and our campus is receiving an infusion of fifteen million dollars, but we have many holes to fill. I remember budget cycles in the 1970s, and the lesson there is that this positive budget climate won't continue."

One of the women leaned sideways and whispered to me, "But that was then; this is now." She and I suppressed a laugh at Toulan's need to dredge up ancient history.

As I listened to Toulan natter on about budget cycles through the 1970s and 1980s, I watched the body language of those assembled. They brought back memories of an unruly group of boys I taught in a freshman social studies class at Wayland High School two decades earlier. The class met following lunch, and the twenty-five boys and six girls were nearly impossible to control. The boys' gangling, hormonal bodies could barely squeeze into their desks. The sugar and other mind-altering substances they ingested during lunch made for a collective high. In the nearly twenty interviews I had had in the past three years, this was the most unruly. It was hard to imagine it was something personal to me, since they knew me only from my résumé and, perhaps, from checking up on me with colleagues around the country. Questions seemed increasingly hostile, painting a picture of administrators in competition over scarce resources. One of the deans and Sylvester quarreled openly about whose faculty was paid the least. The dean of engineering and computer science, Bob Dryden, tangled with Toulan over how Portland State ended up losing some of its share of state allocations to the smaller regional campuses while the flagship universities escaped.

A man with a band of neatly clipped hair above his ears and a youthful face darted from group to group and then sat down on the edge of a seat. His name tag read, "George Pernsteiner, vice president for finance and administration." He gave me a condescending look and asked, "How would you position yourself in relation to the historically favored campuses? How would you respond to challenges from other campuses in the state?" I wondered if Pernsteiner was trying to smoke me out early to see how much I knew about the political terrain of higher education in Oregon. I fumbled around for an answer. The vice president for university relations, Gary Withers, jumped in. "That's not where the problem is, George. Our biggest threat is the alternative institutions that are springing up along every freeway exit."

His remark gave me a few minutes to think. "Well, I'd get to know the provosts on the other campuses and build a collaborative relationship with them."

"Huh." George laughed. "You think that would work? You think collaboration is in their circuits?"

I looked him straight in the eye and asked, "How would you answer your own question?"

"Use your friends in the legislature. It's important for the provost to get resources through a good relationship with the legislature. This is a small state, you have to remember."[1]

It came as a surprise when I was one of four candidates invited back for an on-campus interview. A couple of days later, the president, Daniel Bernstine, a law professor and former dean at the University of Wisconsin, called. He had a reputation as a successful fund-raiser. One of his former colleagues said, "Be careful, or he'll pick your pockets."

"Mary Kathryn," he began, "this is President Bernstine." I cringed at the use of my given name, which I began using out of a wish to get out of Mary Kay's skin as I sent out yet another application.

"Ah, President Bernstine," I said.

"Call me Dan. I just want to introduce myself before we meet on campus. I want to wrap this search up as quickly as I can and get a new provost on board. It's time for some changes in academic affairs. I see from your résumé that you've published more than most administrators. Do you plan to continue your research, should you become my provost?"

A warning signal went up. Did the president and the campus see me as too scholarly? "I've found that continuing to write and publish sends a good signal to the faculty. Of course, as provost, my first responsibility is to do the work of the office and to build a strong administrative team."

"That's good," said the president. "I want the most experienced provost I can find to run academic affairs. Launching the university's first-ever capital campaign is going to take all my time."

The first evening of the on-campus interview, I had dinner with the president at an upscale restaurant in the Vintage Hotel where I was staying. When I walked up to the reservation desk, I saw a well-dressed, short, overweight, dark-skinned man in his early fifties. In a city where whites were more than 75 percent of the population, this was surely Bernstine.

We were shown to a narrow booth for two on a busy aisle with waiters passing on their way from the kitchen. The president and I squeezed into opposite seats. The computer where waiters punched in their orders was within eyesight. The pleasantries of our initial greetings were interrupted by the clashing of silverware and plates dumped into the gray dishpan underneath. What kind of a president would accept such a bad table? Then I remembered a similar covert racism at play when Marc and I and Jamie Jenkins were shown the least desirable table at Chasan's in Los Angeles.

"How did your interviews go today?" the president asked.

"Fine, fine," I said, "although I found my second interview with the deans and vice presidents to be particularly contentious. They were universally negative about the budget and about how the fifteen-million-dollar enhancement from the chancellor's office is being distributed throughout the system."

"Ah, the deans," he said, "they're a challenging group, most out only for their own colleges. I want a provost to free the deans and me to go out and raise money for the capital campaign. If you come here, you'll be dealing primarily with the associate deans."

The deans in California and I had been a tight group, too tight for the paranoid president. Believing that a distant relationship between the chief academic officer and the deans put any provost in an untenably weak position, I said, "I can't imagine not having a close working relationship the deans. Your deans seem at one another's throats. How can you have a healthy academic unit with that kind of culture?"

The president laughed and shrugged his shoulders. "What you see is the culture that's been around a long time."

⋘⋙

I sat at the airport, awaiting my flight back to Orange County, staring at the tall pines on the embankment across the Columbia River. I had forgotten how green and gray predominated in Portland because of the rain. Feeling numb after two and a half days of back-to-back interviews, I found it ironic that I had spent only an hour with the president. A provost served at the president's pleasure. Surely in an arranged marriage, you had more than one hour with the man who would hold such power over your life.

Marc and I had a house rule—we set a fifteen-minute limit on talk that took you into a downward spiral. I checked my watch to see how long I had been engaged in the conversation in my head about the president. Other worries sucked me in. The administration was predominately white and male, although the president wanted to change that. Some people I'd met spoke candidly about the president in less than favorable terms. One person told me at lunch, "I'm not sure the president is going to make it." And what was that academic senate resolution about where University Studies should be housed?

I glanced again at my watch. There were positive things as well. PSU's general education program was truly innovative. It culminated in a capstone course in which seniors formed teams to address a critical issue in the community. It was clear that some of Reardon's success as provost was helping the faculty understand and contribute to the national discourse about student learning. Many of the deans had touted the partnership between the university and the city. The university was a national player in ways Cal State Fullerton wasn't.

When my flight was called, I thought of my upcoming provost's interviews on the East Coast—City College in New York (CCNY) and the College of New Jersey (TCNJ). I knew better than to count on the PSU position being offered to me. A week or so later, after an interview at TCNJ, a highly selective liberal arts college, Marc and I were relaxing in a hotel room on Manhattan's West Side. Marc was surfing television channels, both of us knowing we were near the end of the marathon of interviews that had filled the 1998–1999 academic year. My experience at TCNJ had made me think the position had some promise. In 1996, the campus president and the state legislature had taken an undistinguished comprehensive university, Trenton State, significantly reduced the enrollment, and reinvented the campus as a highly selective liberal arts college. The architecture of the campus, quadrangles graced with traditional Georgian-style buildings from the nineteenth century, added an aura of authenticity. The search committee and the president had been particularly attentive to Marc, taking him to nearby museums, curious about his work and his knowledge of art, and proposing that he teach an art class.

As I dozed off, the telephone rang. "Am I speaking to my next provost?" It was Portland State's president. "I need a decision from you now so I can contact the other three candidates."

Trying to maintain a cool voice, I said, "I need a little time to talk it over with my husband and get back to you."

"The other three candidates need to know as soon as possible. How about tomorrow?"

"I'll need until Sunday," I said. "It's nearly five on Friday in New York."

"OK, if that's the best you can do. By the way, I've appointed *Brianna Feldman as vice provost for diversity and special assistant to the president. I want to get a diversity initiative going. She'll report to both of us. Is that going to be a problem?" I hesitated. How could I possibly respond negatively to an appointment that had already been made? If I objected, I'd be seen as difficult. But if I conceded, I could be seen as weak, too compliant. The compliant girl from the 1950s won: "No, not really."

I placed the phone in its cradle. "Well, he offered me the position, but in the same breath, he told me he'd appointed that woman, Brianna, the high energy one. She'll head up the president's diversity initiative as vice provost. Isn't that a provost's prerogative, to appoint her associates? How could I object to his end run when it was a done deal? At least he told me before I accepted, but it feels like a power play. It suggests trouble. It makes me suspicious of him."

"This makes the College of New Jersey look even better," Marc said. "And they want me to teach in the art department. New Jersey is close to New York. Think of the art, the restaurants, the theater." His voice trailed off. "But its president isn't without her craziness and duplicity either."

"What do you mean?"

"When I was in her office doing that faxing for you, I said to the president, 'Your assistant is really good.' She whirled around toward me and said, 'You're not stealing her from me!' Talk about paranoia. All I could say to her was, 'I'm doing some work for Mary Kay. She still has a job, you know.'"

The next day, Saturday, the president of TCNJ called and offered me the provost's position. But a red flag went up there as well when she asked that I forward the evaluations from my review as Fullerton's provost. I balked at this. Why would she want to see my evaluations when she had already offered me the position? It seemed intrusive to ask for them, even though they had been generally positive. I suspected she didn't trust that I was telling the truth. Weren't the letters of recommendation, the calls she made to those who knew me, and her observations during my interviews enough?

While Marc and I wandered through some of New York's museums, the Guggenheim and the Whitney, I weighed the advantages of my two offers. The deciding factor was that I found Portland State more advanced than TCNJ, where the president was new and about to launch a planning process. There was talk of revising the general education curriculum. I had done planning at Lewis and Clark and CSU Fullerton and didn't think I could muster up enthusiasm for yet another round of that work. The final dinner at the college with the president and the search committee was noticeably joyless: a five thirty meal of institutional food and no wine that was served in a corner of the cafeteria with a seemingly interminable, strained conversation. I found the faculty on the search committee less than interesting. I called President Bernstine on Sunday and said, "You are speaking to your next provost."

Marc and I planned a trip to Ireland in July 1999 to recover from the past year and to arrive rested and refreshed for my new assignment in Portland. The day before we left, as I was deciding about how much rain gear to bring and wondering how Ireland would feel after growing up in St. Patrick's parish, a mission of Ireland in the heart of Nebraska, I heard the telephone.

"Jill Kerr Conway here. I'm calling because Matt Goldstein has resigned the presidency of Adelphi. When we hired him, I told the board that he wouldn't stay, that we should hire you, that he'd move on to something bigger, and he has. He is now the chancellor of the CUNY system."

I looked through the glass doors into Marc's studio, the morning sun illuminating his paintings.

"I'm calling to see if you're available to come to Adelphi, to be our president for this coming academic year. The appointment would be for one year, with the option to apply for the position."

Taking a deep breath, I said, "I would be interested, but I've already accepted an appointment as provost at Portland State. I'll need to honor that."

I hung up the phone and was reminded of a favorite line of a poem in the anthology *The Best Loved Poems of the American People* that my high school friend Kathryn Swanson had given me for graduation: "For of all sad words of tongue and pen, the saddest are these: 'It might have been!'"

<hr>

Before I officially began my assignment in August 1999, President Bernstine went out of his way to bring me to campus for university events that spring, including a foundation board meeting and graduation in June. During the interminable ceremony, four thousand graduates came forward two by two as their names were called by alternating readers, received their diploma, and shook hands with a line of smiling administrators. I sat next to the graduation speaker, Donna Shalala, who was then the U.S. Secretary of Health, Education, and Welfare. "I was scheduled to be the speaker last year, but President Clinton called to see if I would mind waiting a year. You know the answer."

Shalala had an idea a minute for improving things: "You've got to get a handle on this ceremony. It's too loose, too ragged. Look at those lines of students. You need to shape them up." She also dispensed other advice: "Dan is going to need help dealing with the liberal arts faculty. He was the dean of the law school at Wisconsin while I was president. That's very different. But the good news is that he's not afraid of smart women."

However, a conversation several weeks later with a provost colleague in California curbed my enthusiasm. *Nick Longo was an economist with a PhD from Harvard. I remembered the story of his tenure at PSU. Rumor had it that he had been fired for standing up to other provosts in the Oregon system, arguing that his campus had the right to PhD programs in the disciplines, not just in systems science, environmental sciences and resources, and education. And wasn't there a rumor about an affair with one of his vice provosts, a woman who reported to him and who was now his wife?

"Nick," I said, "I just learned that you were provost at PSU. I'm going there in that spot the first of August." He threw his head back and laughed. "You have your work cut out for you. There is a power vacuum in Bernstine's presidency. He has no vision and doesn't work very hard. He doesn't know what the score is. But hey, you can run the place." The meeting was about to begin; I smiled weakly and sat down, my head whirling. Why hadn't it registered earlier that Nick had been the provost at PSU? Why didn't I give him a call before accepting the position? Had his years as an administrator made him cynical, bitter? I hoped the optimism I expressed in my journal, May 29, 1999, didn't prove to be an illusion: "The past year and a half has been filled with anger and disappointment that I hope haven't become a way of life. I want to be successful and feel confident again."

CHAPTER 12

AMONG THE MOST INTERESTING PROVOST'S POSITIONS IN THE COUNTRY

Once I was on campus at Portland State University (PSU) in August 1999, I experienced the high of a new engagement. The university had both national visibility and ties to the community of Portland. Perhaps Tom Erlich, a leader in the student learning movement, was correct in describing my new assignment as "among the most interesting ones in the country."

When I asked Tom later what he meant by his claim, he said, "I came to believe deeply in the initiatives that President Judith Ramaley, Provost Reardon, and their colleagues developed in the early 1990s. Campuses like PSU are the main streets of American higher education. I came to see PSU as a beacon for integrating liberal and professional learning in ways that could ensure success for its graduates in their personal, civic, and social lives, as well as in their careers."

One of my newfound pleasures was the extent to which University Studies had captured the interest of scholars who did research on higher education, such as Alexander "Sandy" Astin of UCLA's Higher Education Research Institute, and Tom Ehrlich, Pat Hutchins, and Lee Shulman from the Carnegie Foundation. PSU's general education program had received funding from the W. K. Kellogg Foundation to advance institutional transformation efforts (1996); the Pew Charitable Trust to Restructure for Urban Student Success (1996); and the ACE/W. K. Kellogg Project on Leadership and Institutional Transformation (1997). The program was also the recipient of several awards, which also increased its national visibility.[1]

I was barely on campus a week when I traveled to represent the campus at one of the foundations' meetings to assess institutional transformation. Much

210

as I looked forward to being a part of the national conversation about higher education, I quickly saw that little attention was being paid by the organization to assess what was being learned on the participating campuses, which included PSU. Most of the authorities at these meetings seemed focused on global questions: What have we learned about higher education as meaning and process? What is the most powerful force for change in higher education? What is unique to high-performing institutions engaged in transformation? My primary question was different: How could it be that a project that claimed to stand for the promotion of social justice through transformation in colleges and universities would pay so little attention to the demographics of students and faculty in all their diversity or the changing discourse in the disciplines?

Marc, who came along with me to a similar meeting some months later, picked up a clue to this dysfunction. Sitting outside the office of our lodging on campus, smoking a cigar after dinner, he saw a project director weaving his way up the sidewalk, arm in arm with one of the program's consultants. She was saying, "You don't know a fucking thing about running a university; you don't know a fucking thing about change." Her laughter drowned out his response.

⋘

Beginning with my on-campus interview, I began to piece together the story of how PSU gained national prominence for its award-winning general education program, University Studies, which was adopted in 1994.[2] But the program was controversial among some of the faculty. A university-wide program, the director reported to the president and the provost. However, it was housed in the College of Liberal Arts and Sciences (CLAS). All the ingredients of a Machiavellian plot were there. The dean of the college suspected that the director of the program cut deals with the provost behind his back. Some faculty grumbled that there was not enough disciplinary content in the courses. Others resented the resources that went to the program to the detriment of academic departments.

The academic senate took action and passed a resolution directing the incoming provost to decide about where University Studies should be housed before January 2000. Reluctant to make such a major decision before knowing campus politics, I nevertheless had no choice but to comply with the senate's resolution. After consulting individually with each of the deans, faculty leaders, and the president, I made the decision to move the program into the provost's office under the direction of an associate provost for undergraduate education, a new position. The most compelling reason I heard from the deans was that it was a university-wide program. I presented my decision to the senate as stipulated, careful to iterate all the consulting I had done along the way. When I finished speaking, I looked out at the members, who were quiet and subdued. As Brianna Feldman said later, "The way you did it did not invoke discussion."

"The senate's directive was for me to decide, not to open up debate," I said.

Just as the meeting adjourned, a biologist, Larry Crawshaw, known for his opposition to University Studies, made his way toward me, taking the steps down two at a time from the back of the large, tiered lecture hall and said (as I recall), "I'm going to bring University Studies down. I'm not sure how to do it because you are very powerful, but I will do it."

"Well, I hope you'll see your way clear not to do that. Make an appointment to talk with me about your concerns. I want to hear what you have in mind to replace University Studies." My meetings with Crawshaw followed a similar pattern. He would sit down and begin, "Your office's commitment to University Studies, particularly Freshman Inquiry, is taking away resources from biology, taking the faculty away from our research and out of our specialized subfields." Pausing for a deep breath, he continued, "In the budget cuts of the early 1990s, we lost faculty positions, resources that were rightly ours, resources used to fund University Studies."

I would counter his arguments. "I asked someone in Institutional Research to track student course-taking patterns in science and mathematics. Look here; look at the data. Students are taking more science-related courses than previously was the case."

He looked at me in silence.

I tried another tack. "True, the campus lost positions in the early 1990s, but it's important to remember that University Studies was begun with new money from state appropriations, and has brought more than four million dollars to the university from external sources since its inception. New faculty positions are available to departments if they commit to full-time faculty participation in the program."

"I don't care about any of that. I think the program is wrong and should go."

"Also, the program's budget is now balanced and producing more dollars through tuition and state allocations than it costs to provide the program. Tell me what you propose in its place." Silence.

A week or so later, Crawshaw came in with a piece of tattered, yellow, lined, 8½-by-11 paper on which he had drawn circles with projecting arrows that seemed to be proposing the old distribution requirements, heavier on the sciences than the humanities or social sciences. At our final meeting, he said, "I'm going to the press."

I didn't take him too seriously but became concerned when a reporter from the *Willamette Week*, an alternative paper that had been published since the 1960s, called to say that a faculty member had contacted him about dissatisfaction with University Studies. "Was I aware of this resistance? Did I believe the program was good for students?" I tried to keep a balanced response, emphasizing that the "resistance committee" numbered between eight and twelve faculty members. I wanted to tell him that I thought this group had done all they could to poison the well of University Studies, that when I met freshmen, I asked them how they liked Freshman Inquiry, and most often received this reply, "Actually, I like it," their voices rising at the end of the sentence as if asking a question. Instead, I said, "I'm in a rush now. Can I call you back or meet with you next week?"

"No," he said, "I think I have enough." He paused. "It sounds to me like a bunch of old white guys resisting."

A warning signal went off in my brain. "You'd better talk to them about their demographics," I said, imagining the headlines if I had fallen for his trap.

On June 7, 2000, a headline in the *Oregonian*, then a daily newspaper that served the entire state, announced: "Faculty, Students Question PSU Undergraduate Course." On the surface, the author worked to exhibit fairness, to present both sides—those who believed the program should be designed to help students become better learners versus those who believed it should teach writing, math, literature, science, art, and other subjects that students need for courses beyond the program. But underneath it all, doubt was cast on the actions of administrators: "In their zeal to impose the program, [they] have hijacked the traditional power of faculty to decide what is taught and how it is taught and faculty . . . bristle at this interference." Even though the reporter had contacted me, I didn't see my perspective in the article.

The next call came as I was leaving my gym, waiting for the light to change so I could cross Fourth Street. My first academic year as provost was over, and I was still standing. "Hi, this is Liz Greene from the *Chronicle of Higher Education*. I'm doing a piece on PSU's University Studies program and some of the questions being raised about the efficacy of the program. I heard from one of your professors, who is interested in presenting the debate from both sides."

"Would that be Larry Crawshaw?"

"I believe that's his name. He says he has thirty-five faculty on his side." I had to suppress the desire to say, *Crawshaw, both sides? That's an oxymoron.*

Greene's voice brought me back, "I'm thinking about visiting your campus."

"We'd welcome you. That should help contribute to a balanced article," I said. "I'd be happy to answer any questions you may have."

"None at this time, but could you send me a copy of your résumé?"

Greene called in July to say she would not be visiting campus. The headline, "An Emulated General Education Program Finds Itself under Attack at Home," heralded her July 28, 2000, article. While giving a nod to both sides, Greene posed the tensions starkly as "heavy attack from dozens of top professors" and stated how the program's "political correctness bothers the student and faculty critics." And later, the article continued, "One of the things that has irked faculty critics most about the University Studies debate is the administration's defensiveness about the program. Instead of engaging in a meaningful dialogue, Portland State has shown 'arrogance and continuing inflexibility.'"[3] Crawshaw went on to say that he and his colleagues have "met with Ms. Tetreault, the provost, and Mr. White, the associate dean, several times, and have felt that their requests for

a deeper discussion of the program's academic merits and for rigorous, independent assessment, aren't given enough credence." Is this what Tom Erlich meant
when he said that my assignment was one of the most interesting provost's positions in the country?

My understanding of this debate was deepened by an email from Judith
Ramaley sometime later.

> What I failed to understand at the time [that I established the program] is
> that beneath the surface of scholarly identity are deeper and less coherent
> elements of core human identity itself—who am I, where do I belong, what
> does change mean to my deeper sense of self? The perceived arrogance and
> favored status of the new order evoked resistance [in some of the faculty]. In
> the very rush to create the new order, the failure to maintain connections, to
> focus on local knowledge, and to re-establish consensus laid the groundwork
> for opposition.

A short time after the *Chronicle* article appeared, I attended a national meeting on general education reform. The president of the Association of American
Colleges and Universities, in acknowledging those in attendance, said, "And of
course we have Mary Kay Tetreault, provost at PSU, the poster child for defending GE reform." I laughed along with the others but wanted to point out that I
thought Greene's article was slanted toward Crawshaw's perspective.

The program weathered these attacks because a sufficient number of faculty
supported it, were able to shift allegiance from their discipline to a university-
wide program that they believed was right for PSU students, and were revitalized
by teaching in it. For some, the time was right when, for example, they were looking for something new after completing a book or because the work informed
their teaching in a broad sense. An English professor, Shelley Reese, who was
on the original University Studies faculty team in 1993 and who taught in the
program until he retired, had this perspective:

> Working on an interdisciplinary team is exciting because another member
> on the team can compensate for my lack of knowledge and can school me
> enough that I can provide a basic view for a freshman. After twenty-five years
> of schooling, a liberal arts college education, and thirty years of teaching, I feel
> mildly offended that someone tells me I don't know enough to teach a fresh-
> man some basic concepts of science or, what's worse, that I don't know how
> to find out how to do so. The opportunity to learn from colleagues and teach
> them, that's what I'd call a new kind of collegiality at Portland State.

Other factors contributed to my position being one of the most interesting in
the country. Coincidental with my arrival, President Bernstine hired the Collins

Group to conduct focus groups in the community as a launch for the university's first-ever capital campaign. The consultants reported that PSU's image of itself was outdated, that there were no tensions between excellent academic programs and student access, and that the community looked to the university for leadership in technology. Other ideas to emerge were the need for an excellent and engaged faculty, scholarships for students, outstanding academic programs, and dollars for bricks-and-mortar growth and repair. They stressed that the university needed to develop a plan for PSU, a statement of where we were headed and where we planned to be in the future. *Wow*, I thought. *Here is an agenda I can put to use, including the assertion that the university needs a new vision statement, an "elevator speech," describing our aspirations.*

The following spring, political dignitaries, faculty, and university administrators sat in the sun on the Urban Plaza for the dedication of the new buildings that housed the College of Urban and Public Affairs. Everything in the plaza signaled a bright future: streetcar tracks ran through it; a colorful car manufactured in the Czech Republic was ready for its first riders. The space was designed on a grand scale.

The then mayor of Portland, Vera Katz, placed the physical space in the city's context: if Pioneer Courthouse Square in the heart of the city was its living room, then the Urban Plaza was its library. Then she held out an inspirational idea: "Portland is a great city, but it needs a great university, and that university is Portland State." This resonated with findings from the Collins Group and connected to an observation I was beginning to hear at community meetings—Portland was the only city of its size with no major research university. When I next returned to my office, I said to Donna Bergh, "Vera Katz gave me an idea that may resonate with people. It's that a great city deserves a great university, that the two are inextricably bound. How about having the theme 'Great City, Great University' for our fall 2000 faculty symposium?"

With the deans' tepid blessing, Donna and I planned a series of events that took up variations on our theme, first at a campus faculty roundtable followed by a public forum on the same subject. At the first symposium, Mayor Katz and President Bernstine were featured speakers on the promise of city and university collaborations. As a symbol of looking outward, we scheduled lunch off campus at the Multnomah Athletic Club, the place where the city's powerful met. And consistent with the city's values, we decided to walk the mile or so from the university to the club, much of the walkway running parallel to the 405 freeway. The dean of Oregon's Graduate Institute, which offered degrees in engineering and computer science, and I fell into walking together. Crippled by polio, the dean swung his arm crutches along as we walked. My fears about what I was launching dissipated with each step. *If he can do this walk*, I thought, *I can certainly face the challenges of getting the faculty and administrators to buy into the theme of the symposium.*

Several events that took up subsets of the Great City, Great University idea were scheduled in subsequent years. For example, one event explored partnerships with the Oregon Health and Sciences University to promote research and teaching; another focused on our K–12 school system and teacher preparation, drawing on lessons learned at the University of Texas at El Paso, nationally known for innovative partnerships that crossed the border into Mexico. A third turned its lens to creative industries in Portland; Will Vinton, the producer of films and commercials such as the one about the California Raisins, dazzled us as we explored how the community could promote workforce development and educational programs and the place of capstone courses in all of this. So as not to privilege the sciences, education, and the arts, we also hosted a faculty roundtable and public forum on the topic, "The Place of the Humanities in the Great City."

There was some resistance to the idea—namely, that a great university was more like Harvard. The then provost of Oregon Health and Sciences University told me that she couldn't imagine what the great university would be. But our theme wasn't about trying to reproduce Harvard. It signaled what we had in mind: helping stakeholders create visions of a twenty-first-century urban university. The idea later stalled not because of faculty resistance but because of inertia among the president's cabinet. In the spring of 2001, I gave an update to

Figure 19. Provost Tetreault with Donna Bergh, executive assistant, 2003

EXCOM, hoping to gain support for furthering the idea of Great City, Great University. Somewhat to my surprise, the director of governmental relations, Debbie Murdoch, whom I felt had the habit of hijacking meetings with conspiracy theories about legislators in Salem or presidents at the other two state universities, said when I finished, "I think we've exhausted that idea. I think it's time to move on." This was the first, but not the last, initiative I spearheaded that she would resist. I looked at the president and then at her. His face remained passive. He said nothing.

At the time, I wondered whether this had ever been one of the president's priorities. I really thought the theme resonated with the situation at PSU, but I couldn't be sure if he also thought the idea had played itself out since he didn't support me against Murdoch's declaration that the idea was dead. Judith Ramaley's insights on core human identity came to mind as I tried to understand Murdoch's position. Once driving to a meeting, she told me the story of how her aspirations to be an academic were short-circuited when the University of Oregon's political science department denied her advancement beyond a master's degree to their PhD program. Perhaps my talk of aspiring to be great university stirred up deep and incoherent elements of her core identity.[4]

National initiatives also fed our sense of what might be possible. PSU, the city of Portland, and surrounding municipalities were participating in a national "Best Practices" program. A team of university administrators, public officials, and business leaders traveled to cities such as New York or Chicago to observe firsthand how their counterparts there had collaborated to address a regional problem. In 2001, the program in Austin seemed of particular relevance to PSU because the University of Texas (UT) had become a national player in engineering, science, and technology. PSU was in the silent phase of our capital campaign; raising funds for a state-of-the-art engineering building had emerged as the campaign's centerpiece. Also, Chantal had returned from her field site, Paris, and was beginning work on her dissertation in Austin. Marc would come with me to Texas, and we three could have some time together after the conference.

The focus of the two days of panels and keynote speakers was Texas's technology miracle. The story began in the 1980s, when an alarm went up that the Japanese were outstripping the United States in engineering and technology. The federal government appealed to universities around the country to address this erosion of America's preeminence, a call backed up by millions of dollars in grants. Many thought a university known for leadership in these areas, such as MIT, Stanford, or perhaps Cornell, was expected to be selected. UT was embarrassingly at the bottom of this hierarchy.

For two days, we heard the story of how those at UT worked to convince key constituencies in the state that the university should be thought of as an economic driver, not just a sports school. To the surprise of many, UT came out on top. They attributed their success to collaborations between the Austin campus and the medical school in San Antonio; support from the state legislature, which endowed sixteen chairs in electrical engineering and computer science; and the participation of the high-tech community. On the heels of that success, the university brought in some of the best talent in the world. The number of endowed chairs rose to thirty-two, and high-tech companies flocked to Austin. With top-ranked PhD programs came incubators and learning labs, serving as catalysts for bringing the community together. Austin was touted as a "hot" place for "cool" jobs.

The clearest message, despite an uncomfortable opinion from entrepreneurs that the university hadn't made much difference, was the importance of collaboration among all the players. We were told not to duplicate what the Texans had done but to figure out what made sense for the players in our region. When it was time for the Portland team—which included President Bernstine, local mayors of Portland and the surrounding towns, entrepreneurs from the high-tech industry in Portland, and me—to meet to discuss what Oregonians might do, the mayor of Hillsboro said, "What makes sense in Portland is sustainability. That is what is beginning to make our region unique." I waited to see if President Bernstine would say anything, and when he was silent, I said, "You're right. It is becoming an idea of great interest among the faculty from a number of disciplines. Initiatives such as this are broader than just engineering and technology."

When I returned to campus, I began to talk with the deans, learning new information. Nohad Toulan told me about the School of Urban and Public Affairs' work in environmental sustainability in China, an initiative of interest to Congressman Earl Blumenauer. The dean of CLAS spoke enthusiastically about an economist, David Ervin, who had funding from both Portland State University and the Wallace Center at Winrock International to study sustainability.[5] The dean of the business school, Scott Dawson, invited me to a breakfast of business leaders whose companies were becoming known for sustainable practices.

I sent out a call for faculty interested in sustainability. When I walked into the president's conference room for the initial meeting, all twenty seats at the table and those around the periphery were taken. Quickly, I noted faculty from engineering, urban and public affairs, the sciences, business, economics, and history. Someone from architecture was sitting near the door.

After giving some background about our experience at the University of Texas, I said, "When our Portland team met near the end of the conference, the mayor of Hillsboro observed that sustainability is what could make the Portland area and PSU stand out above the crowd. As I look around this room, I see it is your issue as well. Bill Feyerherm (the vice provost for research and graduate studies) has agreed to designate five hundred thousand dollars, resources accumulated through indirect costs, as seed money to further this effort—a sum you will all appreciate, knowing how carefully he guards money that is rightfully *yours.*" Laughter rippled around the table, and by the end of the meeting, the faculty were on board and Feyerherm was chairing the initiative.[6]

⋘⋘⋙

As I reflect on my years as provost, I now see that Nick Longo's characterization that there was a power vacuum in Bernstine's presidency was off. He had missed a key element when he attributed the problem to Bernstine: power lay elsewhere. My first day on the job in August 1999, I walked back into the warren of offices that were part of the provost's suite, looking out on the huge trees in the Park Blocks. Dutch elm disease, so destructive in the East, had not traveled over the mountains. While I waited for Donna to get off the telephone, I noticed a long rectangular box of photographs near the Xerox machine, amid the clutter of a stapling gun, discarded papers, and a dirty coffee cup. Headshots were peeking out from another era. When Donna came into the workspace, I asked, "What are these?"

"Oh, beginning in the early 1960s, the president's office took a photograph of each new faculty member. They stopped the practice in the mid-1980s, but everyone hired in that twenty-year period is there in alphabetical order."

My fingers immediately went to the *R*s, and there was Michael Reardon with a youthful, almost boyish face. His discerning gaze was as evident then as it was in the late 1990s. Long hair and mustaches dated some of the young white males, each one looking like the smartest boy in the class. Later, someone told me the faculty at that time had been like a family, supporting one another through early marriages, some divorces, and even death. They took care of one another as brothers might. What held them together and gave them power was their longevity. Presidents and provosts came and went, but they stayed.

I wondered where the photographs of the women who had been hired were. A few images of women I knew were scattered among the men in the photograph box, women such as Nona Glazer, a sociologist whose book *Women's Paid and Unpaid Labor* was talked about in national feminist circles. And there was Nancy Porter, the editor of *Women's Studies Quarterly*. They were the ones who had started the university's women's studies program. But a different photo, framed and hung in the hallway, set me to wondering about the real gender relations at Portland State. Three young women in their early thirties—long legged, slender, attractive, and Donna among them—were seated at a table outdoors in the sun.

"Where was this photo taken?"

"Oh, that was one of the Kellogg Foundation conferences in Michigan to discuss general education reform. You know: What's the rationale behind it? How were we implementing it? . . . We were there with Michael."

"And who are those women with you?"

"Adjuncts who taught in University Studies. God, I can't dredge up their names. Neither is around now."

"Did any other faculty attend?"

"Oh, sure, Michael was there and Chuck White, who directs the program. Among the twenty or so from the campus who attended, many were tenured faculty."

In no time, I would come to see a direct line of power that extended from Reardon to later generations. The brotherhood in academic affairs was as well oiled as an Irish ward in Chicago. If you had the ear of the "alderman"—in this case, the provost—your needs were taken care of. During my time at PSU, three former students in the university honors program, all mentees of Reardon, who directed the program, filled tenure-track positions in the program once they received their doctorates. Another of Reardon's protégées, who had been president of the student body in 1968, a leader of the student power movement, was paid thirty thousand dollars per year to work to ensure that students transferred from Portland Community College to PSU. Despite meeting with him several times, I never did get clarity about his work; his monthly stipend continued. As he explained to me, "It's critical to me personally because my wife has MS, so you can imagine we have lots of expenses." One thing that changed because of my questions and our intermittent meetings was the level of his hostility toward me. The other was that a year later, at the recommendation of Terry Rhodes, the newly hired vice provost for curriculum and undergraduate studies, I agreed to allocate his stipend to University Studies in exchange for him teaching two classes.

One pair of supplicants stood out from the myriad of early "begging" meetings, *Mark Roberts and *Philip Lyons, coeditors of an academic geography journal.

Sitting side by side at the round glass table in my office, their bodies stiff, their mouths set, they handed me several copies of their journal and came quickly to the point. "We're editors of one of the most highly regarded geography journals. Before being here, it was housed at one of the University of California campuses. It was a real coup to bring it to PSU. But it's been a struggle to keep up our reputation for quality; we need an additional seventeen thousand dollars to increase the salary of our office manager and cover benefits."

"That's a pretty hefty amount of money for a journal. What is the university contributing now?"

"Seventy thousand dollars per year." *That's nearly enough for two assistant professor's salaries,* I thought. Working to remain calm, I asked, "How is that amount allocated, and how much is for the office manager?"

"She's currently being paid eighteen thousand dollars for the calendar year, not including benefits. The work of getting a journal out goes on all year."

"That's quite a salary increase," I said.

"It's important to note that the total amount we're requesting now—thirty-five thousand—is for her salary and benefits. She's worth the increase," one of the geographers said. "She's highly qualified; she received her PhD in geography from Ohio State." The faces of both men tightened, showing resolve.

I did a quick calculation and asked, "If eighteen thousand is the manager's salary, how is the additional fifty-two thousand dollars distributed?"

"Well, her benefits, as we said earlier, production, printing, and mailing costs, office supplies, telephone." One of the professors paused and seemed to squirm. "And for enhancements to our salaries. About the time the journal came to campus, we complained to Michael about our low salaries while discussing compensation for our work on the journal. He came up with a creative solution, saying, 'One way to increase your salaries is to add the stipend for your editorial work to your base salaries.' And so a good chunk of the seventy thousand dollars goes to supplement our salaries."

The only response that came to mind was inappropriate. Instead, I merely said, "Let me think about this and get back to you."

When the geographers received my email saying that the best I could do was increase the office manager's salary by 15 percent, or $2,250, they requested another meeting. I reiterated my offer. As they left the second meeting, I overheard one say to the other, "That didn't go very well. At least she did approve our request to promote our office manager to editorial assistant. She doesn't seem to understand the costs of things not going smoothly for us."

⋘⋙

Sherwin Davis, the dean of extended studies, arranged a dinner to welcome Marc and me to the deans' community. As we drove to the restaurant on a warm, early September evening, I said, "I can't decide if I'm feeling anxious or positive about this dinner."

"Remember, you're the boss. This is a dinner to welcome us. Let them welcome us."

The party was in full swing as we descended the steps to the function room in the restaurant's basement. Except for Nohad Toulan, an observant Muslim who didn't drink, the others held wine glasses aloft, moving them slightly to choose one of the appetizers being passed around by a waiter. Marc and I worked our way from one cluster of deans and their spouses to another. While enthusiastic in their initial greetings to us, most made no effort to include us in the conversation.

When the waiter announced that dinner would be served in ten minutes, the deans and their spouses scrambled to the largest table, one set for three quarters of the party. I was surprised that Marc and I had no designated seats, that no one ushered us to a place. When the head table was full, those who were left standing, besides us, were the librarian and his wife, who always looked as though she had just escaped from some harrowing experience, and James Ward, the dean of social work, and his wife. We moved to the smaller table for eight tucked under the stairs. Two empty places at the end awaited the dean of arts, who was expected later.

It seemed like this seating arrangement represented the real power relations in the university. The larger schools were all at the main table: business, engineering and computer science, liberal arts and sciences, and urban and public affairs. The two female deans had outflanked their less aggressive male colleagues. The contrast between the noises emanating from the two tables couldn't have been greater—loud conversations from the main table and bursts of raucous laughter. Voices at the smaller table were softer, polite—almost a mute subculture within a dominant culture.

On the way home, I turned to Marc and said, "What have we gotten ourselves into?"

One thing became increasingly clear. There was an "anything goes" culture among the deans. Previous provosts seemed not to have paid attention to practices some of them had established that ran counter to university policies. For example, instead of appointing junior tenure-track faculty as assistant professors with a six-year probationary period, Dean Toulan appointed them as adjunct faculty for two years. If they were successful, he then placed them on the tenure track. Such uncertainty for junior faculty seemed like cruel and unusual punishment to me. When I asked what seemed to me as reasonable questions—What does the job advertisement say? Will there be a review? Is there a transition year? How does this affect the applicant pool?—Toulan blurted out, "Every time you have a question or produce a new form, we become more bureaucratic." Nonetheless, he began to conform to university policy. One of the deans, who had been a Catholic priest, told Reardon that he left the priesthood because he didn't like the "bishop" telling him what to do. On hearing this story, I said, "And now his bishop is a woman." As a provost hired from the outside, I would have to earn the deans' acceptance.

Donna's earlier remark that my way of being a provost had thrown all the deans off gave me pause. *Better pay attention to them*, I thought, *and get to know them as individuals and understand their culture.* I decided to institute the deans' informals, which had worked to build community and trust among the deans and provost at Cal State Fullerton. When we first gathered at the Arlington Club, I could tell something was up—little eye contact, tense body language. We settled into a cluster of comfortable couches and chairs. I could see the fireplace flickering on the far wall. Founded in 1867, a short walk toward the city from campus through the cultural district at the end of the South Park Blocks, the club still had the feel of a posh men's club of another era. Toulan spoke first: "We need to discuss the president's diversity initiative. You are usurping our authority."

"How so?"

"We're not happy about needing to come to you to ensure that we're complying with the president's wishes. We don't think you should be a part of the process, but if you insist, your involvement should be earlier. We are too far into the process to seek your approval after we've done on-campus interviews." Bernstine wanted to initiate a plan to diversify the faculty, and he liked the recommendation of one of the associate vice presidents. When a department hired an American faculty member of color, it would receive an amount equal to 25 percent of the person's salary as a bonus for three years to spend in any way it chose. Concerned that this gave the deans too much leeway, I had asked the president, "Are you sure you don't want any strings attached?"

"No, none."

When the president's program was announced, I told the deans that I would be part of the process. Once a department had completed interviewing the final candidates and made a recommendation to the dean, it would then be forwarded to me. I would approve their recommendation if the whole process had met the program's criteria for diversity. For example, if they were not recommending a minority candidate, they would need to demonstrate that they had actively sought out those from underrepresented groups. If that were not the case, they would have to continue to search.

The deans' complaint about the process had merit, yet I believed that I had a role in ensuring that we diversified the faculty, so I asked, "What would you suggest?"

"If you must intrude, it should be when we have a list of finalists to bring to campus for an interview." I looked around at the circle of deans and saw that Nohad spoke for everyone there. "I think you're right; let's make that change. Is there still time to do it this year?"

A collective exhale filled the air.

If the deans objected to the process set out for diversifying the faculty, the initiative itself evoked a different kind of resistance from the departments. I was reminded of Judith Ramaley's observation from her time as president of the university about the source of faculty resistance to University Studies and of the elements of core human identity when the chair of the psychology department told me about a discussion that had ensued in his department when the president's initiative was explained.

The chair, Keith Kaufman, a good university citizen and a productive scholar brought to campus from Ohio State to strengthen the department, which was all white and mostly male in early 2000, contacted me:

> I want to tell you about the issues that came up when I described the president's diversity initiative to my faculty. They were silent at first, and then their comments came one after another: "What will happen to us if we're in a culture where diversity is valued?" "What will happen to us when we're forced to hire our fourth or fifth or sixth choice, a candidate who is unprepared?" "I have genuine concern for a person we might bring in. We're a department with

certain strengths and parameters. Aren't we just setting someone up for failure, knowing they'll be stretching?"

The chair went on to tell me how he had emphasized that the president's support money could be used for anything, no strings attached: faculty travel, bringing in visiting scholars in their area of expertise, or supporting networks in the community and the region. The dollars could even be used to support graduate students. Still, they resisted. "Who are we, and what are we going to become? Once we cast a broader net and overlay issues of diversity, we'll dilute the mission of the department."

Kaufman established a team in the department to address these issues, their concerns and worries, and moved his department along so that they were able to make two offers to candidates they interviewed—one, a man of Vietnamese heritage, and another, an African American scholar. In the end, neither accepted PSU's offer. But word had gotten out about the psychology department's team addressing faculty members' concerns, and the chair became a regular on a Diversity Action Team formed by Brianna Feldman. The team was one of several examples of Feldman's high energy when working for the good of the university.[7]

There were successes and failures in other departments as well, examples of biases and fears that emerged when the definition of inclusion changed. The College of Urban and Public Affairs wanted to hire a noted scholar in community health. Once offered the position, he began to negotiate for a tenure-track position in biology for his partner, a recent PhD. When the department was approached with the offer of a position for her, it balked: it didn't want to hire someone it didn't want and was opposed to spousal hires, even though it was university policy. In the end, the department, all male except for the wife of the department chair, relented—chilly at first and cautious at best, only later to realize how brilliant it had been to hire the young woman, who was soon awarded a coveted National Science Foundation Young Scholar's Award, providing research funding for five years. A Latino applicant with a PhD from Harvard was initially rejected by the biology department because he "wasn't good on the phone interview." I forced the department to interview him in person, and in no time, it decided it had achieved a coup by hiring him.

Other diversity hires did not fare so well. The African and African American studies department hired its first woman, a gifted postmodern scholar, an African American. Shortly after she arrived, she made an appointment to see me. "It's not going as I thought it would," she said. "When the chair introduced me to the other faculty, he said 'Finally, we have a departmental wife.'" She left for the University of London within a few years. Only too late did I think to offer to transfer her line to the sociology department, known for supporting women.

It wasn't only men who resisted hiring faculty of color. The theater department hired an Afro-Caribbean woman with a PhD from the University of London.

At first, things went well. She directed a play, *Seven Characters*, brilliantly using masks to reveal constructions of gender, race, and ethnicity. But soon she came to my office to talk about the chilly climate in her department, how the chair, a woman, questioned everything she did. Finally, in exasperation, she confronted the department, saying, "It is clear that it was a mistake to hire me; it is clear that you're not ready for a woman of color in this department." Within two years, she took a position as a voice coach with the Shakespeare Company in Ashland, Oregon.

When I had a free hour at lunchtime with no engagements, I would often take a walk around campus, feeling the ground solid under my shoes. Once outside Cramer Hall, I would take a deep breath and look forward to clearing my head. Most often, I would merely nod at faculty I met along the way. One bright sunny day as I headed out to do some shopping, I heard someone calling my name. It was Keith Kaufman, the psychology department chair.

"I need some clarity on the president's diversity initiative. I understood that if a department hired a person of color, 25 percent of the person's salary would go to the department to use in any way it saw fit."

"Yes, that's my understanding as well."

"Our dean gives the money to a department in one line, and then takes it away in another as part of his budget reductions."

"That doesn't sound right. I'll have Pratt look into it, and if that is indeed the case, I'll talk to the president." James R. (Dick) Pratt was my vice provost for academic personnel and budget.

"Thanks so much," he said, turning back toward the university.

Pratt checked the dean's budget, and the chair's perception was indeed true. When I told the president how the dean was handling his diversity resources, I said, "I know these dollars come out of your budget, but I'd be happy to talk to him to tell him he can't do this." Shaking my head, I continued, "It runs totally contrary to the intention of your initiative."

"Let me talk to him," the president said.

The next time I met with the president, I asked, "So how did things go with the dean?"

"He was adamant that he controls the budget in his school, and that it is within his authority to do what he sees fit with these dollars as well. I'm not going to fight him."

≪≪≪≫

By the spring of 2002, despite the hiccups with the president's diversity initiative, I felt confident and secure in my position: the deans and I were on an even keel, I was instrumental in seeing that University Studies survived beyond the "seven-year shelf life" such programs often have, and the sustainability initiative was humming along. Over the past three years, Pratt, my "main man," and I had formed a productive partnership that included not only budget management but, equally importantly, honest assessments of things that mattered, including campus politics. We discussed, for instance, every tenure and promotion case, made progress on raising faculty salaries to be more consistent with our peer institutions, particularly in disciplines in the School of the Arts, where PSU salaries were the lowest. Pratt, with my support, increased the number of tenure-track faculty when he proposed reallocating funds from the provost's instructional reserves to create twelve new faculty positions. Recently, Pratt characterized our time together this way: "Our working together came down to two important points: clear expectations and trust. I kept your trust, and I knew where the limits were. It's actually the best job I ever had."

Influenced by the work of Al Guskin, former president of Antioch University, who argued that universities had to confront issues about the quality of faculty life, Pratt and I decided that Portland State faculty could benefit from hearing about his thinking, so we arranged for him to visit PSU. During his campus visit, Guskin laid out the problems of higher education: inadequate resources even in good times; changing conceptions of student learning; understanding that technology was now a part of the core, no longer an add-on; and an inability to deal with diversity in constructive ways. His central questions for us were the following: How should we capture faculty time so they'll have decent work lives and be used effectively in student learning? If we were creating the university today, given what we know and currently face, what would it look like? His suggested answer was that we should maximize essential student/faculty interactions by relying on technology, peer interaction, and individual learning.

Guskin's ideas inspired the early adapters on campus, particularly in foreign languages, statistics, math, and psychology, who went on to do significant course redesign, supported by a two-hundred-thousand-dollar grant, written by Pratt, given from the Pew Charitable Fund Course Redesign project.[8] Mostly, these departments redesigned their introductory courses, the bottleneck courses that focused on the mastery of materials and skills, an approach that contributed to student success.

Student enrollment rose sharply in 2002 because of a downturn in the economy.[9] Some believed this was an opportune time to raise our admissions standards for entering freshman. The GPA required for admission was 2.5, even though the students we were actually admitting had an average GPA of 3.0. Officially raising the GPA would align our requirement with our sister institutions in Oregon and overcome our second-tier image. The deans and I did what we usually did and formed a committee, the Student Enrollment Management Team (SEMT) that included senior administrators and a faculty member. Once we decided to raise the GPA to 3.0, I took the proposal to the deans' council and to the academic senate's Admissions Requirement Committee, gained approval, and then went on to the full senate.

The proposal passed the senate 35–20, with three abstentions. It was now ready to go to the chancellor's office for review. When student government leaders got wind of the proposal, they were, to use their words, "outraged." I was first on their list of administrators to lobby. The students were ushered into my office, and after introductions, they testified that they would not have gotten into PSU because their GPAs had been 2.5 or lower. "I appreciate your personal identification with this issue," I said. "Do you know that someone with a GPA lower than the requirement has several routes for getting in to PSU? They could enroll for several courses, do well, and then apply for admission? Or the student can request a special admit?"

"How do you expect a high school kid to know that?"

"That's true. But something else to remember is that freshman applicants who don't meet the minimum GPA are considered for admission based on both their GPA and their scores on the SAT or ACT. It's a combination of the two."

"That wouldn't have helped me," a male student said.

"Why do you feel so strongly about this?"

Emily spoke first. "I'm a second-generation PSU student. My parents went here and told me about the freaky, alternative demonstrations that took place in the Park Blocks. That's what PSU is about. I don't want our alternative image to change."

The president of the senior class, *Judy, a young woman from rural Oregon, spoke next. "I feel strongly about this because I was such a poor student in high school. I didn't get into the University of Oregon."

"Were you also a student leader in high school?"

"I was—I was the student body president. This is all part of my plan to work in government, to get an internship in Salem after graduation."

"I'm going to have an internship in labor organizing," Emily said.

Before leaving, they asked me to encourage the academic senate to rescind its decision and have open hearings on the matter. I told them I didn't believe I had the authority to do so. I ushered them out of my office and wondered to what extent the director of governmental relations had a hand in this profess, as Judy worked in Murdoch's office. The proposed change was sustained and continues today.[10]

Rapid enrollment growth affected faculty work life as well. In October 2002, I met with the dean and directors in the College of Urban and Public Affairs to hear their specific concerns: they expected their enrollment to increase by 11–12 percent in the 2003–2004 academic year. To meet this increase, chairs were relying more and more on adjunct faculty, who tended to come in only for classes and did little of the important business of the tenure-track faculty because they were not paid to do that work. Some of the directors saw faculty morale dipping due to a climate of uncertain budgets and rapid enrollment growth. They felt a need to be clear with their faculty about where the institution was going. "We need to feel that someone is paying attention. The president is the one who matters most."

As a way to get the president's attention on the faculty's thinking about this, I proposed a series of luncheons between the president and the faculty, held at the Arlington Club, a place frequented by university administrators but not the faculty. My hope was that they would feel appreciated once inside the three-story redbrick building, where quiet and privilege reigned. By gathering in one of the private dining rooms, sharpened by crisp white linen tablecloths and napkins and fresh flowers, they would see that those around the table mattered. When I mentioned these luncheons to Chantal, close to finishing her PhD in anthropology, she warned me, "Don't forget, Mom, that narratives of declining morale can be described as 'performance.'" And perform many of the faculty did, airing all their grievances when they had the president's ear. After several luncheons, as the president's irritation seemed to grow with each one, I decided we had heard enough and discontinued them. I was disappointed nonetheless because I had hoped that hearing faculty perspectives would make the president more receptive to the pressures they felt and willing to work with me to alleviate them.

I tried other ways to involve the faculty and to get the president's attention, such as sponsoring a series of focus groups, facilitated by one of the anthropologists, Martha Balshem. She had captured my attention when she said to everyone assembled at an earlier faculty retreat, "The provost needs to reconcile her rhetoric with the reality of faculty's lives. We find increasingly larger class sizes and pressure to produce research." Looking directly at me, she said, "You're trying to turn us into a Research One while we lack the necessary infrastructure: library holdings, insufficient support for released time from teaching, and not enough start-up costs for research, including labs."[11]

The focus groups had high participation—86 percent of those contacted attended. Balshem's summary revealed the faculty's values and points of tension in a much more balanced way than I had expected: faculty felt connected to the university by the values of community engagement and quality teaching and learning. However, they felt Portland State had an identity crisis that created tensions between access to and quality of education and between research and the lack of supportive infrastructure. They felt that institutional direction was needed in maintaining the balance between undergraduate and graduate programs.[12] Despite all this, grant and contract activity soared because the faculty was changing, and new people with new expectations were being hired.

There was a continuum of beliefs among the deans and faculty regarding tenure standards for faculty research and publications. On one end was a dean who said, "You can be a world-class faculty member by doing what the institution wants from you, being an excellent teacher, and holding the promise of becoming a scholar." On the other, the dean of engineering and computer science said, "Good teaching and scholarship are not at odds with one another. If we want departments that offer doctorates, we need to have high expectations for [faculty] publications." I agreed with the dean of engineering.

My first year as provost, I got a request for early promotion and tenure from the first dean quoted above, my initial challenge regarding tenure expectations. The candidate in question had published two book chapters, strikingly similar. I consulted the tenure and promotion guidelines, and he clearly did not qualify for early action. When I told the dean of my decision, he was furious: "He deserves this action because he wasn't given credit toward tenure when he was hired. If you hold to your decision, I am going to schedule a meeting with the faculty, a meeting for you to explain your decision to them. You should know that I supported your hiring as provost. I stuck my neck out for you."

The day of the meeting with the faculty and their aggrieved colleague, every seat in a large meeting room was taken. The low ceiling in the room only added to the tension. I stood in front of the group as the dean said, "We're here to give you an opportunity to explain your recent decision regarding one of our faculty's request for early tenure and promotion." The faculty member in question glared at me from the front row. I looked out at the crowd, seeing anger on their faces. Even though I explained how I had been guided by the university's tenure and promotion guidelines, the temperature in the room continued to rise. No one came to my defense. As I explained my position, which I did not change, I could not discern a nod of agreement. Only later, a senior faculty member whispered to me, "I totally supported what you did in that tenure case. This should have happened long ago."

A regular tenure case in the spring of 2002 was different but also mired in past practices. The case involved a man in foreign languages who had no peer-reviewed publications. I recommended a negative decision to the president. After consulting with Pratt, who agreed with me, and the faculty member's dean, who argued for a positive decision, the president concurred with my recommendation.

The professor appealed my negative recommendation, which set a series of hearings in motion. The first took place in my office with the aggrieved faculty member and the chair of his department. The professor made the case that he had been derailed because the principal investigator of a major grant he had been involved with was bedridden with a troubled pregnancy and he'd had to take over the project (indeed, the report was the one publication credential he had). He had a strong educational background, including an Ivy League undergraduate degree and a PhD from a highly ranked West Coast university. I knew he was a husband and a father. I sympathized with him, but I also felt I had a responsibility to the university. He had just not met the requirements.

The next and final stage was a hearing before a faculty committee. I was subjected to two long afternoons of meetings during which the professor's advocates argued that he deserved tenure because he had been a good departmental citizen. The most troubling aspect of the hearing to me was the parade of his female colleagues who came forth and said, "I was tenured with no more publications than he has." The subtext was, We take care of one another at PSU.

After the hearing, I did not reverse my recommendation to the president against tenure and promotion, but others were at work behind the scenes. A senior faculty member in the foreign languages department, a professor hired in the early 1960s, now in the president's office as his advisor, convinced the president that the professor should be tenured. Pratt, who was most likely contacted by her, came to me and said, "You can't be in opposition to the president." I knew that was true and agreed that the man could be awarded tenure but not promotion. More than a decade later, he is still an assistant professor.

I was criticized for my position with such arguments: the professor was doing what the university wanted by being an excellent teacher and held the promise of being a scholar. I listened to those criticisms but did not agree. I believed it was my responsibility to adhere to the university's tenure and promotion requirements with regard to both teaching and research even though the chain of command forced me to comply with the president's decision. My initial recommendation flew in the face of past practices at the university, and I wondered if my decision threatened some longtime professors who'd gotten tenure on the basis of being good teachers and university citizens rather than scholars. While the majority of tenure and promotion cases were easy recommendations because the applicant met and often exceeded institutional requirements, not all of them did. I believed that it was my responsibility to build a university of quality rather than award tenure to a "good citizen." I agreed with the faculty member who said this shift should have happened a long time ago.

CHAPTER 13

A WILD PATIENCE HAS
TAKEN ME THIS FAR

Follow the Money

As engaging as all the initiatives and routine university business were, my primary responsibility as provost was to ensure that academic affairs got its fair share of resources. In 1999, there was a fifteen-million-dollar, one-time allocation to the base budget that was too good an opportunity to squander. When I asked the president how it would be allocated, he said, "Talk to George."

When I sat down to talk with George Pernsteiner, vice president for finance and administration, I said, "Tell me how we plan to allocate this one-time budget enhancement to the campus."

"Ha," he laughed, squinting his eyes. "A lot of it is going to backfill commitments made when the budget was in serious decline—unfunded items such as faculty salaries, start-up packages to support new faculty members' research, capital construction, and deferred maintenance. And establishing some kind of a reserve for the next time the budget goes south."

"But surely all fifteen million isn't going to be used for those understandable purposes."

"No."

"I'd like your support to go to the president and propose we establish a budget process for all the divisions in the university to put forth their requests."

I went next to Donna. "How does the budget process work here? I'm surprised to see there is no vice provost to oversee the budget in academic affairs." There were vice provosts for international programs, research and graduate programs, and diversity but none for the essential work of academic affairs—budget and personnel.

"Oh, that's simple," Donna said. If one of the deans or an associate provost needed resources, he or she would come to Michael and he'd send the requester to George or *Travis Johnson, his associate, who would decide to fund or not to fund. It seemed to keep everyone happy and explained why the deans were always dropping in on Michael. "It's so different now that you are insisting on a budget process and regularly scheduled meetings with the deans. Frankly, it's thrown them all off."

I decided it was time to fund a position, vice provost for academic personnel and budget, and searched internally to fill it. Strong candidates applied, half of them women, but the one that stood out to me was Dick Pratt, a biologist and then director of the environmental science program, a man with a razor-sharp mind who had come from Penn State. He was known for not suffering fools gladly, and while he wasn't one of the old boys, he had their respect. When I told the president of my choice, he said, "A brilliant decision."

Dick's skill at managing academic affairs' nearly one-hundred-million-dollar budget was put to use immediately. I was beginning to see how resource poor the Oregon university system was. Portland State got just under 20 percent of its budget from state allocations; during my time at CSU Fullerton, it had been more than 65 percent. Often the legislature would not approve the budget until late spring or summer; some years, it was as late as October. Budget planning under such circumstances was an Alice in Wonderland experience, but I believed planning was still needed to bring resource allocations, often part of the begging system, out of the shadows.

The next time I met with the president, I told him about my conversation with Pernsteiner and said, "There's not enough here for the faculty. They need to see some concrete benefits for themselves. I took a tour of the science labs and have never seen anything worse. The equipment is outdated and often nearly nonexistent. We need an open budget process, done in conjunction with finance and administration, to make the best use of these one-time resources. What do you think?"

"Sounds good to me," the president said.

In early January 2000, I presented a detailed process to the president and his cabinet for their approval that would establish the priorities of the university, identify the resources available, and ask each division—the president's office, academic affairs, finance and administration, and university relations—to put forward its requests. The process would culminate in university-wide hearings on the budget. Once I had EXCOM's support, I returned to the deans' council, told them how the budget process would work university-wide, and asked them to prepare written requests for tenure-track faculty positions, equipment, and program development. They were wary. "Who will make the final decision?"

"The president will, after considering each division head's recommendations and, of course, after consultation with the academic senate's Budget Committee."

"But won't it take a long time to hear each dean's requests? In the past when we had a budget process, some of the deans tended to go on and on and on."

When the laughter subsided, I said, "It won't be necessary for each of you to make a presentation on your requests. You will do that here in the deans' council, but I'll do that as provost in the university-wide budget hearings."

Nohad Toulan, the senior dean, said, "This breaks from what we have done in the past. I can remember the last time we had such an increase, in the late 1970s, and—"

"What is important," I said, interrupting him, "is that we reach consensus among ourselves. Once Dick and I have reviewed all your requests, I'll come back with a proposal that prioritizes them. At that time, you'll have the opportunity to make counterproposals." Strikingly missing among the deans was a sense of the chain of command—dean, provost, and president. It was no secret on campus, and indeed nationally, that these deans were a contentious bunch. Tom Erlich early on gave me this advice: "You've got to get the deans to work together, to see that they're in this together, and especially to support University Studies." When I told him of the things I was doing formally and informally to reach that goal, he said, "Give it time. I don't think the president has any understanding of all that needs to be done."

At the next meeting, two weeks later, I presented my proposed allocations and the rationales for each. "Now," I said, "is the time for you to give me your thoughts on my proposal, to object, and to recommend something better." After the deans had each made their case, some suggested that their requests should be lower priority, owing to the poor state of other colleges, and argued that we needed to get students to graduate. Despite their need to be parochial, they worked together, softening their strongly held positions.

A few days later, the room where the university budget hearings were held was abuzz with anticipation. Donna, a master at planning every detail of such gatherings, made sure each administrator and the chair of the academic senate received a large, white spiral notebook. The color-coding of tabs and dividers marked off each division's proposal. Sun reflected brightly off the white plastic budget notebooks, illuminating what I would later see as one shining moment of progress—breaking out of the begging system into a more rational way of doing business. As each division head presented a budget scenario, it was as though the various parts of the university were present in the university commons, working together in all our complexity.

True to his promise to make the capital campaign a priority, the president got EXCOM's support, including mine, to grow university relations' budget. Initially, I worried that the deans and faculty would criticize me for such support. However, at a subsequent planning retreat in February, EXCOM and CADS agreed that building a new facility for the College of Engineering and Computer Science (ECS) was our top priority. Borrowing from the Tour de France by handing over a yellow jersey, the business dean designated his colleague in engineering as the campaign's lead rider, a designation the dean wore reluctantly. With Withers's (vice president for university relations) and the president's leadership and determination, a new facility was built, and several colleges created endowed professorships. The lesson I learned here was that PSU's first-ever capital campaign was primarily about working together across divisions on initiatives so that each college benefited, especially those at the heart of academic affairs—supporting students and faculty and identifying donors for projects such as the ECS facility.

What I didn't know in 2000 was that this would be the one and only shining budgetary moment of my years as provost. In subsequent years, when budget deliberations dragged on in the state legislature or when we were required to cut the budget, I could not get the support of the president or his cabinet for a similar process. "But isn't it more important," I would argue, "to have an open budget process when you're cutting than when you have new resources to allocate?" Despite our earlier success, there was no support among the president's cabinet for such a process when I was provost.

Hard to Get Along With

I had a meeting with the president in the spring of 2002. He eased his body into one of the two chairs in his office and pulled at the creases in his perfectly pressed chinos. The university's alumni magazine, brochures promoting the university, and the *Portland Business Journal* were on the coffee table in front of the couch. A large bookcase took up most of another wall. There were some law journals and pictures of his two children, both recent Brown University graduates. His daughter Quincy was an aspiring New York actor. A signed photo of Miles Davis looked out at me. One of the ways the president generously shared his knowledge of jazz and the blues was to copy CDs for people. When I'd told him I listened to traditional blues for the back-and-forth communication between a singer and the pianist, he gave me discs of two modern vocalists, Eva Cassidy and Rachel Ferrell.

Getting down to the business at hand, the president said, "George (Pernsteiner) is looking for positions outside the university, saying that his reason for doing so is because you're hard to get along with."

Sitting in the other chair, turning slightly to make eye contact, I said, "If there's something I've done to make him say so, I'd be happy to hear his complaints."

"He's registered nothing specific. I think he's trying to make a scapegoat out of you."

Feeling secure, I said, "I know I serve at your pleasure; if you want me to resign, I will." Even though the president had not given me yearly reviews, a Christmas card had arrived with an evaluation of sorts—"Thanks for another great year!"—written in his bold hand.

Figure 20. Celebrating the new addition to Portland State University Library, 2002: President Bernstine, Senator Gordon Smith, Librarian Tom Pfingsten, and Provost Tetreault

Waving his hand aside, he said, "I'm not thinking of anything like that, but I'm going to ask my secretary to set up regularly scheduled meetings among the three of us."

Within several days, George and I were seated with the president in his office. He began, "There is the perception on campus that the two of you don't get along. I'm responsible for the situation. I haven't fostered communication among us, haven't brought us together enough. I see this as the first of a number of regularly scheduled meetings with my two senior administrators. I want frank and honest discussion about where we are headed." I felt the tension in the room relax and was surprised at the president's candor in acknowledging his role.

Before I had a chance to speak, George jumped in. "I'd like to take up extended studies and its role. What is the best model for the future? They should be contributing more to the university's budget."

"We've certainly got issues in that school," I said, "but I believe you know Pratt has been working on the situation, especially to ensure that academic affairs gets its fair share of summer session tuition, where the money is really made." Inwardly, I straightened up and took a deep breath as a feeling of threat came over me. Was George trying to manage academic affairs? Or was he now too cowardly to talk about why he thought I was hard to get along with?

I continued, "The president and I have had discussions about its purpose. We agree that it should be both serving the community and turning a profit, but the vice provost for extended studies does not necessarily share that idea. And, of course, the deans want to run their own self-support programs so that they can maximize their profits."

This discussion came to feel like a fast-paced game of handball, ideas ricocheting off the walls, with George bringing up a new topic at every turn and not responding to my answers: he argued that what we were doing was not sustainable, that we needed to tie enrollment growth to our place in the state university system, and he proposed that PSU become a cross between Babson and Stanford, involved with companies such as Intel and working with legislators who supported us politically. I was reminded of his similar hyperactivity at my airport interview. The president, who had been quiet for most of this discussion, looked at his watch. "Time to head out for my luncheon appointment."

There was no discussion of what was contributing to our "not getting along," no explorations of what would improve our relationship. Now I wish I'd said, "George, I hear that you think I'm hard to get along with. I would welcome hearing why that is so, what the issues are." Looking back, perhaps I was afraid of playing into the idea that I was hard to get along with in the first place, or perhaps I was fearful about what he might say. Our two subsequent meetings followed the same pattern as the first. But then the meetings stopped. I also never asked the president why that was so. I suspect that without knowing how to engage us in any meaningfully directed discussion, he just felt he had more important things to do with his time.

On May 16, 2002, Johnson, Pernsteiner's associate, left a message on my voice mail. "George has an offer from the University of California, one of their campuses—which one I'm not sure. We need to do everything we can to keep him. One reason he's considering leaving is because he's concerned about his relationship with you." I returned the call immediately and left a message on Johnson's voice mail. My next call was to the president to tell him about his news. Johnson never responded to my message. The president, who often joked about having to babysit a difficult Foundation Board member or university dean, did not comment on my call.

Pernsteiner took the job in California. I felt a sense of relief that I shared with Marc: "Now there will be a search, and hopefully I will get a colleague I can work with. The president can build the team he thinks will work." But much to my surprise, the president announced that he had appointed Johnson, without a national search, because he knew the campus and the budget, which was particularly important during yet another time of cuts. I was incredulous. It was widely known on campus that Johnson had recently signed a contract for a similar position at the University of Wyoming. He talked freely about getting faculty status with tenure and about buying a house. But when George took the job in California, Johnson broke his contract and stayed at Portland State.

I had my suspicions about Johnson from the beginning. George had instructed him to help me become familiar with the budget at PSU. Johnson, who had been on campus since 1988, had matured there in a sense, working his way into more responsible positions in finance and administration and completing his doctorate in public administration and policy. He was the quintessential old boy, although he was barely forty when I first met him, known on campus for activities that bespoke a high level of testosterone, like leading high-risk trips with male faculty: spring canoeing in wilderness areas when rapids were the most treacherous, backpacking treks into western mountains, rock climbing, and beer-infused house renovation parties at his cabin in southern Oregon. "Have you noticed," Brianna Feldman said, "that he has no women in his inner circle?"

Johnson's thoughts on how the budget process worked would frequently turn into a narrative of palace intrigue. His face would light up, a smile would cross his lips, and he would straighten up his body. "I don't trust him," he said of one of the deans of arts at our first meeting. "And extended studies. I've been trying to get the associate provost to do things differently for years. She just keeps resisting."

"What worries you about the dean?"

"He's close to a million dollars over budget, and he wants to make PSU a Research One, something like Arizona State."

"I can deal with him," I said, even though I worried about how to handle the dean in a collegial way, "and I thought that George said he was $240,000 in the red."

"Whatever," Johnson said. When I told Dick Pratt of conversations such as this, he said he thought Johnson was someone who thought by talking, throwing ideas out in the process of formation and sharpening them that way but not expressing well-reasoned concepts.

The president held a few meetings with Johnson and me, much worse than those with Pernsteiner because Johnson would take over and talk about his current projects—expanding the university district, just south of the city's central core, and buying up properties as they came up for sale, including a broken-down building that came to be occupied by the art department and a Double-Tree Inn. I could not imagine that renaming it the University Center would improve its national ratings. He talked in an impassioned voice about his efforts to finance and build a new dorm on campus. Unable to get state support, he sealed an agreement with the Foundation Board whereby it would put up the necessary capital and then own the facility. I was made aware of his singular control over the university's budget when he casually told me, "I've spent nearly a million dollars on lawyers' fees to work out an agreement with the Foundation." I wondered why none of these initiatives and their concomitant costs had come before EXCOM or even if and how the president was involved. Using resources in this way meant that they would not be used to support teaching or research.

Worrying that such a question might be seen as questioning the president's authority, I kept silent. I still had faith that he would guide the conversation toward some common purpose.

Johnson's practice of thinking by talking came out in other ways as well. An upcoming reaccreditation visit in the fall of 2004 required extensive forward preparation and planning. There was antipathy to planning in EXCOM, but the president reluctantly agreed to form a committee in January 2002, which I chaired. At my suggestion, the president appointed an influential city politician; Intel Oregon's CEO; key university administrators; highly regarded faculty members from across the disciplines, including one or two I thought needed to be watched; and two students.

Attending the planning meetings infrequently, Johnson began to bring PowerPoint presentations to weekly EXCOM meetings that laid out his vision for the university. "I've been working on my vision of the future, and it just kind of grew and grew." With a shrug, he passed out a sixty-page document that included a mission statement, plans for expanding the university district by purchasing a number of buildings near the campus, reducing the number of tenure-track faculty and hiring adjuncts with increased teaching loads, and "incentivizing the faculty" through salary increases when they obtained external funding. He also had ideas for ways to better serve the business community and to make extended studies more entrepreneurial.

I saw his vision for the university as misguided in light of the planning meetings and said, "As you know from being on the University Planning Committee, one of the things we'll be taking up after we revise our mission and vision is the place of tenure-track faculty." Johnson's only response was to briefly glance at me.

"Your vision is brilliant and exciting, Travis," Debbie Murdoch chimed in. She went on, "Hard to imagine the faculty coming up with something that isn't in their interest."

"I originally started out planning for economic development," Johnson said, "and then it just expanded."

In retrospect, I see my handling of this conversation as a failure on my part to use what I was learning in my research to inform my practice as an administrator. In the summer of 2000, Marc, Chantal, and I vacationed on Cape Cod for several weeks, which gave Frinde Maher and me time to talk about our next book. In preparation for that work, we read *Academic Capitalism*, which sounded the alarm about changes under way that were similar to Johnson's vision: the growing role of corporate values over academic values, the supposed shift in higher education from a social institution to an industry, and the decline and irrelevance of the liberal arts in the face of scientific and technological dominance.[1] Now I wish that I had pointed out that such ideas had been critiqued in *Academic Capitalism* and that I agreed with the authors' worry that all of this posed a threat to universities. I could have recommended that he and others might benefit from reading it. I didn't do so because I only later saw the parallels, but had I seen them at the time, I would have hesitated, worrying that my colleagues on EXCOM would have thought me to be too academic, too resistant to change. Also, I wasn't certain of the president's position on this matter. Looking back, I see that negative assertions about me ("You're hard to get along with") and Marc's observation after hearing yet another of my administrative challenges ("You're too timid") functioned as a form of control. Jane Roland Martin's observation that the academy charged an exorbitant admission fee to those women who wished to belong captured my experience.[2] In retrospect, the fee I paid at Portland State was my firing.

FACULTY DISCONTENT

On May 3, 2004, a sunny afternoon, I walked to the academic senate's monthly meeting. I tried to concentrate on the beauty of the day even though I had been warned about troubled waters ahead by Michael Driscoll, who I had hired to replace Pratt as my associate vice provost for budget and personnel because he seemed like the best choice among the applicants. (Pratt had left PSU in 2002 to be dean of arts and sciences at Idaho State University.) I had denied Mike's request for promotion from associate professor to full professor earlier, and things were still tense between us. His dean made the case that he should be promoted because of his administrative work. Driscoll was still a young man, plucked much too early from the faculty to be associate dean, an appointment that forever derailed his research. When I checked the university's tenure and promotion document, however, there were no provisions for promotion based on administrative work.

The trouble now was that the Education Policies Committee (EPC) was charging that I had violated the academic senate's constitution when I moved management of summer school, which had resided in extended studies, into Driscoll's office. Frowning, I said, "How did I do that?"

He pushed a copy of the constitution into my hands, pointing to Article III, Section 1.

"It says here essentially that only faculty, acting through the academic senate and particularly EPC, has the power to alter the structure of departments or programs."

"But the deans and you agreed that the summer school should be moved from extended studies to your office because the summer quarter is now counted as a fourth quarter because of enrollment targets." Driscoll raised his shoulders and shrugged but said nothing.

Faculty governance at PSU had a culture of live and let live—their colleagues in student affairs were members of the academic senate, and it was not unusual for a fixed-term faculty member to chair the body. Despite this, I knew to tread carefully. In a series of interminable meetings that spring with the chair of EPC, the full committee, and the chair of the senate, I addressed their questions and concerns about the financial implications of the move for departments and faculty salaries. They seemed most worried that there would be pressure to be as innovative in their teaching and structuring of course meetings in the other three quarters as they were in the summer.

Inwardly, I sighed, thinking of Adrienne Rich's poem "A Wild Patience Has Taken Me This Far"[3] before saying, "It is completely within the purview of faculty to decide those issues, no matter what quarter. The president has stressed that he doesn't want us to assume that this is a fourth quarter for the faculty workload. You'll still be expected to teach the three quarters during the traditional academic year."

When it came time for the EPC report at the senate meeting, I drew in my shoulders and thought about how I hated this kind of academic posturing, its legalism, and its attention to rules. No wonder I had resisted mastering Robert's Rules of Order, even though I had chaired hundreds of meetings. I felt as though I wasn't in the room.

The chair began by noting that the report had the unanimous support of the committee and that it was their intent not to be provocative but to maintain the authority and responsibilities of the faculty as guaranteed by the PSU Faculty Constitution. They recommended the formation of an ad hoc Faculty Senate Committee to "begin immediate discussions" regarding the movement of summer session out of extended studies and requested that "the president formally respond to the senate regarding the violation of Article II, Section 1, of the Faculty Constitution inherent in renaming and restructuring the 'School of Extended Studies' to 'Extended Studies.'" Because summer term was fast approaching, they moved to provisionally approve the location of summer session in the provost's office, pending the recommendations of EPC to be made by October 2005.

As a way of reminding them that I was in the room and that my actions did not threaten them, I said, "The president has stressed that he doesn't want us to assume that this is the fourth quarter for the faculty the way other quarters are." One of the senators, who directed a student advising center, said, "Summer session was moved out of academic affairs in 1989, and the senate probably never approved that move." That action had taken place a decade before I became provost.

Grant Farr, the chair of sociology, came to my defense, arguing that the motion was "overly punitive. It seems the administration is working with the committee to resolve the issue, and it serves no purpose to force the president to comment." A geologist weighed in, saying, "I agree in some sense with the previous speaker, but authority was taken from the faculty, and this is a shared governance issue that needs to be resolved."

The chair spoke again, "The reason for the motion is to emphasize to the administration as a whole that the academic senate recognizes that the constitution has been violated, and we would like, to the extent possible, for that not to happen again." Throughout the discussion, the president made no comments.

When the meeting adjourned a few minutes later, I was stunned at this carefully orchestrated move to put the constitution, the president, and me in opposition to one another. Wanting to flee, I knew I had to attend the reception that followed.

Searching quickly for a friendly face, I spotted Farr at the reception and walked toward him. He gave me a friendly hello and then said, "I don't want to be seen talking to you too long."

≪≪≪≪≫

May 14, 2004

1:15 p.m. Email from the president's secretary to the president's executive committee. "The president has canceled this Monday's EXCOM meeting. See you as scheduled next Monday."

1:16 p.m. Email from the president's secretary to me. "Hi, Mary Kay, The president would like to meet with you Monday morning."

I read the two emails and became suspicious. Why was the president canceling his senior administrators' regularly scheduled meeting to meet with me? Recent happenings made me uneasy. The previous week, I had chaired the meeting, something the provost did in the president's absence. During the meeting, his secretary had stuck her head in the opened door and, pointing to the vice president for university relations, said, "The president is on the phone."

Strange, I'd thought, *I'm the person in charge when the president is away. It must be something about the capital campaign.* When the vice president returned twenty minutes later, her face was drained of color. Whatever the president had said was a shock.

As I dressed Monday morning, I put on a black opal pendant, a gift from the president the previous Christmas. Half in jest, I hoped it would ward off any evil that might befall me. At the least, it would remind the president that he had some obligation to be loyal. When I walked into the president's office at nine, he was not at his desk but standing on his balcony, smoking. As I watched him put out his cigarette, I sank into my usual seat in his meeting area, wondering if this was going to be as bad as I feared. I smiled to myself, remembering all the ways I had evoked his high-pitched laugh.

When the president sat down, he said, "I'm going to have to have a difficult conversation with you. Several faculty have asked for an appointment with me, but I'm not meeting with them. There is talk of a vote of no confidence, and I don't want you to go through that. I'm not sure the deans would come to your defense."

Ha, I thought to myself. *I know who the faculty members are who want to see you*—an engineer (who would later be appointed provost), a psychologist, and a biologist, all close friends of Travis Johnson. When Dick Pratt left, he had given me a long letter about issues in his domain as well as academic affairs as a whole. To my surprise, he'd written that some of the faculty—namely, the three who wanted to see the president about me two years later—had talked about a vote of no confidence for him.

"Should I tell the president about this?"

"No," Dick said, "I wouldn't. I don't think it is that serious."

I brought my attention back to the president. "What are the reasons for this?"

"It is primarily because of some of the promotion and tenure decisions you've made." All with your concurrence, I should have said. "We serve in these jobs when we have the faculty's confidence, and I'm afraid you have lost that. What happened at the academic senate meeting earlier this month is an indication of that. I didn't want to give in to Travis's demand that a condition of his staying, rather than going to the University of Wyoming, was contingent on your going. So I've decided it is best that both of you go and that I start fresh with a new administrative team. You will have a sabbatical with full pay next year so you can work on your book."

Not again, I thought, *not again*. "I was planning to retire next year, but I decided to wait to tell you this summer. You know, of course, that if you announce your retirement too soon, you're a lame duck." *Which isn't as bad as being a dead duck*, I thought.

The president had a look of surprise on his face.

"No one ever gave me any help to succeed," I said.

"I know that."

I felt completely alone. I didn't think I could win in a fight for my position without the president's backing. And on some level, it didn't seem worth fighting for, trying to convince the president to retain me until I retired. True, the deans might not come to my defense. I felt some solace when Nohad Toulan, who was Johnson's mentor, told me later, on hearing of my stepping down, "I had no idea the president would do something like this."

When I told a friend, Renate Powell, someone with no association with the university, whose husband had given me the swagger stick in 1987, that I would be stepping down as provost, she said, "I know; there was an article in the *Willamette Week* today."

When I looked at the article several days later, "Doing the PSU Shake," I recalled a remark that the director of governmental relations, Debbie Murdoch, had made: "Zach Dundas just loves Travis." Zach was a reporter at the *Willamette*

Week, an alternative newspaper known for character assassinations, and the author of this particular article.

"In the small world of Portland State University, it was as if Alan Greenspan and Colin Powell had quit on the same day. On May 17, Portland State announced the resignations of vice president, Travis Johnson, the finance czar called the 'resident genius' behind the school's rapid growth, and Provost Mary Kay Tetreault, its controversial academic chief."

In the next five paragraphs, Johnson, described as "the rainmaker," was touted for his achievements. "[With his] aggressive construction agenda and his uncanny knack for working with a broad cross-section of people . . . [he] will be an enormous loss." an executive at the Portland Development Commission was quoted as saying, referring to Johnson's new assignment in Wyoming.

And toward the end of the article, "Tetreault [is] known for tightening Portland State's tenure process and bolstering its research credentials. . . . Her relationship with the faculty has been tense from early on. Recently she clashed with the faculty senate over procedural matters—a sign, some say, that profs had lost patience with their boss—and she reportedly butted heads with Johnson as well."[4]

I suspected Johnson was feeding Dundas information and probably had been much of the time I'd been at PSU, considering how well he came off in the article. Later, I subsequently learned of the extent to which Johnson had worked with key administrators to undermine me. Some weeks after the article, the vice president for university relations relayed a conversation she'd had with Johnson. He'd told her he had one thing to work out so he could stay at Portland State—my firing. The vice provost for extended studies told me that Johnson would come into his office daily, railing against me and saying what a terrible administrator I was. He concluded this information, saying, "Finally, I said to him, 'Look, I report to her. I don't want you to speak ill of her again.'" I never knew exactly why Johnson was so hostile toward me. It could have been because in his free and easy way of dealing with the truth, he saw my refusal to be swayed by bluster as being an impediment to him getting his way. Or it could have just been that he disliked working with women.

A few days after it was announced that I was stepping down as provost, Marc and I made our way to a hotel downtown, where a retirement dinner was being held for the dean of the School of Social Work. As we waited for the traffic light, I spotted a table outside Jake's Grill, next door to the hotel, which presented a tableau of power relations at Portland State. Clustered around a small table having drinks were the president; Reardon, who would be stepping in as interim provost until a new hire was made; my executive assistant; and the dean of engineering and computer science. How I wished I'd had a camera. It was a tableau of male privilege, right down to the attractive younger woman, my executive assistant.

It was the kind of male privilege that was tribal and cliquish, with the informal rules of power relations made by them.

"Look at that," I said to Marc, once we greeted them and passed by, repeating what I'd said only a few weeks before, "It's like something out of an Irish ward in Chicago."

~~~

The Foundation Board meeting in early June 2004 was held in the student union, in a room with no windows.⁵ Once inside the door, squinting at the harsh fluorescent lights overhead, I saw clusters of people talking in animated ways, mostly Foundation Board members, who numbered about twenty-five. The president and his executive team were ex officio members of the board, and they were milling about as well. Wondering which group to approach—surely they had heard that Johnson and I were leaving—I decided instead to sit at the large rectangular table where the meeting was soon to begin. An alumna of the business school, a woman with a sunny face free of wrinkles and a cloud of gray hair, was in a circle dominated by Travis Johnson. She gushed about how his innovative practices were serving the university. To me, she was the embodiment of the values of the board; I saw the majority of them as fiscal conservatives and entrepreneurs who subscribed to corporate values over academic ones; a university education was primarily preparation for a job.

On the agenda was an item titled "Administrative Changes," with the president's name on the same line. *Yikes*, I thought. *He may ask me to make a few remarks.* I began to jot down the ideas I wanted to include. When we reached the president's report, he began, "I've decided it is time to form a new administrative team—one that can start fresh together, one that will be compatible. As you may know, Mary Kay will be leaving to complete her book *Privilege and Diversity in the Academy*, and Travis has accepted a position as chief financial officer at the University of Wyoming. Let me give them a chance to make a few remarks. Mary Kay?"

At least he didn't say I've resigned to spend more time with my family, I thought. I remained sitting, raising my voice to be heard around the table in the cavernous room. Taking a deep breath, I thought, *Be positive. Be professional.*

"It's been a privilege and an honor to serve as provost at Portland State for the past five years. I take pride in the accomplishments that the deans, the faculty, my associate provosts, and I, in collaboration with the president, have been able to do. For example, since the summer of 2000, we have been working on the idea of 'Great City, Great University,' designed around the idea that a great city and a great university are inextricably bound." I went on to highlight some of the faculty round tables and public forums that were held, interspersing stories of faculty enthusiasm.

"Now other major efforts and achievements include engaging in a planning process that developed a vision and values statement, identifying the marks of our baccalaureate graduates, and establishing a system of program reviews for the academic departments every five years. And if that weren't enough to keep us busy, we've done enrollment management and taken on a series of initiatives of special interest to the president: diversifying the faculty, internationalizing the campus and the curriculum, and assessing student learning. All of these efforts are documented in our electronic portfolio, which will house our work in preparation for our ten-year accreditation visit."

I looked at the chair of the Foundation Board and nodded to indicate I was finished, proud of these achievements. But I wondered if they mattered to anyone besides me. Those around the table were still; no one made eye contact.

Next came Johnson's turn. He stood up and backed away from the table, his shoulders hunched forward, straining the seams in his suit jacket, his voice quavering for a moment until he gained control.

"Portland State has been the center of my life for the past sixteen years. I've grown up here, gotten my doctorate here. I've done everything I could to expand the university district, to work with you to build dorms, parking lots, and green buildings. I never thought I'd get the chance to do such things. I'm just a country boy from a Texas farm." With that, his finger brushed against his nose, and he said, "PSU has meant more to me than any other place I've been. I'm going off to Wyoming, but I shall return. I shall return to Oregon."

FACING MYSELF BACKWARD

As I bring this memoir to a close, I am reminded of the words of a Lewis and Clark student, Noreen Nakagawa, who was inspired by Emily Dickinson's poem "Before I Got My Eye Put Out."[6] She wrote,

> Before I got my eyes put out I like as well to see—As other Creatures, that have Eyes and know no other way. But looking at [poem 327] it's problematic, there is a price to pay, and it isn't always voluntary. Infinite wisdom seems to come from suffering through enforced pain. You can run around in ignorant bliss until something breaks through this level of illusion, takes out the "eye" that makes it possible for you to view the world this way and once you see through it, you can't go back, trying to face yourself backwards would strike you dead.

Facing myself backward as I wrote this memoir did not strike me dead. It has made it possible for me to see anew the world I was born into, a world and a religion that expected women to marry, raise children, and stay at home. It was also a world that held out the promise of a liberal education: becoming a whole man.

My world changed as I worked among the priests in Oklahoma with their message of social justice and calls to reform that medieval institution, the church.

Their message took on new meaning once racial justice was added to the equation, made particularly urgent for me when I moved to the South Side of Chicago, studied at the University of Chicago, and taught in all-black high schools during the height of the civil rights movement.

My world changed again in the 1970s, not only as I discovered feminism and women's history but also as Marc and I went about unlearning our own sex-role socialization. For me, it was the recognition that my future depended on me taking responsibility for who I was in the world. To paraphrase Gloria Steinem, I became the man I wanted to marry. Feminism also gave me a way to channel the anger I felt at women's subservient position into intellectual work, writing articles and books, turning ideas over and over, the greatest privilege of all. It also gave me a feminist community and a feminist research partner, Frinde Maher.

When I first drove up the hill to Lewis and Clark College, I was in a state of ignorant bliss, knowing little about what I was getting myself into. Yet I learned many important things as a faculty member there—how to engage in the essential work of teaching and research, internalizing the belief that becoming accomplished and successful at both were reasonable expectations. I also came to see the importance of having an institutional perspective as I served on the college's Mission and Planning Committee. The men who were my colleagues there, especially the department chairs in graduate programs, taught me not only how to be a chair but how essential academic values, competence, and creativity were to that work.

In light of the ten years I served as a provost, I can imagine that today's aspiring administrators might have questions similar to those of my editor: What is a provost supposed to do? What was being an administrator like from my perspective? Why were such things important to me and to the overall university? How is this a story of change in higher education?

In pondering these questions, I see that I had a split vision on that work. One eye was an administrative one, focused on what a provost was supposed to do—build a team and articulate the mission, vision, and priorities that inform activities from teaching and research to community engagement. Of primary importance was ensuring that academic affairs received its fair share of resources to do that essential work and, once acquired, that the budget was managed fairly and openly. My decision to give the deans at Cal State Fullerton the authority and responsibility over their faculty dollars and equipment budgets confirmed my belief that by putting that responsibility on them, there would be better budget management.

Serving as provost in two large comprehensive universities taught me to respect and implement the chain of command, never forgetting that I was the "boss." Yet I also knew how dependent I was on associate provosts, the deans, and department chairs for ensuring that things ran smoothly on the canyon floor. They saw, for example, that the classes students needed to graduate were scheduled and held, enrollment targets were met, faculty tenure and promotion reviews were conducted, research grants were written and submitted, reports were written, and accreditation requirements were adhered to. Early on, I decided that I needed to ask: What should I be doing and what should someone else be doing? Appreciating the value of what others thought was brought home when Tom Klammer and Soraya Coley came up with the idea of holding a retreat for deans and department chairs to further the work of institutional planning at CSUF. Their idea paved the way for department chairs to be instrumental in implementing the university's mission and vision.

This same eye came to see, sometimes the hard way, that my most important relationship was with the president to whom I reported. I knew never to upstage nor to surprise my presidents by moving forward without their knowledge and support, even though President Gordon at times didn't see my behavior that way. However, I was sometimes not sufficiently mindful of this as I engaged in the heady satisfaction of working with others, particularly at Cal State Fullerton, to forge new interpretations about how to work together and realize our ideas for a university for the twenty-first century.

Finally, this eye paid attention to my colleagues in each president's cabinet—the vice presidents for finance and administration, for student affairs, and for university advancement. While we knew that our various divisions were often in competition for resources, we also knew that we needed to work as a team for the good of the university.

And what of the other part of my split vision? Inspiration came from feminist thinkers such as Adrienne Rich, who held out the idea of imagining and working toward a woman-centered university and how things might be different if women were in positions of responsibility and authority.[7] This eye gradually came to see that Rich's idea was inspirational in theory but complex when put into practice. Ironically, I was able to enact Rich's idea while a faculty member at Lewis and Clark in ways that I could not in my administrative assignments. My decision to be silent about the workings of gender at my first dean's convocation at Cal State Fullerton was the correct one because I ran the risk of alienating too many department chairs if I had done so. The warning some months later from a female faculty member that I would be seen as "a one-issue person" if I brought in one of the authors of *Women's Ways of Knowing* as a speaker caused me to step back and let others take the lead.

Imagining a woman-centered university was insufficient in another way; the workings of race and ethnicity also needed to be taken into account. I learned about this beginning with my assignment as a social studies teacher on the South Side of Chicago in the 1960s. It deepened as I served under four black presidents during my seventeen years as an administrator in higher education. The importance of expanding how I thought about diversity was clear once I was in California. The "new" ethnic student majority at CSUF in 2017 was Hispanics

(40.8 percent), followed by Asians (20.5 percent) and whites (20.4 percent).[8] A student of European and African American ancestry, who characterized herself as having made it in an institution that wasn't made for her, inspired me to work with others to think about how to create universities made for an increasingly diverse student body.

Emboldened by feminist colleagues at Lewis and Clark, I resonated with Jane Roland Martin's depiction of women in *Coming of Age in Academe* as newcomers reluctant to act and think like the natives. Yet as Noreen Nakagawa knew, there was a price to pay, a price I chronicle throughout my story. Acting and thinking in ways different from the natives, particularly at Portland State University, had its costs. I now see that some of my positions—for instance, initiating an open budget process, resisting the culture of begging and favors to insiders, and adhering to written tenure and promotion guidelines—threatened the ingrained male power structure (to paraphrase the feminist scholar Beverly Guy-Sheftall). However, despite the costs, my experiences also came with many benefits: a high salary, the chance to work with wonderful teams and individuals on the day-to-day business of academic affairs and initiatives I valued, status in the university community and beyond, opportunities to travel, and a national platform that led to many positive friendships.

But it was in my research that I could see and report how some were acting and thinking differently than the natives, as Frinde Maher and I worked on *The Feminist Classroom* and *Privilege and Diversity in the Academy*. Yet in some cases, I could enact lessons I was learning from doing this research—namely, the shift from teaching to learning. This led me to see the value in Don Schweitzer's draft for a mission statement: Learning is preeminent at Cal State Fullerton. But mostly I believed that I would jeopardize my position as a dean or provost if I expressed the things I was learning. It was better that I kept silent.

Perhaps I was too much of a true believer, shifting my faith from Catholicism—believing there is but one truth out there—to other beliefs: feminism, antiracism, and university reform. Maybe the things I was asking faculty to do stretched their own tolerance too much. The values I learned at the University of Chicago may have been misplaced on the campuses where I worked, which were less richly funded and most often had faculty members with higher teaching loads. Some of my actions were ones that could endanger relationships and threaten survival, as the psychologist Carole Gilligan wrote—for instance, the tenure and promotion recommendations I made to President Bernstine.

I don't know that I have gained "infinite wisdom" by looking back at my life. But I have learned that I can face myself backward despite the pain. Seeing the joy that has been a part of my life—namely, Marc and Chantal's love and support—is also a part of the wisdom, which has not wavered over the years. Chantal is now a tenured linguistic anthropologist at Michigan State University, married and the mother of a son to whom this book is dedicated. On the occasions when my brothers and sisters and I come together, we're reminded of how the capacity to laugh, something we learned from our father, is a saving grace. Life has brought me things I couldn't have imagined—the privilege of leading an examined life in higher education and being an essential part of teams that imagined a university of the twenty-first century.

NOTES

PREFACE

1. Gail Collins, *When Everything Changed: The Amazing Journey of American Women from 1960 to the Present* (Columbus: Little, Brown, 2009).
2. Mary Karr, preface to *The Art of Memoir* (New York: Harper Collins, 2015), xviii.
3. In cases where I used a pseudonym because I was unable to obtain permission or decided to do so for reasons of privacy, I have placed an asterisk by the pseudonym the first time it appears.

CHAPTER 3 — NESTLED IN THE BOSOM OF CATHOLICISM

1. This is a mass offered for the soul of a dead person, most likely in purgatory, to intercede with God for admission into heaven.
2. An Irish political movement founded around 1905 that is dedicated to the reunification of Ireland and the end of British jurisdiction in Northern Ireland.
3. Being in a graduating class of thirty-six students enhanced my chances for success.
4. The Sodality is an association that fosters in its members' devotion to the Blessed Virgin Mary and seeks to make them devout Catholics.
5. Several years later, I was contacted by one of the nuns from the Mount, who asked if I was interested in returning to Atchison to become a full-time recruiter for the college. I was surprised they would consider having me back as a role model, considering my past behavior. But perhaps it was a generous example of their belief in redemption.

CHAPTER 4 — WANDERING IN THE WILDERNESS

1. Newman Centers administer to Catholic students at non-Catholic universities. Activities at these centers usually include Mass, social get-togethers, discussion groups, and in the 1960s, social justice projects.
2. A low-water bridge provides a roadway when the water is low; when there are high flow conditions, the water runs over the roadway and can be dangerous when a car attempts to cross.

CHAPTER 5 — FINDING LOVE AND WORK

1. A university supervisor was assigned to each intern, with the expectation that he or she would observe the intern's teaching several times during the year. Mine sat in on one of my classes, but I never received an evaluation. Rumor had it that he observed a fight among the students and, feeling threatened, never returned.

2. When I returned from France, I did substitute teaching until I obtained a teaching position at John Marshall Harlan High School in an affluent African American neighborhood south of Parker.

3. The Committee on Social Thought is an interdisciplinary PhD program. Its guiding principle is that the serious study of many academic topics and of many philosophical, historical, theological and literary works is best prepared for by a wide and deep acquaintance with the fundamental issues presupposed in all such studies.

4. Pre-Cana Conferences are still required today, although online programs have emerged as an alternative for those who cannot easily attend one in a parish.

5. Naomi Weisstein, "'How Can a Little Girl like You Teach a Great Big Class of Men?' the Chairman Said, and Other Adventures of a Woman in Science," in *Working It Out*, ed. Sara Ruddick and Pamela Daniels (New York: Pantheon, 1977), 241–259. I also communicated with Jesse Lemisch, Naomi's husband, on August 6 and 8, 2018.

CHAPTER 6 — BECOMING THE MEN WE WANTED TO MARRY

1. Gloria Steinem, "Leaps of Consciousness" (Women and Power Conference, September 2004, New York).

2. I recall no issues around my teacher certification. Most likely my MAT degree and nearly five years teaching experience gave me the necessary qualifications.

3. Alan Feldman, "Before the War," in *The Personals* (New York: Yarrow Press, 1982), 12–13.

4. Interview with Hazel Rose Markus, Stanford University, May 9, 2005. See also Susan Fiske and Hazel Rose Markus, *Facing Social Class: How Societal Rank Influences Interaction* (New York: Russell Sage Foundation, 2012).

CHAPTER 7 — MY LEWIS AND CLARK CHAPTER CONCLUDES

1. Janice Law Trecker, "Women in United States History High School Textbooks," *Social Education* 35, no. 3 (1971): 249–260, 338.

2. Mary Kay Thompson Tetreault, "The Treatment of Women in U.S. History High School Textbooks: A Decade's Progress," *Women's Studies Quarterly* 10, no. 3 (Fall 1982): 40–44.

3. James A. Gardner, *Legal Imperialism, American Lawyers and Foreign Aid in Latin America* (Madison: University of Wisconsin Press, 1980).

CHAPTER 8 — A DEANERY OF MY OWN

1. Adrienne Rich, "Toward a Woman-Centered University (1973–74)," in *On Lies, Secrets, and Silence: Selected Prose 1966–1978*, ed. Adrienne Rich (New York: W. W. Norton, 1979), 125–155.

2. Chancellor Tim White and the California State University Board of Trustees have appointed a historic 52 percent of CSU women presidents—twelve of twenty-three are women—a record unsurpassed by any other state college system (email communication from Ellen Junn, August 22, 2018).

CHAPTER 9 — SECOND CHANCE TO BE A PROVOST

1. The Faculty Fellows Program was a yearlong residency in the provost's office for a person who wanted to learn about higher education administration. The fellow worked on special projects of her or his own design or those assigned by the provost. For instance, Coley worked on enrollment management and planned special events such as a department chairs retreat and a symposium that brought Al Guskin to campus to talk about the changing roles of faculty members.

2. Stanley Woll, "The Sound of One Voice Dialoguing," *Senate Forum* 11 (Fall 1996): 10–12.

CHAPTER 10 — OPPORTUNITIES AND AMBITION
OVERSHADOWED BY AMBIVALENCE

1. This was a school offering courses and certification to high school graduates who were preparing to be teachers, especially elementary school teachers.

2. Boxer, a feminist historian, was provost at San Francisco State University from 1989 to 1996.

CHAPTER 11 — SHIFTING MY GAZE FORWARD

1. Recently, a colleague, Dick Pratt, pointed out the fallacy of this thinking. It was the president who worked the legislature for funding, not the provost. Yet Pernsteiner's comment about "friends in the legislature" made sense in the context of Oregon, a state with a small population where it is common to know your legislators. Also, formulas, especially enrollment ones, drove the bulk of resources; the state did not pay for capital construction.

CHAPTER 12 — AMONG THE MOST INTERESTING
PROVOST'S POSITIONS IN THE COUNTRY

1. These awards were the Pew Leadership Award for the Renewal of Undergraduate Education (1996), the Corporation for National Service Award for Commitment to National Service (2001), and the Theodore M. Hesburgh Award for Enhancing Undergraduate Teaching and Learning (2002).

2. See Mary Kathryn Tetreault and Terrel Rhodes, "Institutional Change as Scholarly Work: General Education Reform at Portland State University," *Journal of General Education* 53, no. 2 (2004): 81–106.

3. Elizabeth Greene, "An Emulated General-Education Program Finds Itself Under Attack at Home," *The Chronicle of Higher Education*, July 28, 2000, https://www.chronicle.com/article/An-Emulated-General-Education/6662.

4. Affirmation that the idea lived on was demonstrated by an agreement signed by Mayor Sam Adams (2008–2011) and President Wim Wievel titled "A Great City Needs a Great University."

5. See Jennifer H. Allen and David Ervin, "Building Sustainability Scholarship: Lessons from Portland State University," in *Let Knowledge Serve the City*, ed. B. D. Wortham-Galvin, Jennifer H. Allen, and Jacob D. B. Sherman (New York: Greenleaf, 2016), 1–20.

6. Recently Feyerherm attributed the culture of cross-disciplinary collaboration across departments and colleges at PSU to a statewide higher education system that historically required approval from the chancellor's office to initiate any doctoral program. The two "senior" institutions, the University of Oregon and Oregon State University, precluded any traditional science or social science PhD programs, forcing PSU to operate with two interdisciplinary programs: environmental studies and system sciences. Because the chancellor's

office funneled state higher education investments to the senior campuses, PSU was forced to pool resources across academic units. Thus Feyerherm's job was to provide resources that were needed for campus-level initiatives such as sustainability. For instance, twenty-six faculty submitted a proposal to the National Science Foundation (NSF), making the case that an electron microscope (EM) was essential to their research. When NSF turned them down, Feyerherm and others worked with a local company, one of the top international EM manufacturers, to buy the machine. This and other related purchases attracted other top faculty and made capabilities available to local businesses such as Intel (emails from Bill Feyerherm, August 30, 2018, and September 21, 2018). The restrictions on disciplinary PhD programs began to change in 2000, as a number were added in engineering and the sciences.

7. See *Connecting the Dots: Portland State University in the Twenty-First Century*, a publication chronicling all that was being done in academic affairs at that time. It was originally issued in September 2002 and was revised in January 2003.

8. The Pew funds came via the Center for Academic Transformation at Rensselaer Polytechnic Institute.

9. The year 2002 marked the beginning of enrollment increases that lasted for a few years. One of the reasons often given for this was a downturn in the economy and an increase in students entering community colleges, followed by transfers to four-year institutions. This also had an impact on master's program enrollment, and demographic trends pushed high school graduating classes up. The university saw some flattening before 2010, when there was another increase, but since then, enrollment, which was 27,670 students in 2017, has vacillated (depending mostly on the economy) with periods of up, flat, or down numbers.

10. Because there were so many avenues for students to reach PSU, this GPA requirement seemed irrelevant to some. At this time, the campus admitted about one thousand freshmen and graduated two thousand seniors.

11. At this time, the Carnegie Classification of Institutions of Higher Education had abandoned Research One (R-1) for "research extensive," institutions where doctoral programs were widespread among disciplines, and "research intensive," institutions where doctoral programs were only offered in limited fields. The R-1 moniker continues to this day, however, even though Carnegie abandoned it in the 1990s.

12. Balshem was part of a faculty team that included Kerth O'Brien, Leslie McBride, and Peter Collier.

CHAPTER 13 — A WILD PATIENCE HAS TAKEN ME THIS FAR

1. Sheila Slaughter and Larry K. Leslie, *Academic Capitalism: Politics, Policies and the Entrepreneurial University* (Baltimore: Johns Hopkins University Press, 1997). See also Frances A. Maher and Mary Kay Thompson Tetreault, *Privilege and Diversity in the Academy* (New York: Routledge, 2007), 2.

2. Jane Roland Martin, *Coming of Age in Academe: Rekindling Women's Hopes and Transforming the Academy* (New York: Routledge, 2000), 115–121.

3. Adrienne Rich, *A Wild Patience Has Taken Me This Far: Poems 1978–1981* (New York: Norton, 1981).

4. Zach Dundas, "Doing the PSU Shake," *Willamette Week*, May 26, 2004.

5. The PSU Foundation is responsible for raising and managing private resources to support the mission and priorities of the university.

6. Frances Maher and Mary Kay Thompson Tetreault, *The Feminist Classroom: Dynamics of Gender, Race, and Privilege* (New York: Basic Books, 1994), 105.

7. Adrienne Rich, *On Lies, Secrets and Silences: Selected Prose 1966–1978* (New York: W. W. Norton, 1979).

8. California State University Fullerton, "Fact Sheet," 2016, http://news.fullerton.edu/_resources/multimedia/factsheet.pdf.

INDEX

Names preceded by an asterisk (*) indicate a pseudonym.

Adler, Louise, 153
adolescent rebellion, 40–42, 45, 49–52
Allen, Father Daniel, 59–60, 67–69
Alva, Sylvia, 152–153
American Educational Research Association national meeting (1984), 113–114; Women Educators' Research Award, 113
ancestors and relatives, 18, 25; Haselhorst relatives, 23–24; Thompson relatives, 18–21, 24–25
Astin, Alexander "Sandy," 210
Atwell, Margaret, 179

Baker, Sister Imogene, 44, 48, 51–52, 55, 56
Balshem, Martha, 228, 254n12
Banta, Mary Ann: catechetical work, 63–64; Oklahoma norms, 62–64; pastor management, 64–65; volunteer partner, 60–64
becoming a whole man, 44, 51, 54, 56, 71, 193–194, 245
Berg, Dennis, 149
Bergh, Donna: budget processes, 231–233; differing provost styles, 222; Great City, Great University initiative, 215–217; power relations, 219–220; staff networks, 202
Berkson, Dorothy, 113
Bernstine, Daniel, as president: administrative changes, 241–243; "Best Practices" program, 217–219; budget deliberations, 231–234; capital campaign, 214–215; diversifying the faculty, 222–225; faculty concerns, 227–228; Great City, Great University initiative, 215–216; managing vice presidents, 234–239; orientation to

Portland State University, 208–209; power vacuum, 209, 219; provost search (1999), 201–207; tenure cases, 228–230
Blumenauer, Earl, as congressman, 218
Boston University, 6, 8, 11, 102–103
Boxer, Marilyn, 190, 253n2 (chap. 10)
Boyum, Keith, 149
Brennan, Dennis, 80
Brewery Arts Complex, Los Angeles, 199–200
Broad, Molly: advocating for women, 179, 190–191
Buck, Vincent, 191
Bullard, Carolyn, 126–127

California State University, Fullerton: budget resources and negotiations, 149–150; founding, 134; introduction to, 132–134, 150–151; President's Advisory Board, 161–162, 164, 170, 186, 189; student and faculty diversity, 151–153; University Planning Committee, 163–165; Western Association of School and Colleges accreditation (1990), 148
California State University, Fullerton, School of Human Development & Community Service (HDCS) dean, 1987–1993: associate dean to, 135, 144–146; Center for Collaboration for Children, 147–148; chain of command, 138–139, 141–142; collaborating and new possibilities, 142–143, 148–149; department chairs, 135–136, 146–147; executive assistant of, 141–142; faculty retreat (1990), 147; job description

California State University (*continued*)
and appeal, 131, 133–134; President Cobb's
influence, 132–133, 136, 150–153; resource
allocations, 136, 145, 149–150
California State University, Fullerton,
School of Human Development &
Community Service (HDCS) provost,
1993–1998: Academic Affairs retreat,
166–168; canvas of academic programs,
172; Deans' Council, 162–163, 165–166;
fired, 189–192; implementing planning,
165–170; job description, 159–161; keeping
track, 161–162; resource allocations, 162,
170–172
California State University System: founding, 134; presidential appointments, 252n2
(chap. 8); provosts' collegiality, 184–185;
system-wide budgeting, 144–145
Cambridge Adult Education Center, 88
career choice, 56
Castro, Donald, 191
Catholicism: Calvert House, 70–73, 78–79;
college, 8, 39–40, 42–45, 48–49, 54; Extension Lay Volunteers, 59–69; heritage,
24, 27–28, 31–33, 59, 74, 85–86, 126, 190;
religious retreats and sexuality, 38–39;
salvation, 248; Sinn Fein, 33; St. Patrick's
Parish, 31, 33
Century of Struggle, 89, 97
Champagne, Lucille, 96–97, 101
Chapter 622 / Title IX coordinator, Massachusetts Department of Education,
104–106
Chicago, 56–57, 68–71, 74–75, 105, 150, 217,
247
Chronicle of Higher Education, 5–6, 213–214,
253n3 (chap. 12)
civil rights: Civil Rights Act of 1964, 58;
movement, 71, 76, 86, 246
Clapp, Michael, 147, 149, 161
Clark, Marge, 7, 11, 120–122
Cobb, Jewel: administrative hires, 171, 175;
chain of command, 138–139, 141–142;
diversifying the faculty, 151–153; job offer,
136; mandatory retirement, 154; public
persona, 132–133; restricting campus
contacts, 190; workings of class and race,
150–153
Cole, Johnetta, 151, 178
Coleman, Jack: accounting books, 159;
administrative style, 136, 150, 162–163;
approval for research time, 139–140; chain
of command, 139–140; retirement, 155;
school funding, 136; Western Association

of School and Colleges accreditation
(1990), 148
Coley, Soraya, 152–153, 166–168, 247
college years, 1956–1961: choices, 39–40;
disappointing return, 48–49; expectations
and reality, 42–45, 47–49, 50–52, 55
Collins, Gayle, ix
Collins Group, 214–215
Conway, Jill Kerr, 193–194, 208
Corey, Jerry, 135, 143
Crawshaw, Larry, 212–214
Cross, Amanda, author, 10

Darney, Virginia, 129
Davis, Sherwin, 221
Dawson, Scott, 218, 233
Deakin, Michael, 78
Dias, Sally, 105
Dixon, Marlene, 83
Dodds, Dinah, 9–10
Donnelley and Sons, R. R.: employment,
57–58; gendered expectations, 57–58, 60
Dowdall, Jean, 197
Dowling, Annie and Tom, 21–22
Driscoll, Michael, 239
Dryden, Robert, 204, 228–229
Duke, Dan, 16, 109, 128

Eder, Sid: orientation to MAT program,
2–4; role in search process, 6–9; teaching
assignments, 14
Encyclopedia Britannica, 56
Erlich, Tom, 201, 210, 214, 233
Ervin, David, 218, 253n5
*Evans, Ralph, 181
Extension Lay Volunteers: activist priests,
67–69; introduction of program, 59–61;
life as a volunteer, Oklahoma City, 65–67;
life as a volunteer, Skiatook, OK, 60–65

Farr, Grant, 240–241
*Feldman, Brianna, 207, 211, 224, 237
female friendships, 26–29, 39–42
feminist pedagogy, 114–117, 182; national
interest, 114, 156, 183; negative factor in
presidential search, 192; voice, 152; writing
The Feminist Classroom, 138–140, 248
feminist phase theory, 114–115, 120, 144
Feyerherm, Bill, 218–219, 253n6
Fideler, Elizabeth, 88–89
Fideler, Paul, 89
Fort Riley, KS, 25–28, 34
Framingham, MA, 87–89, 100, 176; Chil-
dren's Center, 91

Freud, Lucien, 137
Freud, Sigmund, 12, 36, 93, 102

Gardner, James, as president of Lewis and Clark College: credentials, 122, 252n3 (chap. 7); graduation (1984), 125; Mission Planning Committee (MPC), 122–125
Gardner, Sid: Center for Collaboration for Children, 147–148
Garza, Ana, 152
Gemelch, Walt, and department chairs' retreat, 166–167
gender expectations: consciousness, 112, 152, 188, 190, 196; Lewis and Clark College, 8, 110–111, 125, 127–129; of the 1950s, 38, 138; of the 1960s, 57–58, 65, 67, 93; Portland State University, 219, 225; scholarship, 112, 114–115, 183; silences, 144, 247; traditional roles, 57–58, 74, 93–94, 101–102
Germany, 1957–1958: defining experience, 30, 45, 47–48; dreams of returning, 45; dull days and romantic nights, 45–48
Getty Museum, 198
Gilligan, Carole, 248
Glazer, Nona, 219
Goldstein, Matt, 193–194, 196, 208
Goldstein, Phyllis, 99–100
Gomez-Amaro, Rosa Maria, 154
Gordon, Milton, as president of California State University, Fullerton: administrative reviews, 186, 188–189; controversial candidate, 154–155; deans' council, 162–163; dual realities, 180–182, 184–187, 188; funding initiatives, 169, 186; help in dealing with president, 187–188; most important relationship, 182, 190, 247; offers provost's position, 154, 158, 182; President's Advisory Board, 161–162, 164, 170, 186; University Planning Committee, 164–165
graduate studies: Boston University, 6, 8, 11, 102–103; Clark University, 102–103; Harvard University, 102; University of Chicago, 1, 5, 8, 11, 15, 73–75, 89, 120, 246, 248
Grant, Grace, 129–131
*Great Lakes University, 193, 195–196
Guskin, Al, 226
Guy-Sheftall, Beverly, 158, 248

Hagan, Willie, 186, 188
*Hansen, Jane, 110–111
Harvard University: Gutman Library, 5; Schlesinger Library, 97–98
Haselhorst, Dorothy Thompson, 22–23, 26–28, 30

Hass, Ray, and California State University, Fullerton, mission planning, 164, 168, 174
*Haverford, John, 49–50, 52
high school, 1952–1956, 33, 36, 161; Tom Austin, 36–39, 47; Mary Anne Broderson, 41–42, 52; Barbara Fitzpatrick, 40–43, 52; Judy Hansen, 26, 38, 40–42; Bob Mueller, 37–38, 52–54; Willa Jean Pease, 40–41; sex education, 38–39; Kathy Swanson, 38, 40–42, 52, 67, 99, 208
high school teaching: John Marshall Harlan High School, 252n2 (chap.5); Parker High School, 74–77, 88; Wayland High School, 90, 96–97, 102, 104, 106, 196, 203–204
Hutchins, Patricia, 210

Institute for Educational Management, 175–177
institutional planning: California State University, Fullerton, 163–170, 173–174, 247; College of New Jersey, 200, 207–208; Lewis and Clark College, 122–125, 128–129, 246; Portland State University, 217–219, 237–239

*Jenkins, Jamie, 175–176, 186–187
*Johnson, Travis, 231–232, 236–239, 242–245
Junn, Ellen, 152–153, 173, 252n2 (chap. 8)

Katz, Vera, as mayor, 215
Kaufman, Keith, 223–224, 225
Kennedy, Louanne, 193, 198
Killilea, Mary Ann, 81
Kirschner, Susan, 10, 110
Klammer, Tom: Educational Policies Fellowship Program (EPFP), 149; implementing mission planning, 166–168, 247; offers advice, 190, 197

Lambert, Father Rollins, 71
Lange, Jack, 47, 49
Lerner, Gerda, 7–8, 10, 110
Lewis and Clark College, 1–2, 6, 11–14; feminist research group, 113; Graduate School of Professional Studies, 124–126, 128–129; master of arts in teaching (MAT) program, 1–4, 6–9, 11–12, 120–122; Mission Planning Committee (MPC), 122–125; tenure-related reviews, 17, 109, 117, 118–120; teaching assignments, 14–16; women's interest groups (WIGs), 10; women's studies seminar, 10, 109–111
*Longo, Nick, 209

Luecke, Monsignor Sylvester, 65–69
*Lyons, Philip, 220–221

Magnusson, Paul: advocate and mentor,
  2, 11, 117, 125–126, 138; hiring new dean,
  125–126; interview, 8; staffs Mission Planning Committee (MPC), 122–123
Maher, Frinde: critics of one another's
  work, 112–113; *The Feminist Classroom*,
  140, 248; feminist community, 246;
  feminist pedagogy, 114–117, 139; graduate
  school colleagues, 103–104; preparation
  for next book, 238; wedding, 183
Manhattanville College, 61
Martin, Jane Roland, 239, 239n2, 248
Massachusetts Department of Education,
  105
May, Ruth, 152
McAlpin, Mary Margaret, 79–80
McDonough, Father Tom, 71–72, 81
McFerrin, Bobby, and parents, 150
McIntosh, Peggy, 111–112
"MG man," 72–73, 79
Minicucci, Cathy, 104–105
Montano-Harmon, Maria R., 152–153
Morgan, Douglas, 118–119, 125–126
Mothers and Others, 89
Mount St. Scholastica College, 40, 42–45,
  48–52, 54–55, 103
Munitz, Barry, 190–191
Murdoch, Debbie, 217, 227, 238, 242

Nakagawa, Noreen, 152, 245, 248
Nebraska, 1, 25–26, 31, 64, 195, 208; class dif-
  ferences, 104. *See also* North Platte, NE
Newcomb, Sherri, 161, 171
New England Coalition of Educational
  Leaders, 107–108
Newton, MA, public schools, 5, 108
Nicholson, Debbie, 75
North Platte, NE, 18, 20, 26–27, 31, 36, 51,
  53, 80

Oder, Barbara, 103
O'Grady, Patsy, 61–62, 64
Oklahoma, 60, 77, 245; Collinsville, 64;
  Oklahoma City, 59, 65–69; Skiatook, 60;
  St. William's Parish, 60–64
orphan trains, 21
Osage Indians, 61, 63

Paget, Roger, 126–127
parents. *See* Haselhorst, Dorothy Thompson; Thompson, John

Parker, Michael: associate dean, 135, 143,
  144–146, 162; culture of school gradu-
  ations, 141–142; enrollment management, 145; knowledge of California State
  University funding, 144–145; marketing
  school, 148–149; rumors, 140, 158
Parks, Rosa, 150
Patrick, John, 15, 74, 87–88
Pernsteiner, George: frank and honest
  discussions, 235–236; hard to get along
  with, 234–236; questions during Portland
  State University provost interview, 204;
  resource allocation, 231–232; University of
  California appointment, 236
Porter, Nancy, 112, 219
Portland State University: admissions standards, 226–227; advice, 208–209; budget
  negotiations, 232–234; capital campaigns,
  214–215, 233–234; *The College That Would
  Not Die, 1946–1996*, 201–202; *Connecting the Dots*, 254n7 (chap. 12); costs and
  benefits of belonging, 239, 242–245, 248;
  Council of Academic Deans (CADS),
  205–206, 222–223; course redesign project,
  226; faculty discontent, 227–228; faculty
  diversity initiative, 222–225; gender
  relations, 219–220; Great City, Great
  University initiative, 215–217; national
  "Best Practices" program, 217–219; President's Executive Committee (EXCOM),
  217, 232, 234, 237–239; provost's search,
  200–207; quality of faculty life, 226–228,
  254n11; retention, tenure and promotion,
  228–230, 239; sustainability initiatives,
  218–219, 218n5; University Studies, 206,
  210–214
Powell, James, 138
Powell, Renate, 242
Pratt, James R. "Dick": budget management, 253n1 (chap. 11), 225–226, 232–234;
  course redesign and faculty development,
  226; insights, 237, 242; leaves Portland
  State University, 239, 242; strongest candidate, 232; tenure and promotion, 229–230
presidential aspirations: airport interviews,
  192; American Council on Education
  National Identification Project (ACE
  NIP), 177–178; aspirations and ambivalence, 179, 192, 196–198; women presidents, 178, 196
Presidential Commission on the Status of
  Women, 58
presidential finalist: Adelphi University,
  193–194, 208; Fort Lewis College, 194–195;

*Great Lakes University, 195–196; Southern Illinois University, Edwardsville, 193; State University of New York, Brockport, 178–182, 189

provost interviews, 200–201; College of New Jersey, 206–207; Portland State University, 201–208

Putnam, Anne, 195

racism, 77, 96, 205, 248

Ramaley, Judith: role model, 178, 210; University Studies, 201, 214, 223

Ramirez, Judith, 135, 145–146, 152

Rand McNally, publisher, 99–100

Reardon, Michael: "bishop," 222; brotherhood in academic affairs, 219–220; budget management, 231–232; candidate interview, 202–203; historian, 202; longevity, 219–220, 243; University Studies, 203, 206, 210

Reese, Shelley, 214

research projects: dissertation, 106–107; feminist pedagogy, 114–117, 139–140; feminist phase theory, 114–115, 120, 144; *Women in America: Half of History*, 6, 10–11, 96–100, 106, 110, 120; women in U.S. history textbooks, 112–114, 120

Reynolds, Ann, 154

Rhodes, Terrell, 220, 253n2

Rich, Adrienne, 133, 240, 247, 252n1 (chap. 8), 254n3

Riesman, David, 176–177, 197

*Roberts, Mark, 220–221

Ross, Diane: introduction to California State University, Fullerton, 132, 134; the power of new ideas, 147

Royce, Ed, 177

Samuelson, Jerry, 150, 163

Sandler, Marty, 98–99

Savage, David, 7–8, 10, 110

Schaeffer, Sue, 187–189, 191

*Schlageter, Tom, 96–97

Schmuck, Patricia, 115, 176

Schmuck, Richard, 176

*Schneider, Marlene, 48–51, 59–60, 66–68

Schon, Donald, 128, 136, 143

Schwartz, Father Elmer, as pastor of St. William's Parish, 60–65, 69

Schweitzer, Don: as California State University, Fullerton, provost, 155, 179; decorating, 159, 172; guarded colleague, 156–157; mission statement, 164–165, 248; silence and dysfunction, 150, 162; untimely death, 157–158

second women's rights movement, 86, 91, 104, 106, 115, 120, 196

Seitz, Martha, 27–29

Shaheen, Raja, 61–62, 64

Shalala, Donna, 208–209

Shavlik, Donna, 177–178

Shulman, Lee, 210

Silverman, Robert, 114

Skeehan, Father William, 59–60, 69

social class, 26, 30, 53, 104, 104n4, 130, 150, 155

split vision on provost's work, 246–247

Stanley, Sheila, 98

Stark, Michael, 12

St. Benedict's College, 40, 47

Stovall, Eula, 134–135

Stratton, Michael, 195

Sullivan, Father John, 59, 68–70

Sullivan, William, 129

Sutphen, Sandra, 151, 173

Sylvester, Robert, 203–204

Takaka, Ronald, 151

Tarule, Jill, 145–146

Taylor, Barbara, 178–179, 181–182

Teacher Standards and Practices Commission (TSPC), 2–3

Tetreault, Chantal: adolescence, 16, 96, 117–119, 136; birth, 85; childhood, 2, 4–5, 88–89, 91, 95–96, 101–102, 104, 113; college and graduate school, 137, 157, 217, 248; loss of Catholic heritage, 85–86; one whole happy family, 18, 106, 109, 120, 185, 197, 200, 238; performance, 228

Tetreault, Marc: artwork, 2, 13, 105, 137, 141, 148–149, 199, 200, 207; best advisor, 97, 119, 121, 133–134, 190, 236, 248; Catholicism, 85–86, 126; coping and making do, 198–200, 206, 243–244; gender roles, 93–95, 239, 246; graduate school, 81, 84, 87; high school teaching, 87; loyalty, 87, 185–186, 188, 248; marriage, 80–81; parenting, 5, 90–91, 100–101, 117–118, 137; reproduction, 81, 101; supporting my searches, 181, 194–195, 207; taking risks, 106; team effort, 11, 221; travel, 156–157, 176, 211, 217, 238; work, 4, 16, 101, 105, 129

Thompson, John, 21–22, 25, 26, 28–30

Thompson siblings, 18, 21, 30, 249

Thorne, Barrie, 128

Tierney, Dennis, 129, 131

Toulan, Nohad: budget climate, 203, 222; diversifying the faculty, 222–223; provost's firing, 242; provost's search committee chair, 203; sustainability, 218

Trecker, Janice Law, 112, 112n1
TSPC. *See* Teacher Standards and Practices
  Commission

Vatican II, 60, 67, 78, 81
Voice of America, 52, 56
Voigt, Deborah, 172
Vura, Dolores, 149

Wagner, Pat, 169–170
Wallace, Jim, 118–119
Ward, James, 203, 221
Ward, Patricia, 48

*Warren, Joe and Nancy, 94–95, 101
Weisstein, Naomi, 83–84, 252n5
Wellesley College Library, 98
Westerman, Father Robert, 62–64, 69
White, Tim, as chancellor of California
  State University, 252n2 (chap. 8)
*Wilson, Robert, 12–14, 17, 122–123
Withers, Gary, 204, 233–234
Woll, Stanley, 173–174, 253n1 (chap. 9)
women-centered university, 133, 247
Wright, Jerry, 152

Zuniga, Carmen, 157

ABOUT THE AUTHOR

MARY KAY THOMPSON TETREAULT is provost emerita at Portland State University in Oregon. She is also the author or coauthor of several books, including *The Feminist Classroom: Dynamics of Gender, Race, and Privilege.*